SEXUAL ATTRACTION
IN THERAPY

SEXUAL ATTRACTION IN THERAPY

CLINICAL PERSPECTIVES ON MOVING BEYOND THE TABOO – A GUIDE FOR TRAINING AND PRACTICE

Edited by Maria Luca

WILEY Blackwell

This edition first published 2014
© 2014 John Wiley & Sons, Ltd.

Registered Office
John Wiley & Sons Ltd, The Atrium, Southern Gate, Chichester, West Sussex, PO19 8SQ, UK

Editorial Offices
350 Main Street, Malden, MA 02148-5020, USA
9600 Garsington Road, Oxford, OX4 2DQ, UK
The Atrium, Southern Gate, Chichester, West Sussex, PO19 8SQ, UK

For details of our global editorial offices, for customer services, and for information about how to apply for permission to reuse the copyright material in this book please see our website at www.wiley.com/wiley-blackwell.

The right of Maria Luca to be identified as the authors of the editorial material in this work has been asserted in accordance with the UK Copyright, Designs and Patents Act 1988.

Library of Congress Cataloging-in-Publication Data
Sexual attraction in therapy : clinical perspectives on moving beyond the taboo : a guide for training and practice / edited by Maria Luca.
     pages cm
  Includes bibliographical references and index.
  ISBN 978-1-118-67434-5 (cloth) – ISBN 978-1-118-67433-8 (pbk.)   1. Psychotherapy–Practice.
2. Clinical psychologists–Training of 3. Psychotherapists–Sexual behavior.   4. Psychotherapist and patient.   I. Luca, Maria, 1956– editor of compilation.
  RC465.5.S48 2014
  616.89′14–dc23

                                    2013036259

A catalogue record for this book is available from the British Library.

Cover image: Kazimir Severinovich Malevich, Torso, 1928-32, oil on canvas (detail). State Russian Museum, St. Petersburg, Russia / The Bridgeman Art Library.
Cover design by Simon Levy Associates

Set in 11/13.5pt SabonLTStd by Toppan Best-set Premedia Limited
Printed in Malaysia by Ho Printing (M) Sdn Bhd

1   2014

Dedication
To Stefanos, Andreas, Marianna and Maria

Contents

Notes on Contributors

Anthony Arcuri, DPsy, is a Counselling and Clinical Psychologist who has completed Doctoral studies in Counselling Psychology and has practised psychotherapy, conducted research and taught across various settings. He currently operates a private practice in Sydney, Australia.

Michael D. Berry is a PhD candidate and counselling trainee, working in the Department of Clinical, Educational and Health Psychology at University College London. His work examines the use of dynamic psychotherapies in treating sexual and relationship issues, and appears in sex therapy journals, psychology journals and psychoanalytic publications. His research is supported by a grant from the American Psychoanalytic Association.

Richard Blonna, EdD, is a university professor with over 30 years of experience teaching human sexuality. He is a Board Certified Coach (BCC), Counselor (NCC) and Health Education Specialist (CHES) and the author of the best-selling college textbook, Blonna, R., & Cook-Carter, L. (2013). *Healthy sexuality* (2nd ed.). Dubuque, IA: Kendall-Hunt Publishers. His groundbreaking new book, Blonna, R. (2012). *SEX-ACT: Unleash the power of your sexual mind with acceptance and commitment therapy*. Charleston, SC: CreateSpace Publishers, is the only book devoted entirely to applying acceptance commitment therapy (ACT) to improving one's sex life.

Mark Boyden, MBA, Dip (Marketing), MA (Psychotherapy), MBACP & UKCP Accredited Psychotherapist. He completed his MBA at Oxford Brookes, and the advanced management programme from Templeton

College at Oxford University. He followed a series of psychotherapy trainings, including cognitive analytic therapy (CAT), and worked as a psychotherapist at Guys Hospital for 3 years. His clinical experience includes work with teenagers and young adults and psychotherapy through new media. Prior to training in psychotherapy, he ran complex departments in both private and voluntary organizations as well as two businesses. He is an Associate Member of the Institute of Management Consultants. Mark spent 7 years in France working for the Aga Khan Development Network. He maintains a private practice based at various London locations and in Dorset.

Malcolm Cross, PhD, was formally Dean of Students and a Reader in Psychology at City University London. He was elected Chair of the Division of Counselling Psychology of the British Psychological Society (BPS) Division in 2007–2009. He has worked as a senior manager in the higher education and not-for-profit sectors and served in a voluntary capacity on a range of BPS committees over the past decade. He is also a council member of the Health Professions Council. He has authored and edited three books and numerous chapters and peer-reviewed publications. He is regular contributor to print and broadcast media in the area of gender and masculinity.

Steven M. Harris, PhD, LMFT, is Director of the Couple and Family Therapy Programme at the University of Minnesota. He has also been practising as a marriage and family therapist for over 23 years. He has conducted research and presented on the topic of sexual attraction in therapy throughout his career. One focus of his research agenda is on the ethical delivery of mental health services with particular attention to the dynamics of sexual attraction.

Maria Luca, PhD, is Reader in Psychotherapy and Counselling Psychology and the Head of the Reflections Research Centre at Regent's University London. She teaches modules on sexual dynamics in therapy, assessment and formulation, and grounded theory. She has extensive clinical experience as a psychotherapist in the British National Health Service and has a small private practice in London. Maria gained her PhD from the University of Kent at Canterbury and is a registered psychotherapist with the United Kingdom Council for Psychotherapy and an accredited supervisor with the British Association for Counselling & Psychotherapy. She is editor of the book *The therapeutic frame in the clinical context – Integrative perspectives.* (2004). London: Brunner-Routledge, and author of book chapters and articles in journals. Among other publications on the subject, she is author of (2003) 'Containment of the Sexualized and Erotized Transference', *Journal of Clinical Psychoanalysis*, Vol. 11 No. 4.

Desa Markovic, DPsy, is Programme Director of the Masters in Psychotherapy & Counselling, Regent's University, London. She is a systemic Family Therapist, supervisor and trainer for over 20 years in the United Kingdom; she also qualified as a psychosexual therapist. She has written and published, taught, presented and practised clinically in the context of integrating systemic and sex therapy and has created a model of integration of systemic and sex therapy developed through many years of working with clients presenting a wide range of sexual issues. Some of her more recent articles on the subject were published in the *Australian and New Zealand Journal of Family Therapy* and *Sexual and Relationship Therapy Journal*.

Anna Marshall, DPsy, is a counselling psychologist registered with the health professions council. Anna gained her BSc (Hons) in Psychology from Royal Holloway, University of London, her MSc in Health Psychology from City University, London, and her PsychD in Counselling Psychology from the University of Surrey.

Doris McIlwain, PhD, is Associate Professor in Psychology at Macquarie University, Australia, teaching personality and philosophy of psychoanalysis, supervising many postgraduate students and clinical interns alike. Researching emotion and personality, she profiles narcissism, Machiavellianism and psychopathy in terms of affective personality dispositions. She is interested in self-reflective awareness of the bodily broadcast and pursues this new interest exploring colonizing the body via participant observation and experimental research into the practice of yoga. An enduring interest is in charismatic leader–follower relations, and she has a book on that subject and an encyclopedia article in press. She has published in psychology and philosophy journals as well as literary journals like *Meanjin* and *Artlink*. She does yoga, throws pots, loves poetry and has a small private practice.

Martin Milton, DPsych, CPsychol, CSci, AFBPsS, UKCP Reg, is Director of Counselling Psychology programmes at Regents University London. He also runs an independent practice in psychotherapy and supervision. He is a counselling psychologist chartered with the BPS, a BPS registered psychologist specializing in psychotherapy and a UKCP registered psychotherapist. Martin gained his BA from the University of Natal (Durban), his BA (Hons) from the University of South Africa, his MA (Antioch) from the School of Psychotherapy and Counselling Psychology at Regents

College and his DPsych from City University (London). He is author of several articles, chapters and books.

Kirsten W. Murray, PhD, is an associate professor in The Department of Counsellor Education at The University of Montana. Her interests include supervisory practices and sexuality competencies for counsellor training. She has taught graduate-level courses in subjects of supervision and sexuality for counselors and has been a clinical supervisor since 2002.

John Nuttall, PhD, is Head of the School Psychotherapy and Psychology at Regent's University London and also lectures at the University of Greenwich. He is an honorary psychotherapist and Chair of West London Centre for Counselling, and is a UKCP and BACP accredited psychotherapist, a Certified Management Consultant, and Chartered Marketer. He has written widely on management and psychotherapy and his PhD focused on the process of personal psychotherapy integration. His special interests include psychotherapy integration, organization theory and the provision of psychotherapy in the community.

John Penny, DPsych, is a chartered psychologist. Following a successful career in teaching and educational management, and having achieved his Chartership as a Counselling Psychologist, John worked in the prison service and in the British National Health Service before establishing a successful private practice. He now divides his time between psychotherapy, psychological assessments, supervision work and writing.

Andrea Sabbadini, C. Psychol., is a Fellow of the British Psychoanalytical Society, its former Honorary Secretary and its current Director of Publications. He works in private practice in London. A former director of the Arbours Training Programme in Psychotherapy, he also taught at Regent's University London for 20 years. He is currently a Senior Lecturer at University College London, a trustee of the Freud Museum, a member of the IPA Committee on Psychoanalysis and Culture, the director of the European Psychoanalytic Film Festival and the chairman of a programme of films and discussions at the Institute of Contemporary Arts (ICA). He was the founder editor of *Psychoanalysis and History* and is currently the Film Section editor of *The International Journal of Psychoanalysis*. He has published in the major psychoanalytic journals, and has edited *Il tempo in psicoanalisi* (1979), *Even Paranoids Have Enemies* (1998), *The Couch and the Silver Screen* (2003), *Projected Shadows* (2007) and *Psychoanalytic Visions of Cinema* (2007).

Paul Smith-Pickard, DPsych, is an existential psychotherapist in private practice. He is a former chair of the society for existential analysis. His interest in embodiment, sexuality, addiction and radical approaches to therapeutic practice are reflected in various book chapters, journal articles and conference papers he has written and delivered. He spends his time between his home in Dorset and his home in Greece, where he is a visiting lecturer in existential thought and practice at *Gignesthai* in Athens.

John Sommers-Flanagan, PhD, is Professor at the Department of Counsellor Education at the University of Montana. He is a Psychologist, Counsellor Educator, author of 'How to Listen So Parents Will Talk', 'Clinical Interviewing' and 'Tough Kids and Cool Counselling'.

Juliet Soskice, MA, graduated from Oxford University and worked in advertising and the civil service before training at the School of Psychotherapy and Psychology. She now has a psychotherapy practice in central London.

Tina M. Timm, PhD, is an associate professor in the School of Social Work at Michigan State University. Licensed as both a marriage and family therapist and a clinical social worker, she has spent her 20-year career focusing on clinical issues related to sexuality. Her training as a sex therapist provides a unique perspective on sexual attraction in conjoint therapy.

Michael Worrell, PhD, is Programme Director and Consultant Clinical Psychologist, Royal Holloway University of London & Central and North West London Foundation NHS Trust, Postgraduate Training Programmes in Cognitive Behavioural Therapy; responsible for overall management, Academic and Clinical Standards across the full range of Postgraduate Programmes including the Postgraduate Diploma/MSc in CBT, The IAPT High Intensity training programme and the Development of Post Graduate Certificate courses in CBT Supervision Skills. Both diploma programmes are Level 2 Accredited programmes with the British Association for Behavioural and Cognitive Psychotherapies (BABCP). He is author of several articles and chapters.

Acknowledgements

All anthologies are collaborative enterprises, including this one. All contributors have worked diligently to make this project viable, and I feel incredibly fortunate to have worked with such erudite scholars. My deep thanks go to my family, friends and colleagues for supporting my work on this volume. I would like to say a special thank you to Michael D. Berry for his assistance in formatting the manuscript and to John Nuttall and Stelios Gkouskos for their comments on my co-authored chapters. Thank you to my students, my clients and supervisees who are always important sources of inspiration. Finally, I would like to extend my thanks to Darren Reed (Senior Commissioning Editor), Karen Shield (Senior Project Editor), Olivia Evans (Editorial Assistant), and the rest of the publishing team for seeing the manuscript through to publication.

Editorial Introduction
An Encounter with Erotic Desire in Therapy

Maria Luca

This book is a study of sexual attraction. Anyone who studies sexual attraction will know that no particular discipline has claim over the subject. Hence, philosophers, anthropologists, sociologists, psychologists and psychotherapists all have much to reveal about the topic. We all in our own ways attempt to reduce such an irreducible human experience and give it the substance our intellect hungers for. This book has no intention of embarking on reductions. This book is situated in the various ways it seeks to begin with the therapy subjects, as they relate to each other in ordinary therapeutic relationships, that is, as involved in particular sexual attraction situations. It is within this space that erotic desire appears demanding a response.

The present collection was inspired by my experience as a supervisor, clinician and teacher of psychotherapy. Having witnessed the unsettling journeys of clinicians in their attempts to grapple with their own sexual attraction to a client or know how to handle a client's sexual desire, I decided it was time to give it the unique place it deserves. As Giles (2008) states:

> It does not take particularly great powers of observation to see that sexual matters are everywhere, that sexual meanings infiltrate and imbue our daily interactions, that sexual glances are forever being made, that sexual fantasies quietly attend our dealings with numerous people, that a person's gender and sexual attractiveness fundamentally determine how we react to him or her . . . (p. 2)

To this it could be said that the therapy consulting room actors would not be immune. After all, therapy is a microcosm of the wider world and human actors are subjects who relate to each other with the agency characterizing their existence as a whole. The chapters included here offer different perspectives on the handling of sexual attraction in therapy. Despite differences in theoretical approach, style, angle and methodology, these perspectives share a common thread that binds them together in their attempt to move beyond the taboo and reveal the consequences on therapy of the neglect surrounding this subject.

Therapists' encounter with erotic desire is never quite one of clear recognition, but more a play at the edges of knowing. As Oliver (2005) puts it, 'our part is not knowing, but looking, and touching, and loving' (p. 72). When we stumble upon the novel territory of desire, we may become blinded by its forcefulness and intensity, thus fear it and run as far away from it as possible. Despite the increasing proliferation of therapy modalities, there is a wide gap in the much-needed multimodal discourse on the topic. The book provides such discourse through giving supremacy to embodied and relational theoretical constructions of sexual attraction, illustrating through clinical material what clinicians of different modalities make of a phenomenon surrounded by much taboo. Thus, the book is about an embodied encounter and handling of desire for therapeutic means. As intimated by Mann (1997), 'The purpose of the erotic bond is that it deepens the individual's capacity for connection and relatedness to others as well as to him or herself' (p. 2).

Recent literature makes it known that 'therapists lack the language to engage with sexual material. Thus, instead of working with such issues, therapists responded to patients in ways that were rejecting, judgemental, condescending or moralistic, thereby bringing the therapy to a premature end' (Lichtenberg, 2008, p. 141). To this end, this collection, attempts to provide a way of talking about sexual desire that harmonizes with actual therapy experience, seeking to overcome the practical limitations and consequences of a common therapeutic avoidance, connected with this subject. Recent literature (Celenza, 2010; Mann, 1997) has notable exceptions in the recognition that the erotic in therapy can be transformational.

In the words of Jeanrond:

> Human desire for the other arises out of the experience of difference or radical otherness. No experience of love can ever remove from us our individuality and our personal journey towards death, but it can make that journey through life, toward our individual and personal deaths, different. Love has the potential to transform our lives (Jeanrond, 2007, p. 254).

In this introduction, I begin by giving an example from my own journey in recognizing and handling desire for the benefits of a client. This is intended to give a flavour of how the book opens the therapy consulting room space to the gaze of you, the reader, inviting you to encounter desire through the contributors' unique perspectives.

An Entry from My Therapeutic Diary

Albert, a man in his late 30s, in the fourth year of his psychotherapy, who was suicidal, had a systematic mistrust of the world; in fact, he hated it and wished he had not been born. He provided numerous rationalizations of the world he constructed in his mind, full of egoistic people that should be dead rather than 'on the loose, causing misery around them'. There was nothing in his life that had meaning except Ginger, his cat. Although he was successful in his job, his narrative revolved around conflicts with others and his sessions were populated by descriptions of nasty, selfish, greedy, disgusting 'bastards' who had no interest in others. Albert waged a war against the world. I worried sometimes that one day someone out there might attack him, especially during one of the 'road rage' incidents where he would get out of his car screaming abuse at a driver who attempted to overtake him from the inside lane. He admitted hating himself too and hating the mother he had not seen for many years through his own choice. Albert's mother tortured him emotionally and often disappeared, leaving him to fend for himself from as far back as he could remember. She told him that he was conceived in an act of rape, the impact of which was evident in Albert's hatred of the world and of himself. His sense of aloneness and a feeling of not belonging to the human race were key presenting concerns, but he mostly feared that his murderous rage would land him in prison, and he'd much rather be dead than trapped.

Albert waited with indifference for his death. In fact, this was his only consolation in life: that his rage and hatred for the world would one day come to an end; in his mind, 'the sooner the better'. His suffering tormented me and his dismissal of my tenderness for him, was disconcerting. He had no love for anyone and expected no love. For him, love was an alien concept; he was on the outside of it. The space he inhabited demolished hope for human empathy and understanding. There was no one coming towards him, no one interested, only silence and a dark void. Whenever he made telephone contact with me to cancel a session, something he rarely did, he would pre-empt the conversation with 'It is Albert, your client'. He believed I had not held him in mind and that he was just a name on my psychotherapy list.

When sufficient meaning had been made of Albert's predicament, particularly his coming to terms with a cold, rejecting mother, and much cathartic work was out of the way, he confronted the cold, rejecting internalized mother and the rage associated with her he became accessible. I felt more connected with him. He no longer fought to keep me at a distance. In fact, he arrived for sessions with a warm, big smile on his face, telling me how much the sessions meant to him. He could hardly wait to come to his sessions. I also enjoyed sessions with him. He was endearing and my tenderness for him had increased enormously. I listened out for the whispers that revealed the presence of self-worth, to prepare Albert for a self-validating life, a life without the constant shadow cast upon it by death. In one of his sessions, Albert announced that each time he walked out the consulting room door, he no longer felt he went straight over a cliff. The world inside the therapy room and the world outside were not so vastly different anymore.

Albert began to share his feelings about me more openly. His statement to me, 'I like to rest myself in your thoughts', resonated with a sense that he had achieved the emotional connection he so craved for. The arrival of sexual dreams where the woman he so desired scorned and ridiculed him did not surprise me. Although Albert allowed himself to feel loved by me, developmentally he was not ready to own his potency as a man. For him, potency was equated with violence and intimacy with rejection. He recognized that he was anxious that women would reject him or worse, he might harm them. In his fourth year of therapy, as he was leaving his session, Albert accidentally brushed himself against me and apologized profusely. I was able to acknowledge his need for warmth through touch and did not reject him. On another occasion, again as he was leaving his session, he kissed me on the cheek and said, 'I've been wanting to do that for a long time'. While Albert previously kept his erotic desires for women and for his therapist at bay, both to protect himself and his therapist, through a process of differentiating himself from a hateful mother, he could get in touch with his sadness. This paved the way for deeper work, where Albert's loving sentiment accompanied by sexual desire manifested in his openly flirtatious and seductive behaviour towards me. During this phase of the work, I, too, felt Albert as an attractive and desirable man and took this to be an indication of a transformational therapy experience, where his previous absence or *lack of* a loving and lovable self was now more fully embodied in a mutual encounter with desire. Albert's aggression and rage captured in his wish to be dead had softened and his self-hatred transformed into feeling worthy of another's love. He soon met a young woman with whom he formed an intimate relationship.

The man described in the above-mentioned illustration exemplifies that sexual attraction, if handled with sensitivity, can be liberating and transformational for a client. If a therapist can embrace the client's as well as her/his sexual desire and facilitate the development of intimacy in a 'measured', embodied fashion, with sentiment and feeling, not pure technique or avoidance, the therapy becomes a vehicle for an authentic, relational and transformational therapy experience.

Anyone who studies psychotherapy, clinical and counselling psychology will recognize something of themselves in this book. Those with curiosity about sexual attraction in a therapeutic relationship will learn that, despite the fears and anxieties such a topic may evoke, the topic is situated in the lives of clinicians; it is therefore a normal, albeit intensity-infused subject. No particular clinical discipline has exclusive claim on this topic. Hence, all clinicians of different disciplines and theoretical orientations have something to say about this pressing topic. To avoid missing out on the valuable understandings of clinicians generally, I have undertaken to be as inclusive as possible, by inviting scholars from different disciplines and perspectives to contribute chapters from their own unique theoretical, clinical and research vantage points. Almost without exception, the authors have worked diligently under the scrutiny of the editor to revise their work to bring it to its present quality. I am grateful to all contributors for their commitment to do justice to such a complex therapeutic manifestation.

My interest in the topic has been evolving for many years since my own very first experience of a seductive male client expressing sexual desire towards me when I was an honorary psychotherapist. I became worried and wondered whether I had the capacity not to make a mess of his therapy, with my anticipated anxiety that if I did, there was a risk of a premature ending to the work. Luckily, my then supervisor helped me recognize the clinical significance of the manifestation of my client's sexual desire so that I could manage the intense feelings it evoked in me. Of paramount significance was my learning that therapy involves an intersubjective connection between two people and that it should not be surprising that sexual desire may emerge as part of the intimacy continuum.

The ideas in this book have been developed through mine and my collaborators' teachings, practice and research of sexual attraction in therapy. I have personally learned a great deal from supervising students' projects, particularly those linked to sexuality and sexual attraction. My readings and writings of erotic, erotized, sexual and sexualized transference and countertransference topics have guided my understanding and practice for many years. However, I feel that the field is now in need of furthering our understanding of sexual attraction in therapy, from a new vantage point and from a variety of perspectives.

I have benefitted from discussions with friends, colleagues and students alike, and in the process, I have come to think about the experience of sexual attraction in therapy as normal and often an inevitable process of healing. So, why should it matter so much how sexual attraction in therapy is experienced and managed by therapists? Having often witnessed how such an experience evokes powerful feelings of fear, anxiety, shame and guilt in therapists, often to the detriment of the therapy process, I believe we need to give the topic the centrality it deserves to help us move beyond the taboo and learn to manage such situations more effectively.

The book's intention is to help students, researchers and those in clinical practice understand the permutations of sexual attraction and learn to embrace it as a manifestation of the human condition, not to avoid or fear it but to attempt to capture its essence as a meaningful occurrence of therapy relationships with transformational potential. The book is peppered with case vignettes and clinical examples. These are developed to help readers see how an idea translates into practice. It also raises important questions rather than answers to invite the reader into deeper reflective practice. Each chapter offers insights on what sexual attraction is, as well as clinical strategies for working with it. Together, they reveal the endless complexity and richness of perspective on sexual attraction. Rather than sum up a single perspective and widen its field, the diversity of this volume seeks to promote new perspectives on sexual attraction, new ways of thinking and new ways of working with it.

The topic of sexual desire and attraction is an existential concern as it is rooted in our everyday life. Sexuality, sexual desire and their manifestation in relation to another are givens of our existence. They are at the core of our human connectedness, no matter how difficult to define. I believe that if we accept sexual attraction as an intrinsic aspect of our fundamentally human condition, then it follows that it would naturally find its way into the consulting room. The book will provide highlights from the consulting rooms of many, while at the same time restricting the content and disguising the agents so that confidentiality and anonymity remain intact.

I hope that the book is received as a torch for further innovative and creative psychological investigations on sexual attraction in therapy.

Maria Luca
June 2013

References

Celenza, A. (2010). The guilty pleasure of erotic countertransference: Searching for radial true. *Studies in Gender and Sexuality*, *11*, 175–183.

Giles, J. (2008). *The nature of sexual desire*. Plymouth: UPA.

Jeanrond, W. G. (2007). *LOVE ENLIGHTENED – The promises and ambiguities of love*. Retrieved from http://www.catho-theo.net 6 pp. 253–281, http://www.catho-theo.net/Love-enlightened.

Lichtenberg, J. W. (2008). *Sensuality and sexuality across the divide of shame*. New York: The Analytic Press.

Mann, D. (1997). *Psychotherapy, an erotic relationship*. London: Routledge.

Oliver, M. (2005). *New and selected poems* (Vol. 2). Boston: Beacon Press.

Part I

Relational Perspectives on Sexual Attraction in Therapy

1

'Hot Cognition in Sexual Attraction'

Clarifying, Using and Defusing the Dionysian in Cognitive Behavioural Psychotherapies

Michael Worrell

A young-ish male therapist walks downstairs to meet a new client for an initial assessment session. The setting is a shabby NHS out-patient psychology department. Sitting in the waiting room is a well-dressed young female client who regards the approaching therapist with a detached look of mild curiosity. The therapist greets the client and asks her to follow him upstairs to the consulting room. The client says nothing and follows as directed. The therapist has already noted that this new client is well dressed, composed and out of place in this grey and grubby environment that the therapist has increasingly come to experience as oppressive.

Upon sitting down in the comfortable but worn chairs, the therapist somewhat lazily starts the session with the usual enquiry "so . . . what is it that brings you here today?". The client does not respond immediately with the usual rush of description regarding anxiety or low mood but instead looks into the distance in an apparently reflective manner. The therapist thinks to himself "how interesting . . . she seems pretty reflective . . . really composed . . . she looks a bit European . . . quite sophisticated." He sits up straighter in and pays more attention. There is some sense of discomfort as well, a vague anxiety. Finally, the client responds. "You know . . . sometimes I think there is nothing at all going on inside my head . . ." instantly the spell is broken . . .[1]

[1] All case materials presented in this chapter are fictional.

Sexual Attraction in Therapy: Clinical Perspectives on Moving Beyond the Taboo – A Guide for Training and Practice, First Edition. Edited by Maria Luca.
© 2014 John Wiley & Sons, Ltd. Published 2014 by John Wiley & Sons, Ltd.

Russ (1993), writing from a psychodynamic perspective, suggests that 'Sexual Drama infuses therapy'. Is sexual attraction between a therapist and a client a phenomenon encountered in cognitive behavioural therapy (CBT)? If one were to judge this according to the amount of theoretical or research literature devoted to this topic within CBT, in comparison to the psychodynamic literature, one would conclude that it is either nonexistent or of such small significance as to not warrant attention. In fact, at the time of writing, there appear to be no substantive theoretical contributions nor research reports that specifically address sexual attraction between therapists and clients within CBT. Possibly, the domain of sexual dynamics in therapy is one that has been seen by CBT therapists as the preserve of the psychodynamically inclined, an area of enquiry that has long ago been demarcated as alien territory. In seeking to address the topic of 'sexual attraction in CBT', it is useful to briefly outline some of the essential aspects of CBT that will function as part of the context for how sexual attraction might be disclosed and responded to. A consideration of some of these features may also go some way towards explaining the lack of attention given to this phenomenon by CBT therapists.

What Is CBT?

The field of the cognitive and behavioural therapies has expanded considerably in recent years and it has become increasingly difficult to make generalizations that would cover all its variations of theory and practice. CBT is increasingly an umbrella term for a range of approaches that share a concern with developing an empirically grounded approach to psychotherapy. In this chapter I will primarily be concerned with discussing what might be referred to as 'Beckian' CBT, that approach to CBT developed by Aaron Beck and his colleagues (Beck, 1976). This seems to me to be appropriate, given that Beckian CBT is likely the most widely practised form of CBT worldwide and also the version of CBT that has been the most productive in terms of research and theory development. Beckian CBT can, in some senses, be regarded as the 'standard version' or 'mainstream CBT'. Perhaps the most important feature of CBT in regard to the present topic, and the feature that has led to the most criticism and challenge from therapists of other orientations, is the relative importance placed on the therapeutic relationship. In contrast to relationally oriented forms of psychotherapy that see the relationship between client and therapist as the primary, if not sole, driver of beneficial change, CBT practitioners regard a good therapeutic relationship as *necessary* but not *sufficient* for beneficial change to occur. CBT has tended to place a strong emphasis on specific technical interventions and skills as the primary driver for therapeutic outcomes. The therapist in CBT explicitly takes up a role of collaborating with clients to identify new cognitive and behavioural skills that may be of benefit in addressing the difficulties the clients experience in their day to day lives. In contrast to approaches to psychotherapy that seek to create and subsequently manage a particular type of relationship, that for its effectiveness needs in some important senses to be seen as separate and different from the client's everyday life (a container or vessel that needs to have strong boundaries to eliminate potential contaminants from the 'outside world'), the CBT therapist's focus is primarily upon what is happening 'outside' of sessions, in the client's everyday world. In fact, CBT therapists will very frequently venture into the client's world in a direct fashion, whereby therapy sessions (such as exposure work for phobias) may take place in the clients home, in a supermarket or in a crowded lift.

Therapy sessions in CBT are usually highly structured, with a clear agenda set at the beginning of sessions, and efforts made at the end of sessions to review what has been covered and to seek clear and direct feedback from clients regarding how the session was experienced. This emphasis on structured sessions and an active–directive stance of the therapist, has led some to criticize CBT therapists for apparently taking up an 'expert position', seeking to control clients and to teach them how to think or how to behave. In response, CBT therapists have argued that, in fact, what is sought is a highly collaborative relationship with clients where there are two experts present. The client is seen as an expert on his or her own experience, thinking and feelings, and the therapist is an expert in general patterns and strategies that have been found to be helpful. The task, as seen by CBT therapists, is to engage with the client in a joint effort to work on those areas of living identified by the client as problematic. CBT, on the whole, also tends towards a short- to medium-term intervention with sessions ranging anywhere between 6 and 24 sessions.

Brief Encounters: Does Sexual Attraction Show Up in CBT?

The previously mentioned, admittedly brief and incomplete, characterization of standard CBT serves to provide some context for understanding how sexual attraction may show up or, perhaps far more frequently, may not show up (explicitly) in CBT. It is possible that dilemmas around sexual attraction between therapist and client are far more likely to become activated in therapies that are of a long-term duration and in which the therapist takes an explicitly relational focus. It is possible that the highly focused and structured nature of CBT functions to prevent sexual attraction from coming to the awareness of the therapist or the client, or, at most, serves to keep such phenomena safely in the background. It is possible but, I suspect, highly unlikely. Any consideration of one's own experience of the vagaries of sexual attraction indicates that this can show up in a wide range of contexts and does not require a specific time context. Where would the field of romantic literature be without the concept of 'Love at first sight'?

I am unaware of any research that reports on incidents of CBT therapists experiencing sexual attraction in therapy (either client attraction to therapist or therapist towards client) or data on how CBT therapists respond to and manage such experiences. Rodolfa et al. (1994), however, report on a survey of over 900 members of the American Psychological Association. While they obtained a typically low return rate of 43%, the findings are striking in that only 12% of respondents indicated that they had never experienced sexual attraction towards a client in therapy. These authors do not report on the theoretical orientation of the respondents; however, it is reasonable to suppose that at least some of these practising psychologists will have been working from a CBT orientation. If we assume that CBT therapists are as likely to encounter the phenomenon of sexual attraction in therapy as are other therapists, it is also reasonable to assume that this experience provokes for them the same anxieties and concerns as that which has been reported in the literature for practising therapists more generally (Pope, Sonne, & Holroyd, 1995).

The experience of anxiety (as well as a wide range of other emotions) is highly understandable when encountering phenomena of sexual attraction in therapy. There is now a very widely shared understanding among psychological therapists of all orientations that actual sexual contact between therapist and client is likely to be highly damaging to the client, is an abuse of the power relationship between therapist and client, and, in addition, is in direct violation of professional ethical codes. While CBT training in the United Kingdom will routinely cover the ethical dimension of practice, it would be unusual, in my experience, for the topic of sexual attraction in therapy to be delivered as part of formal lectures or workshops. The result, particularly for beginning CBT therapists, is likely to be the activation of anxiety when this phenomenon is encountered as it will be experienced as 'This is not who and how I should be as a CBT therapist!' A particularly useful concept in contemporary CBT is the notion of 'thought–action fusion' (Wells, 1995). This concept refers to the beliefs clients (or therapists) may hold about the operation of their own minds. This can refer, for example, to beliefs such as 'if I experience a thought, image or feeling, this must mean something about me, it means that I must want to do this thing and am in danger of doing so'. Such beliefs have been found to be particularly important in obsessional difficulties. While it will be understandable to experience a degree of anxiety in response to sexual attraction for a client (or being the recipient of sexual attraction from a client), this anxiety is likely to be that much stronger and distressing to the degree that the therapist's reactions demonstrate thought–action fusion. Efforts to avoid or suppress thoughts have also been found to have a counterproductive effect in that this serves to increase the salience and frequency of the avoided thoughts (Wells, 1995). Of course, as will be discussed further, sexual attraction may not be reducible to thoughts.

It is likely to be beneficial for CBT therapists that the topic of sexual attraction is more frequently raised in training in order to support therapists to respond appropriately and effectively if and when this is encountered. In my view, a range of recent developments within CBT have extended the range and flexibility of this model and provide a framework that may allow for theoretical and research work to be conducted on this topic.

Developments in CBT: Integration and Expansion

As the theoretical and research base of CBT has continued to be developed, and as the approach has been extended to work with clients presenting with more complex and enduring difficulties (such as clients experiencing difficulties that result in them being diagnosed as having 'personality disorders'), there has been significant reconsideration of some basic principles. Perhaps the most significant of these has been a deepened appreciation for the role of the therapeutic relationship and emotion.

While CBT has maintained its perspective on the therapeutic relationship as being necessary but not sufficient for beneficial change, the emerging research, from within CBT, has indicated that the therapeutic relationship holds far more variance in terms of outcome than had been appreciated (Waddington, 2002). Contemporary CBT can be seen to be moving beyond a somewhat 'black and white' approach that contrasts technique with relationship to a perspective that acknowledges that all technical interventions can also be seen as relational interventions. There is a recognition also that the appropriate application of CBT strategies can also help to support the development of optimally supportive (and challenging) therapeutic relationships. Additionally, contemporary CBT has placed a greater emphasis on emotion in therapy such that the 'cold and intellectual' discussion of cognition is seen as insufficient and that, instead, the focus of work must be on 'hot cognition', that is, cognition that is closely tied to client emotion. A related development has been those efforts directed to integrating a more interpersonal perspective within CBT. Safran and Muran (2000), for example, have argued convincingly that the core beliefs and schemas highlighted by CBT as being implicated in forms of psychological suffering are inherently interpersonal and concern self–other relationships as much as self–self relationships. The purpose of this chapter is not to review these or a range of other equally relevant developments in depth. However, it does seem to me that theoretical and clinical developments that open the possibility for CBT therapists to consider the therapeutic relationship, emotion and interpersonal experience in more depth also open the way for a consideration of sexual attraction in therapy.

While current developments in CBT may potentially make room for thinking about the phenomena of sexual attraction in therapy, might it not also be that doing so in any depth may also provoke further challenges for CBT theory and practice? In my view, the development of a CBT perspective on sexual attraction in therapy challenges CBT to consider in greater depth its perspective on 'embodiment' and the relative emphasis it has placed on the 'computer metaphor'.

Computer Love

A primary metaphor for CBT has been the 'mind as computer' as it has also been for cognitive science more broadly. Clark (1995), for example, asserts that a fundamental postulate of CBT is that all acts of perception, learning and knowing are the products of an active 'information processing system' that selectively attends to the environment, filters and then interprets the information impinging upon the organism. Such 'processing' of information is seen as evolutionarily adaptive. In psychopathological conditions, aspects of the information processing system are seen as having become 'distorted', biased or maladaptive, leading to experiences of emotional, behavioural and relational distress. The role of the CBT therapist is seen as assisting the individual to clarify their current patterns of information processing and to modify this through a range of strategies that encourage individuals to take on a more 'scientific' stance towards their own experience. Clark further states that in CBT:

The therapist and patient collaborate to identify distorted cognitions, which are derived from maladaptive beliefs or assumptions. These cognitions and beliefs are subjected to logical analysis and empirical hypothesis testing which leads individuals to realign their thinking with reality (Clark, 1995, p. 155).

As Safran (1998) has noted, the mind-as-computer analogy has been a highly productive one in cognitive psychology; however, this should not detract from a consideration of the ways in which the mind, and inter-personal experience, is not computer-like. I would suggest that troubling or disturbing instances where a therapist encounters sexual attraction in therapy are likely to be one of those occasions where the person-as-information processing system is likely to be found seriously wanting (reports of individuals who appear to develop attachment relationships with their computer equipment and hand-held devices notwithstanding). Indeed, in situations such as this, and many others besides, the therapist is likely to be confronted with the irreducible embodied nature of human interpersonal existence. Consider the following.

Collaborative Colin (CC) has been working with an older female client on her long-term problems with recurrent depression. He has taken an evidence-based approach and emphasized behavioural activation as well as cognitive disputation strategies, all of this to good effect. The client, who has been single all her life, has responded well to the emphasis on increasing her socialization; however, this has also brought to the fore her long-term anxieties and disappointments about relationships with men. Colin has noted that, as therapy has progressed, her self-presentation has improved. He has noted her wearing perfume and has complemented her on her improved self-care. Towards the end of a particularly productive session she looks CC directly in the eye and states 'I wish I could just take you home with me.' This statement and the look in her eye have an immediate physical effect on him. It feels like her statement is a physical caressing of his face and he experiences himself as both attracted and repelled at the same instant and is unable to say anything. In response to the attraction he feels shock and disbelief, and to the repulsion he feels a sense of guilt and struggles not to express either emotion in his bodily gestures or gaze. He mutters something about the value of her learning to become her own therapist and the session ends.

While in the previous example there are clear indications of interpreta-tive processes or cognitions, can the interaction or experiences described be reduced to the operations of information processing without something central being lost? Sitting with a client in CBT is not an experience of one information processing system encountering another for the purpose of some form of reprogramming, it is rather an embodied experience of being in the presence of another. The embodied nature of the therapeutic encounter is primary; the statement 'I wish I could just take you home with me' may indeed be offered and experienced as a caress of the face.

It is possible that a CBT perspective on sexuality and sexual attraction in therapy could be advanced by considering an integration of insights and perspectives from a wide range of sources. Some mainstream CBT practitioners, for example, have asserted the need to develop cognitive models of transference and countertransference (Guidano, 1991). Others have drawn upon insights from attachment theory and evolutionary biology and neuroscience (Gilbert, 2010). In my view, an alternative source to both challenge and develop a CBT perspective is that of existential phenomenology, and it is to a consideration of this possibility that I will now turn.

Existential Insight on Sexuality

Why seek to draw upon the insights of existential–phenomenological thought to clarify and expand a CBT perspective? Why not draw instead upon psychoanalytic thought and practice or some other form of psychotherapeutic thinking? As Ottens and Hanna (1998) state, at first sight, existential thinking, and the existential versions of therapy inspired by such, seems at opposite ends of the therapeutic spectrum to the behavioural and cognitive psychotherapies. However, there are, in fact, many points of potential contact principally surrounding the focus on 'meaning' in understanding psychological distress; in fact, Clark, Beck, and Allford (1999) have suggested that CBT finds its most compatible philosophical base in the field of existential phenomenology. Thus, it seems entirely reasonable to consider what an existential–phenomenological perspective on sexuality might provide for CBT practitioners wishing to consider the phenomenon of sexual attraction in therapy.

The contribution of existential–phenomenological philosophy, and existential therapies derived from this, to CBT practitioners is, in my view, the foregrounding of the inevitable aspects of human existence itself, or the 'givens' of existence. This includes the inherently 'interrelational' basis of human existence (the centrality of context), the unavoidability and indeed centrality of anxiety for human existence and, as is most relevant for the present discussion, that human existence is always embodied and sexual (Cohn, 1997; Spinelli, 2001). Admittedly, existential therapists themselves, such as Spinelli (2001), have noted that an existential perspective on sexuality has been curiously neglected (again perhaps due to a sense that this field is somehow owned by psychoanalysis). Nevertheless, a consideration of the work of one existential philosopher, Merleau-Ponty (1982), seems to offer avenues for development. As Spinelli writes, in taking a phenomenological approach to sexuality, Merleau-Ponty is setting aside analyses that principally focus on issues of gender and socialization as well as analyses that might focus on biological imperatives such as developmental or evolutionary theory.[2] The question for existential phenomenology is 'what is the essence of human sexuality?' Merleau-Ponty's philosophy places particular emphasis on the embodied nature of human existence. In this perspective, the body is not regarded as a 'thing' to which a consciousness is somehow attached or which acts as the vehicle for an encapsulated mind (or information processing system), but rather human existence is irreducibly an 'encarnated consciousness'. The body, for Merleau-Ponty, is the configuration through which our dialogue with the world is manifested. Sexuality, in turn, rather than being something that can be reduced to the effects of physiological or biological drives, is inherently 'intersubjective' in nature. As Spinelli writes:

> How we are, sexually, and what we enact sexually, therefore become statements not of reproductive drive but of our willingness, hesitation, delight and anxiety to explore the 'being-with' of self and other (2001, p. 8).

From this perspective then, sexuality and embodiment are 'givens' of human existence, an inevitable aspect of the context for human existence, implicitly present, if not explicitly clarified, in all psychotherapeutic encounters. Thus, 'sexual attraction', just as much as experiences of 'sexual repulsion' or 'sexual indifference', can be understood as a relational expression concerning, for example, 'who one wishes to be' in the world, and who one believes 'one cannot or should not be' in relation to self and other, topics discussed more fully in Chapters 3 and 5. How might such an existential perspective on sexuality inform a CBT perspective on sexual attraction in therapy?

---

[2] This in no way should be taken to mean that such considerations as gender and socialization should be considered of less importance for the present topic. The fact that the overwhelming number of instances of actual sexual contact between a therapist and a client occurs between a male therapist and a female client is sufficient justification for an in-depth and critical look at this aspect.

'Emotion Schemas' and Responding Flexibly or Inflexibly to Sexual Attraction in Therapy

Earlier CBT models have stressed the experience of emotion as being primarily an *outcome* of cognitive processing. Emotion is thus seen as, in some sense, secondary to, and consequential to, interpretative processes. Contemporary cognitive models, such as the 'metacognitive' model of Wells (1995) and the 'emotional schema' model of Robert Leahy (2002), have sought to extend this perspective. Leahy's model, for example, has sought to integrate insights from emotion-focused therapy (Greenberg & Paivio, 1997), which itself draws upon insights from existential philosophy as well as the humanistic models of Rogers and Fritz Perls. In this perspective, emotional experiencing and emotional processing in therapy is prioritized as it is argued that emotions are in themselves a form of information processing in which the experiencing of emotion allows an individual to access the meaning of events. Here, emotion is regarded as a 'prime mover' of cognition and not just a consequence of 'cold cognition'. Leahy's model attempts to integrate this insight into CBT and stresses various forms of cognitive and emotional processing, as well as behavioural coping styles, which come 'online' once an emotion becomes foreground for an individual. Emotions, including those centred on sexual attraction, thus become a 'given' of experience that an individual will subsequently process via 'emotional schemas' or beliefs, rules and action plans regarding what emotions may mean and how emotion should be responded to. Thus, once an individual experiences sexual attraction in a specific context, for example, they may then respond to this experience in accordance with a range of rules, beliefs and action tendencies. The model stresses both adaptive and maladaptive processes of emotional regulation and processing that may allow individuals either to experience their emotions as valuable, if at times distressing and disturbing, windows to insight about what is important, true or needing attention in their lives, versus anxiety- and distress-provoking experiences that are responded to with strategies of distraction, suppression and avoidance. How might such 'emotion schemas' and associated processes play out in instances of encountering sexual attraction in therapy? Let's consider the following.

Rational Ray (RR) has been a CBT therapist for over 10 years and comes from an impeccable academic background. He prides himself on the technical proficiency of his work and is fully convinced that therapeutic outcome is driven by the therapist's adherence with specific intervention protocols and procedures. RR has been working with a young female client presenting with a blood injury phobia. She is a post-graduate physics student. Highly verbal and intelligent, she understood the CBT model and treatment plan very quickly and was highly motivated for treatment. RR found himself looking forward to the therapy sessions as a highlight of his working week. He felt more alert and awake in sessions with her and worked in a particularly focused way to help this 'ideal client' overcome this one area of difficulty in her life that seemed to be holding her back. He was vaguely aware that he gave additional attention to how he dressed on her therapy days and he always managed to find the time to prepare for her session. He found himself thinking about her between sessions but quickly dismissed these thoughts other than to note 'ah yes . . . maybe we should try this new CBT strategy that I read about recently'. Therapy was very successful and the client left very happily. RR also felt very pleased and yet was aware of a sense of loss at the end of therapy and experienced a depressed mood for several weeks afterwards that he found difficult to conceptualize or communicate.

Perfectionistic Pat (PP) is a trainee CBT therapist. She loves CBT for its structure and evidence-based procedures and has worked incredibly hard in her training. She always prepares for therapy sessions and is also always well prepared for supervision, frequently bringing audio recordings of her client work for the supervisor to provide feedback on. She has been working with Bruce, a man in his mid-30s working in banking. He is a well-dressed, well-spoken and high-achieving individual with high expectations of CBT and his therapist to help him overcome a recently developed difficulty with social anxiety during work presentations. PP has received lots of positive feedback from her supervisor about the work that she has done with Bruce, and there has been significant progress. In a group supervision session PP states that she would like to bring back Bruce for discussion again and prefaces this with the statement 'You know . . . my guy . . .'. The supervisor notes this statement, and then during a playback of the last session, the supervisor (male) asks PP about her personal response to Bruce. It seems clear to the supervisor that the interaction between the two had bordered on being flirtatious. Presented with this feedback, PP experiences embarrassment but, not wanting to seem an 'avoidant' supervisee, acknowledges that she does indeed find her client 'a little' attractive and was aware of trying really hard to be a perfect therapist for him. After this supervision session, PP ruminates a great deal about this. She is flooded with negative thoughts along the lines of 'How can I be attracted to my client? This is just awful. I must be some sort of immoral individual in danger of acting out'. Her work with Bruce becomes bogged down as she attempts to rigidly adhere to the protocol and gives little room to enquiring how Bruce is experiencing their work together. In subsequent supervision sessions, she avoids speaking about Bruce, is notably withdrawn and her performance in training seems to decline. The supervisor struggles to understand what may be happening to this previously bright and engaged student.

Undeniably Straight Stan (US) is a CBT therapist in a primary care setting. He enjoys CBT but prides himself on having something of an 'integrative attitude' and likes to feel that he is person-centred and offers an authentic relationship with his clients, even when doing technical work like exposure. He has been working with Joe, a gay man with a degree of obsessions and compulsions around sexual thoughts. Joe is a very athletic and handsome man who shares US's interests in Rugby. US enjoys working with Joe and often feels that, had they met outside therapy, they could have been friends as they share many values and interests. During one session, where US had asked Joe to say out loud a range of sexual fantasies that Joe often responds to by forms of 'neutralizing' thoughts, US, to his surprise and alarm, finds himself becoming sexually aroused in a direct and undeniable fashion. US quickly brings the exposure work to a close, suggesting instead that Joe do this as a written assignment rather than live in the therapy. After this session, US goes home and has several glasses of beer and watches the Rugby but finds himself becoming irritated with his team's performance. In subsequent sessions with Joe, he becomes far more directive and structured, and therapy is brought to something of an abrupt ending several sessions later.

Enlightened Arnold (EA) has been a CBT therapist for over 10 years working often with highly distressed individuals, many diagnosed as presenting with 'personality disorders'. He feels himself to be 'burnt out' and is aware that his relationship with his partner has been suffering for several years and that they are disengaged from each other. He has struggled with his experience of burnout as he has always believed in the importance of providing therapy to this client group and he feels himself still committed to his high ethical standards. He has also over the last few months stopped doing many of the nonwork activities that he used to enjoy and has socialized less with friends. He has been working with Justine, a young woman with many features of borderline personality. She has been openly flirtatious with him in sessions and has sent provocative emails and text messages to him between sessions. He cannot now remember why he had thought her having access to his work mobile would be appropriate. Despite his high ethical standards, he finds himself thinking of her between sessions and has even had several obviously erotic dreams about her. His daytime fantasies have sometimes featured this client and involve themes of 'running away' as well as 'rescuing her from all this'. His is aware of finding her flirtatious remarks enjoyable, especially her remarks about him being a 'special therapist'. EA starts to recognize that this situation is now complex and risky for himself and his client. He takes the step of speaking to a trusted female colleague who listens carefully but also strongly confronts him about his need for much closer supervision of this case (he had not brought the case for supervision for several months). He also takes the risk of talking with her about his sense of burnout and his concerns about his relationship with his partner. The conversation is anxiety provoking for EA and he asks his colleague to recommend him to an individual therapist as he thinks this might be helpful both professionally and personally.

The above-mentioned examples illustrate several of the processes highlighted in Leahy's emotional schemas model. For example, RR demonstrates difficulties in 'emotional comprehensibility' whereby he shows deficits in an ability to recognize and make sense of his experience. This is also demonstrated with PP, who reacts to her experience with cognitions such as 'I should not be feeling this way, my feelings don't make sense'. PP also responds with processes of rumination that effectively block her ability to learn from her experience as well as cognitions that provoke guilt and shame responses that express the stance 'This is not who I should be, who I am allowed to be'. The case of US can be seen to illustrate the dimension of 'controllability', which refers to the degree to which individuals experience their emotions as something that could potentially overwhelm them. UC experienced the novel experience of homosexual arousal both as a challenge to his self-concept and also as an experience that could be overwhelming and needed to be managed with avoidance, suppression and substance use to numb his experience. By contrast, in the last example of EA, the factor of 'validation' is evident, where the therapist has the expectation that 'my emotional responses are understandable and will be received and understood by others'. This also illustrates the factors of 'acceptance' and 'simplicity versus complexity', whereby EA is able to both be open to his emotional experience of sexual attraction, rather than attempting to dismiss or 'get rid' of this, as well as a sense that there is a degree of complexity in his emotional response that requires reflection rather than impulsive action. Leahy also introduced into his model a concept derived from the existential model of Viktor Frankl, that of 'higher values'. In Leahy's model, this refers to the possibility that through the clarification and validation of emotional experience, individuals are also able to clarify what for them are important life values. This could potentially be seen to be operative in the case of EA, where he is willing to take the anxiety-provoking step of disclosing his experience to a colleague and being willing to experience her challenge of him, a challenge that would result in him needing to take further steps to address avoided areas in his life, in the interest of him staying true to the high ethical principles that he has chosen for his work.

The cases of RR and US discussed earlier are ones that might never have been discussed or considered in supervision or in an alternative consultative process. In the case of RR, it might also be that the experience of sexual attraction, which remained always a background one, did not in any way impede the effectiveness of the CBT intervention. The other cases, with the exception of EA, illustrate varying degrees to which the therapists' difficulties of 'staying with' and processing their experience, impacted upon the therapy in potentially unhelpful ways. Ideally, these would be experiences that the therapists concerned would feel able to bring to CBT supervision in the expectation that the supervisor, and the model itself, will have helpful things to say. Such explorations in supervision could include, for example, the clarification of how the experience of sexual attraction in therapy has confronted the therapist with 'possibilities of being' that are a challenge to the therapists' currently maintained view of themselves and others or are expressions of 'who and how I would like to be or be seen as being'. Contemporary third-wave approaches to CBT such as acceptance and commitment therapy (ACT) would also offer the therapists strategies of becoming mindfully aware of such experiences as well as being able to effectively 'defuse' from such thoughts and emotions in the service of staying committed to the values of providing safe and effective therapy for the client under challenging circumstances.

In order to promote this, in my view, there is more work to do in the field of CBT training and supervision research and theory development to support this. Potentially, this work will also further challenge and open up CBT to insights from sources outside of the current model.

CBT Training, Supervision and the 'Person of the Therapist'

Over the last several years, there has been a rapid expansion of CBT training. At the same time, there has been recognition within the field that there has been insufficient research and theory development in the areas of CBT training and supervision. What are the best training methods to develop effective and interpersonally skilled CBT therapists, and what supervision models and methods best support this development both for novice and experienced therapists?

A notable recent contribution towards developing a CBT perspective on how effective therapists develop has been Bennett-Levy's 'declarative–procedural–reflective' model (Bennett-Levy & Thwaites, 2007). Consistent with other models of therapist development, this model has stressed the centrality of 'reflection' and the necessity of therapists being able to both be open to, mindful of and accepting of their own experience as a potential source of learning. This model also distinguishes between what are referred to as 'declarative skills', which are skills and knowledge related to theory and models and techniques that can be learnt from reading, books and research, and 'procedural skills' that refer to, often implicit, 'when–then rules' for how to apply knowledge and skills in practice. According to Bennett-Levy, the key process that allows for the transition of declarative knowledge to procedural skills is reflection.

An additional novel contribution of this model is the emphasis it places upon 'the person of the therapist'. In this model, the training and supervision of CBT therapists also need to attend to the emotions, beliefs and 'rules for living' that are expressive of who the therapist is apart from their professional role. Bennett-Levy also argues that a key set of skills that has traditionally been ignored in CBT training is that of 'interpersonal perceptual skills'. This again refers to the embodied presence of the therapist and his or her relative level of skill in being able to perceive and process, in a thoughtful manner, the embodied presence of the client and the impact that this has upon them as they are interacting.

In my view, this model opens up the possibility for CBT therapists to pay far greater attention to phenomena such as encountering sexual attraction in therapy than has previously been the case. This move towards a more interpersonally attuned and embodied understanding of therapeutic practice is also consistent with Bennett-Levy's suggestions for far greater attention to be paid in the training of CBT therapists to processes that focus on the person of the therapist. Bennett-Levy has suggested a process of 'self-practice/self-reflection' that involves CBT therapists employing CBT strategies to explore, open up and challenge their own beliefs and experiences.

Clinical Strategies for the Management of Sexual Attraction in Therapy

Should CBT therapists, introduced at the very beginning of this paper, practise a form of self-practice/self-reflection on their briefly experienced encounter with attraction, they could potentially do the following:

1. Complete a self-monitoring record on the experience in which they clarify and describe the thoughts, feelings and behaviours that emerged in this incident.
2. Submit the various thoughts clarified, and possible implicit meanings within these, to various forms of reflection and questioning including, for example:
    i.   What were the qualities expressed by the other in this encounter, and in this context, that were associated with the experience of attraction?
    ii.   To what extent do these qualities express possibilities and challenges for me in terms of 'who I would like to be/not be/should not be' in the world?
    iii. What was my response, cognitively, emotionally and behaviourally to the experience of attraction? What did I 'do with it'? Did I attempt to avoid, distract and get rid of this, or did I elaborate, ruminate or focus on this experience? What does my response to this experience express in terms of my beliefs of concerning what is allowable, proper, appropriate, irrelevant, and so on?
    iv.   What might the possible effect of this experience be on how this relationship is experienced by the client as well as me? How might I respond in the way that both facilitates engagement with my client, client safety and my own consistency with my chosen values for my work as a therapist?
3. Consider discussing these reflections and challenges in clinical supervision in either a peer or consultative framework.

There are indeed a wide range of potential forms of reflection and challenge for therapists to consider that can support them in considering factors related to the context for this experience, factors related to their clients and factors related to themselves. Additionally, this opening up of CBT to consider the value of working on the 'person of the therapist' also makes some room for considering the possible value of personal therapy for CBT therapists.

Most definitely, this provides some support for CBT supervisors to pay increasing attention to supervisees' relational experiences that emerge in the course of their practice. In the case of 'perfectionistic Pam' discussed earlier, we saw the possibility of the phenomenon of sexual attraction in therapy becoming clarified in supervision. Contemporary CBT approaches would recommend a form of 'interpersonal formulation' as an appropriate response, particularly in instances where some form of relational phenomenon is experienced as 'blocking therapy'. For example, Leahy (2007) has suggested that such instances can be formulated in terms of therapist–client schematic matching and mismatching. In this example, it could potentially be the case that Pam and her client present with matching schemas around needing to appear 'efficient, effective and hardworking', and the experience of mutual attraction can be contextualized and understood in this light. Unfortunately, the understandable responses of guilt, shame and embarrassment, combined with processes of worry and rumination and avoidance, shut down the possibility of further exploration. In my view, such a shutting down of exploration would become less likely should CBT practitioners continue in the project of advancing the model towards a more relational perspective, even if such an exploration may provoke uncomfortable experiences of anxiety expressing the dilemma 'Is this who and how we should be as CBT therapists?'.

In sessions on 'Ethics in CBT', I sometimes ask trainees to imagine that CBT was a person. What sort of person would they be? What values and virtues would they embody? This generally leads to much laughter and some 'venting' of current frustrations regarding their relationship with CBT. Words such as 'cold', 'rational', 'structured' feature strongly as well as words such as 'committed', 'scientific' and 'collaborative'. I usually end this exercise by asking them that if they indeed met such a person as CBT, would they care to go out on a date with him (CBT is usually but not invariably imagined as male)? Mostly, our man CBT ends the session without a date. To be fair, the same question asked regarding all the other known forms of psychotherapy also leads to a dearth of date possibilities as each is found to be an unstable and unsuitable character. The characteristics attributed to CBT would be understood by the philosopher Friedrich Nietzsche as expressions of the 'Apollonian' character type (Nietzsche, 1993). This he contrasted with the 'Dionysian' character that embodies such qualities as 'spontaneity', 'chaos' and 'passion'. Potentially, the move towards some of the so-called third-wave CBT approaches such as ACT opens the model towards a more Dionysian perspective. CBT is unlikely to lose its Apollonian values or character; however, finding a place to reflect upon and to work with the Dionysian aspects of existence appears as a potentially enriching, if challenging, path for CBT to take.

References

Beck, A. (1976). *Cognitive therapy of the emotional disorders.* New York: New American Library.

Bennett-Levy, J., & Thwaites, R. (2007). Self and self-reflection in the therapeutic relationship: A conceptual map and practical strategies for the training, supervision and self-supervision of interpersonal skills. In P. Gilbert & R. L. Leahy (Eds.), *The therapeutic relationship in cognitive behavioural psychotherapies.* New York: Routledge.

Clark, D. A. (1995). Perceived limitations of standard cognitive therapy: A reconsideration of efforts to revise Beck's theory and therapy. *Journal of Cognitive Psychotherapy, 9*(3), 153–172.

Clark, D. A., Beck, A. T., & Allford, B. A. (1999). *Scientific foundations of cognitive theory and therapy of depression.* New York: Wiley.

Cohn, H. (1997). *Existential thought and therapeutic practice: An introduction to existential psychotherapy.* London: Sage.

Gilbert, P. (2010). *The compassionate mind.* London: Constable.

Greenberg, L. S., & Paivio, S. (1997). *Working with emotions.* New York: Guilford Press.

Guidano, V. (1991). *The self in process: Toward a post-rational cognitive therapy.* New York: Guilford press.

Leahy, R. (2002). A model of emotional schemas. *Cognitive and Behavioral Practice, 9*(3), 177–190.

Leahy, R. (2007). Schematic mismatch in the therapeutic relationship: A social-cognitive model. In P. Gilbert & R. L. Leahy (Eds.), *The therapeutic relationship in cognitive behavioural psychotherapies.* New York: Routledge.

Merleau-Ponty, M. (1982). *Phenomenology of perception.* London: Routledge.

Nietzsche, F. (1993). *The birth of tragedy: Out of the spirit of music.* London: Penguin Classics.

Ottens, A. J., & Hanna, F. J. (1998). Cognitive and existential therapies: Toward an integration. *Psychotherapy: Theory, Research, Practice, Training, 35*(3), 312–324.

Pope, K. S., Sonne, J. L., & Holroyd, J. (1995). *Sexual feelings in psychotherapy. Explorations for therapists and therapists in training.* Washington, DC: American Psychological Association.

Rodolfa, E., Hall, T., Holms, V., Davena, A., Komatz, D., Antunez, M., & Hall, A. (1994). The management of sexual feelings in therapy. *Professional Psychology, Research and Practice, 25*(2), 168–172.

Russ, H. G. (1993). Erotic transference through countertransference: The female therapist and the male patient. *Psychoanalytic Psychology, 10*(3), 93–406.

Safran, J. D. (1998). *Widening the scope of cognitive therapy: The therapeutic relationship, emotion and the process of change.* Northvale, NJ: Jason Aronson.

Safran, J. D., & Muran, J. C. (2000). *Negotiating the therapeutic alliance: A relational treatment guide.* New York: The Guilford Press.

Spinelli, E. (2001). *The mirror and the hammer: Challenges to psychotherapeutic orthodoxy.* London: Continuum.

Waddington, L. (2002). The therapy relationship in cognitive therapy: A review. *Behavioural and Cognitive Psychotherapy, 30*(2), 179–191.

Wells, A. (1995). Meta-cognition and worry: A cognitive model of generalized anxiety disorder. *Behavioural and Cognitive Psychotherapy, 23*(3), 301–320.

2
Sexual Attraction in the Therapeutic Relationship
An Integrative Perspective

John Nuttall

'Therapy is at its core an intimate relationship which explores some of the most profound questions we have to encounter as human beings' (Orbach, 1999, p. 1). Some argue that the presence of Eros in the therapeutic relationship has been ignored for too long (Clarkson, 2003a; Gerrard, 1996; Mann, 1997), and it remains an issue that many find uncomfortable and even taboo. Notwithstanding this, 73% of practitioners reported clients expressing sexual attraction for them and 90% have reported sexual attraction for a client (Pope & Tabachnick, 1993). The pervasive view that this is detrimental to therapeutic outcome probably dates from the case of Anna O (Freud & Breuer, 1895), in which Freud considered erotic attraction to be a form of resistance to treatment. The corresponding countertransference was considered in more damning light – as unanalyzed aspects of the therapist (Freud, 1915). Recently, Target (2007) argues that contemporary approaches in psychotherapy have moderated the centrality of drive theory and sexuality in the aetiology of psychological disturbance, replacing them with concepts of relational conflict and deficit. Discussion of the erotic in this context is more about the use of sexuality as a defence against narcissistic wounds. Nevertheless, psychoanalytic theories of sexuality and erotic transference phenomena have overshadowed views of the

Sexual Attraction in Therapy: Clinical Perspectives on Moving Beyond the Taboo – A Guide for Training and Practice, First Edition. Edited by Maria Luca.
© 2014 John Wiley & Sons, Ltd. Published 2014 by John Wiley & Sons, Ltd.

humanistic and integrative world, and Hargaden and Sills (2002) argue that humanistic critique has resulted in an equally inappropriate denial of the deep meaning of the erotic in therapy and, in contrarian fashion, declare, 'the erotic contains within it the archetype of the universal striving for wholeness' (p. 84). Jung noted this symbolic meaning in his linking of this striving with the alchemical metaphor and the erotic depiction of the transference relationship in the *Rosarium Philosophorum* (Jung, 1969).

Can the erotic be acknowledged without overt psychoanalytic theorizing or without it becoming so symbolic that the therapeutic relationship becomes desexualized completely (Renn, 2013)? When asked to give an integrative perspective, I feared the prospect of trying to develop one. I consider psychotherapy integration a personal process rather than a position or end point. I therefore needed a framework that expressed the concept of 'integrating' rather than 'integrative'. I decided Clarkson's (2003b) five-mode approach to relationship might elucidate how sexual attraction and the erotic can be explained or understood from a nondoctrinaire and integrating perspective.

Clarkson's approach is a framework for integration rather than a model of integrative therapy that posits a pluralistic view of the therapeutic relationship based on the discourse repertoires of a wide range of therapeutic approaches. These repertoires are the working alliance, the transferential relationship, the reparative or developmentally needed relationship, the person-to-person relationship, and the transpersonal relationship. The strength of this framework lies 'in the articulation and layering of many different theoretical angles' (Hawke, 1996, p. 406), which allow for different priorities and emphasis. Although the erotic could be seen as a sixth mode, the lack of professional discourse about its positive qualities excludes it from the repertoire of relational possibilities that contribute to healing. Notwithstanding this, I think it is possible to demonstrate that Clarkson's framework can help elucidate erotic attraction in therapy and focus the associated imperatives, admonitions and values. The five modalities 'are not developmental stages but states . . . often subtly "overlapping", in and between which a client construes his or her unique experience' (Clarkson, 2003b, p. xxi). I review each modality and use them to elucidate vignettes of Eros in the therapeutic relationship I have experienced as a psychotherapist and/or supervisor. By this, I hope to identify the skills and insights that constitute good management of sexual attraction in the therapeutic relationship, and I have offered some specific interventions at the end of each section that might be appropriate to each modality.

The Working Alliance

This is the bond that enables a client and a therapist to work together, 'even when the patient or client experiences some desires to the contrary' (Clarkson, 2003b, p. 35). It contains the contractual arrangements concerning competencies and boundaries, attendance and cooperation, and, occasionally, to control destructive behaviours (Stuart, 2010). The parties are 'joined together in a shared enterprise, each making his or her contribution to the work' (Gelso & Carter, 1985, p. 163), and it should be free of ulterior motives that would jeopardize beneficial outcome. Bugental (1987) writes, 'the therapeutic alliance is the powerful joining of forces which energises and supports the long, difficult and frequently painful work of life-changing psychotherapy' (p. 49). Gerrard (1996) argues that such a powerful joining of forces can only happen 'when a patient can arouse our deepest loving feelings (not empathy)' (p. 163). She connects primary love and infantile eroticism with the more mature secondary love and sexual arousal of adulthood, and is emphatic that both are present in loving relationships. Mann (1997) asserts, 'the erotic pervades all psychoanalytic encounters and is largely a positive and transformational process' (p. 1), placing the erotic firmly within the working alliance. In contrast, Rogers (1951) describes a rather pragmatic approach when a client expressed her wish to have sex (p. 211). While expressing understanding of the client's desire, the counsellor simply declined. Berne (1973) is equally straightforward when referring to sexual games as a means of gaining social and existential advantage over others. There is no sense of the erotic representing a powerful joining of forces or of it having the 'transcendent quality' that Kernberg (1992, p. 279) and other psychoanalytic writers expound.

These definitions confirm the omnipresence of the working alliance – it is not just the contract but the ongoing cooperation and management of the relationship by both parties. Whatever the view of sexual attraction theoretically, imperatives of the working alliance demand that it be managed for the benefit of the client, and professional ethical codes expect this. Sexual attraction, either way, must not be enacted as this constitutes misunderstanding of the roles tantamount to that raised by Ferenczi (1949) in the 'Confusion of the Tongues between the Adults and the Child'. The reaction to a client's overt sexual attraction may be, on the one hand, feelings of being appreciated, special, flattered or, on the other hand, feeling under threat, mistaken or insulted. The client may have similar reactions to such attention from the therapist. Neither of these extremes can be engaged, but the 'good enough' alliance will allow empathic recognition of the client's feelings without inducing further regression that might lead to obsessive eroticism or damaging shame. Striking this balance is a delicate process.

A middle-aged woman was referred for depression associated with the death of her estranged partner some years before. Betty felt 'weighed down' by the guilt of separating prior to his death. She reported having had violent parents, and all her life she 'had chosen passive men' unlikely to be aggressive and felt devoid of support throughout life. She blamed herself for all her misfortune and described herself as intolerant and harsh like her mother.

About session six, she expressed interest in my personal situation and asked what I was doing over the holiday. She said, 'you remind me of someone', thought I might be a Buddhist and worried about her teenage son not having good male role models in his life. I felt idealized and flattered, and later she asked if I would meet her for coffee. She proclaimed, 'I want to help others and I have a streak of goodness in me', and I sensed a strong identification with me as she said, 'I wish I had your insight'. I felt she was seeking a supportive father and a partner that could fulfil her needs. This attraction supported the working alliance as it encouraged attendance and gave potency to my interventions. Nevertheless, I felt fragility in the relationship – perhaps like that with her father.

I decided to confront the idealization while affirming Betty's feelings as normal given the intense nature of therapeutic encounters. I was aware of how 'stupid' her father made her feel as a child and wanted to avoid repeating the trauma. I disclosed that I had a sense of her attraction for me and expressed how I valued her honesty in expressing and sharing her feelings. We discussed how her feelings related to the material she was bringing and how I complemented her childhood need for supportive and understanding parents and her desire for a new partner and role model for her son. As I declined social contact, she recognized my role as bringing her this insight and to support her mourning of these desires rather than erroneously fulfilling them. I affirmed that far from being stupid, her desire represented the very core of the work and that acknowledging it, and understanding its meaning, although anxiety provoking, was essentially the working alliance we agreed. Three key interventions are important in this relational mode:

- Value the client's integrity in expressing their feelings
- Validate the client for complying with the spirit of the working alliance

- Verbalize how risking such expression of feelings strengthens the therapeutic relationship and trust.

The Transferential Relationship

The transferential relationship is probably the modality most written about in regard to sexual attraction. It has its theoretical base in psychoanalysis, and Freud (1905) first defined transference as a process 'in which a whole series of psychological experiences are revived, not as belonging to the past, but as applying to the person of the physician at the moment' (p. 116). The physician may respond with attitudes related to their past or evoked by the transference – the countertransference (Clarkson & Nuttall, 2000). 'Transference is everywhere and unavoidable' (Clarkson, 2003b, p. 79) and leads to unwarranted and inappropriate interpersonal attribution that can interfere with the working alliance. Transference experiences are revived, usually early familial and relational paradigms that were unrequited and laden with anxiety and ambivalent feelings. As adults we might unconsciously construe or engineer life events to symbolically represent these early situations so that they might be resolved or relived as familiar attitudes in highly anxious situations – a phenomenon known as the 'compulsion to repeat'.

McDougall (1995) asserts that 'Human sexuality is inherently traumatic' (p. ix) and 'profound ambivalence complicates the attachment and attraction to our parents' (original italics, p. xiv), who constitute our first love objects. Laplanche (1995) further elaborates that psychosexual attraction is derived from converted frustration at the loss of the object, which is then a sought-after fantasy that in reality cannot be refound. Target (2007) suggests that such innocuous frustration can be inadvertently eroticized by the caregiver, while actual infant sexual excitement is usually unacknowledged, uncontained or even shunned. The result is a 'psychosexual core which is unstable, elusive and never felt to be really owned' (p. 517) and adult sexual relations are posited as a means of stabilizing this elusive core. Klein (1997) described this scenario in the 'Origins of Transference', where 'the infant has from the beginning of post-natal life a relation to the mother which is imbued with the fundamental elements of . . . love, hatred, phantasies, anxieties and defences' (p. 49). This has implications for sexual attraction in therapy where a balance between being a sought-after fantasy or an uncontaining object needs to be managed.

Richard, a young gay man, was HIV positive and referred to a much older gay therapist by a befriending agency. He was acutely distressed and wanted to explore his childhood, his promiscuity and aggression in relationships, and his feelings of worthlessness. As a child, he suffered parental physical abuse, especially from his father. His mother could also be 'grotesquely angry' and would report his bad behaviour to his father. In his teens, he would go cottaging and met an older man with whom he had regular 'sexual, but loving relations'. He said sadly, 'I just wanted some love'. His depression related to his unhappy childhood and, following infection, his precarious future. As his blood results worsened, he faced anxious decisions about drug therapy, which evoked 'the return of the bad object' (Fairbairn, 1952; Nuttall, 1998). He felt 'knocked down' by HIV and, taking on the burden of badness, he said in tears, 'I feel as though I've failed; the virus is the ultimate failure. I've always failed; at relationships, job – a sorry pathetic life really. Whenever I get things together, I spoil it'.

Richard was a handsome and pleasant young man. He mitigated his badness by being 'a perfectly presented package', polite, well mannered and charming, just as his mother demanded of him as a child. He was highly seductive and increasingly attractive to the therapist, who reported to me, his supervisor, the desire to 'give him a blow-job' as he sat opposite with open legs. This was reflected in the transference, as Richard said, 'being here for this hour is the safest place to be', and asked the therapist to be his mentor. Challenge to this mitigating defence such as feeling belittled at work, poor blood results or a simple rebuke evoked rage that destroyed any goodness and left him feeling depressed and unloved. The therapist felt wary about making interpretations for fear of provoking an angry reaction, and to reflect the client's underlying desire for emotional contact seemed potentially seductive and submissive. The therapist judged it best to avoid reference to such desires as they might constitute a defence against deeper issues – such as loss, dread, anger, hope (and ultimately longing) of the kind Klein and Laplanche refer to.

However, this avoidance led to some undesirable acting out. As the erotic transference was at its height, the client attended with little to say interspersed with periods of silence and sulking. As this seemed purposeful, the therapist raised his own sense of being excluded from something. The client responded that 'because you're not gay you won't understand' and said he saw the therapist 'as an authority figure' and 'someone I shouldn't upset'. Soon after the client admitted his sexual involvement with an agency worker and was anxious about the therapist's reaction – the client feared the therapy might be terminated.

This questions what can be reparative in such highly cathected contexts and is an issue associated with counselling in gay befriending settings. Much depends on the therapist's experience and judgement of how concrete the client's thinking is with respect to the treatment process. The therapist's judgement seemed sound, notwithstanding the seductive nature of the client and the weakness of the worker. However, this vignette raises the issue of what kind of intervention would avoid enactment in the transferential relationship, and the following are probably the general aspects to bear in mind:

- Acknowledge the client's anxiety about having feelings of attraction.
- Relate the feelings to the broader issues being raised in the therapy.
- Link the relational pattern with other relationships in the client's life and explain the transference process.

The Reparative or Developmentally Needed Relationship

In this, the therapist intentionally provides a replenishing experience where there was failure in the original parenting provision. This mode is generally unavoidable 'because most human beings come for help as a result of their failure to avoid regressing out of the here and now of their current adult reality' (Clarkson, 2003b, p. 129). Ferenczi (1949) advocated the therapist playing a new model parent to avoid evoking the original trauma, although with some expressed reservations in the 'Confusion of the Tongues between the Adults and the Child'. Winnicott (1988) conceived a similar approach in the 'holding environment' of the therapeutic setting. The Cathexis School of Transactional Analysis advocates reparenting to replace dysfunctional relational patterns (Widdowson, 2010). Cognitive analytic therapy similarly identifies and challenges outmoded 'reciprocal role procedures', and in object relations therapy, when the therapeutic relationship 'becomes a new internal object relationship, the patient is fundamentally changed' (Scharff & Scharff, 1998, p. 236).

This modality usually follows the transferential situation, and managing and elucidating the meaning of the desire for intimacy and sexual attraction are part of the reparative process and the reworking of environmental deficits. This may involve the capacity to love the client (Gerrard, 1996) and make it possible to transform repetitive archaic longings into mature love of another. Outcome studies suggest it is the quality of the relationship that is reparative with the therapist opening up new relational possibilities for the client (Hubble, Duncan, & Miller, 1999), and Mann

(1997) believes the emergence of Eros 'signifies the search for a new transformational object' (p. 24). Continuing with Richard's case, I elucidate the developmentally needed mode.

Throughout this period, the therapist's countertransference vacillated between the erotic, the irritable and the needed mentor. Supervision identified the erotic and irritable feelings as *reactive complementary identification* with a father confused by his own feelings for his son. And the strong desire to be his mentor seemed complementary to the client's fantasy of the ideal father he longed to have. The therapist was also aware of elements of *proactive* countertransference that represented his concordant identification with Richard's 'sad little boy'. When the rejecting father transference was ascendant, the therapist felt desperation at not being able to assuage the client's pain and dread. In avoiding either rejecting or seductive interpretations, the counsellor felt as if he were walking on eggshells. Supervision suggested this might be Richard's experience of his family life: terrified to show emotion for fear of violence, leaving him with suppressed fear and rage, and a need to find love elsewhere. Klein (1997) might have described this matrix as the transfer of a 'total situation' (p. 55) from Richard's past into the present.

Understanding the transference and the acting out helped determine that it might be helpful to enact the role of mentor, provided this did not involve judgemental innuendo or yielding to the client's seductive ways, either of which might lead to malignant regression. This required, in the Jungian sense, delicate elucidation of the origins of trauma and its manifestation in therapy, with education of how the client might build new ways of adapting and thinking when events evoked bad feelings. The therapist recognized how important constancy in the relationship was for Richard and how this involved the concurrent use of the person-to-person relationship, which is described later. However, the therapist was left with residual empathy for the 'sad little boy' – probably the dominant feeling that Richard himself found intolerable. A mentoring-type relationship that represented a stable new object helped Richard place his sexual desires, emotional needs and aggression in context and led to a trusting relationship that brought fuller conscious mourning of his childhood and his current existential plight. This can be achieved by exploring the meaning of the attraction in a constructive and reparative way:

• Explore the context and range of feelings and thoughts about the attraction.
• Credit the client for acknowledging and discovering his or her capacity to have such strong feelings.

- Reflect on how the therapeutic relationship can be seen as a model for other intimate relationships.

Richard's desires for love must be seen as a quality that is real in all human beings. The desire to love, know, be known and loved by another often signifies a person's underlying wish for growth and individuation. This is the aim of therapy and in such a setting, feelings and desires develop between two mature adults that are not only transferential and developmentally needed but also real experiences.

The Person-to-Person or Real Relationship

'To find a genuine "good object" in one's analyst is both a transference experience and a real life experience. In analysis as in real life, all relationships have a subtle dual nature' (Guntrip, 1986, p. 467). Mann (1997) goes further:

'In my opinion the erotic transference, in particular the love components, are as real as love experienced outside the analytic setting. That is to say transference love is real love . . . It is because the erotic is real and not a facsimile that something dynamic can be made from it' (p. 11).

The person-to-person or 'real' relationship is most celebrated in humanistic and existential approaches to psychotherapy and 'the extent, level and the quality of this vector can vary enormously. It can be a rare moment or a few transactions . . . or it can be a substantial part of therapy' (Clarkson, 2003b, p. 159). It is a way of relating subject to subject and 'the therapist helps to heal by developing a genuine relationship with the patient' (Yalom, 1980, p. 45). It might not come kindly to the client as it involves some resolution of the transference and in some senses failing the client (Winnicott, 1988, p. 8). It is usually signalled by the client's real interest in understanding themselves and is paralleled by a change in the way they perceive the therapist and a growing ability to tolerate frustration and disappointment in the therapist and, as a corollary, to tolerate reflection on their own reality. When this stage is reached, there is a sense of enjoyment and increased rapport between client and therapist. This might not be experienced as overtly erotic or sexual, but it certainly infuses the work and relationship with a libidinal energy and bond that Fairbairn (1952) termed 'mature dependence'.

One controversial signpost of the real relationship is the therapist's self-disclosure of personal material or, more appropriately, feelings and thoughts generated by the relationship with the client. This must always be in the service of the therapy and not an enactment of the client's need to familiarize the session or socialize with the therapist.

> Sometimes as therapist, you will find yourself feeling protective, or irritated or impotent and suspect that it is because you are being constellated according to the client's old patterns of relating. In this case, it can be useful to find a way of gently giving the feedback to the client. This may be done entirely in the here and now, so that the client understands the effect that he is having on (at least) one person in his world (Joyce & Sills, 2001, p. 51).

However, Bugental (1987) warns:

> Disclosure of hostile, resentful, punitive, *erotic, seductive,* and competitive feelings in relation to the patient must be undertaken only when there has been careful preparation of the patient and when the therapist has taken time apart . . . to examine his own needs, motives, and intentions (p. 143).

Such a mutative moment occurred with Richard.

As the working alliance grew, Richard focused on understanding his emotional and affective experiences rather than acting out. This increased dialogue was marked by two events that gave the therapist the opportunity to challenge Richard's idealized perceptions of him. The first came several sessions after Richard reported his sexual liaison. Richard expressed regret and relief that the therapist was not so angry he would end the therapy and felt 'remarkably understood by someone who wasn't gay'. The therapist suddenly felt conscious of not being authentic and of not genuinely honouring the human being sitting opposite him, and wanted to correct the client's assumption. Equally, he recognized the client's need to have his gay being understood and acknowledged, perhaps by a 'straight' father figure. The therapist was concerned that to 'come out' might be either sexually arousing for the client or, at this late stage, insulting, as the client might feel deceived – evoking the family paradigm of his growing up. However, the therapist felt the misconception should not continue.

The dilemma was brought to supervision. Both considered the therapeutic relationship was at a coincidence of the reparative and person-to-person modes. The dilemma was similar, in principle, to that faced by Richard as a child, in his teens and again on his diagnosis. It is an existential issue familiar to gay men of a certain generation and by HIV-positive gay men today. Who can I tell, who will have sympathy, and will anyone love me if they find out? The therapist reflected on his attraction for the client and his fear that self-disclosure might not only spoil the unspoken *frisson* that existed but also rupture the working alliance. Nevertheless, the therapist decided to share with the client the paradox it represented for him and how he felt about it. He took the risk of inviting Richard into a dialogic relationship that he considered would be helpful so he could learn that the therapist too did not have all the answers to life's dilemmas.

The situation raises an interesting issue for all therapists. To not disclose might have allowed the client to feel acceptable and assuaged the deficits of the past. The danger in leaving it there is that the past might not have been properly 'repaired'. The client might not have mourned the deficit or learned that life has its dilemmas and pain. This represents what Jacobs (1989) described as moving back and forth between I–it and I–thou modes, between the reparative mode and the person-to-person mode. 'The most important therapeutic implication is that the therapy must take place within a dialogic relation if it is to be true to the ontic possibilities of contacting' (p. 64). In one seminar, Clarkson emphasized, 'psychotherapy is not an immunization against everyday life, nor a vaccination against the turmoil and turbulence of existence. Pain hurts. People you love die, leave or betray you'. The following offer some general principles to engage in this mode of relationship:

- Explore the client's wishes and thoughts about your reaction to sexual advances; declare your reactions when this feels appropriate.
- Be clear that a romantic relationship cannot occur, and explain that therapists too often have strong feelings for clients that cannot be enacted.
- Discuss the difference between feeling sexually attracted and overt sexual behaviour.

The imperative of the person-to-person relationship is 'Simply stay with your intention to meet honestly with your client, and trust that what you create between you will be fertile ground for growth' (Joyce & Sills, 2001, p. 55). This concept of growth introduces the transpersonal relationship.

The Transpersonal Relationship

This 'refers to the spiritual, mysterious or currently inexplicable dimension of the healing relationship' (Clarkson, 2003b, p. 20). This is the mode of relating that Jung was one of the first to acknowledge in the modern therapeutic tradition (Walsh & Vaughan, 1996). The transpersonal may be discerned in the concepts of *Eros* and *Thanatos* in psychoanalysis, the actualizing tendency of the humanistic school, and even in the nature of schema in cognitive psychotherapy. The transpersonal evolved from the humanistic psychology tradition inspired by James, Jung, Assagioli, May, Maslow and others, and this perspective provides the capacity to deal with paradox, ambiguity, incertitude, contradiction and simultaneity in human interaction. It differs 'not so much in method or technique as in orientation and scope' (Boorstein, 1996, p. 3). As Jung (1995) wrote, 'it is important to have a secret, a premonition of things unknown. The unexpected and the incredible belong to this world' (p. 390).

The transpersonal dimension sees sexuality and the erotic as something deeply spiritual and creative. It represents the individual's striving for wholeness and connection with other sentient beings and may be conceptualized as the birth to new possibilities and an expression of potential. Kernberg (1992) affirms that 'erotic idealisations may inspire artistic or religious expression . . . and give sexual love a transcendent quality' (p. 279). In this vein, 'It may be more useful to consider love less as an aspect of relationship and more as an event of the soul' (Moore, 1992, 78). And yet, as Rumi (1994) expounded, 'Love comes with a knife, not some shy question; and not with fears for its reputation' (p. 27). I should like to describe one such 'birth to new possibilities', typical of several clients, which resulted in a positive outcome.

A man of early 30s was referred because of aggressive behaviour when 'disrespected' in social and familial situations. This had placed his marriage and children in jeopardy, and he felt guilty and suicidal as 'he was letting people down'. The initial triage suggested his attendance might be erratic and his ability to engage in therapy dubious, and I expected to meet an avoidant and arrogant man. Yet, when I met him, I instantly liked him. I found him attractive and sexy and fantasized about his being gay. He talked about difficulties with his parents and how he was never clear where he stood in the family hierarchy with older and younger sisters. He was often left alone to entertain and fend for himself and felt ignored by his parents and sisters. He recalled having tantrums until he got the things he wanted, but as the therapy progressed, he acknowledged this was not what he really needed and he felt a sense of recognition hunger and a lack of valorization. His mother told him that, as a child, he always 'wanted something' when she was feeding his younger sister. Unable to tolerate the sadness and envy, he mitigated his badness by becoming the family hero – protecting his honour, his sisters and his friends. This often resulted in violent behaviour followed by self-recrimination and depression, often tempered by alcohol. Well into the contract, he reported despondently that his mother did not believe he was in therapy despite his changed behaviour, and he said sadly, 'she can't credit me with doing anything positive'. He continued to get into minor quarrels defending the honour of others in deep identification with their imagined hurt. This seemed a projection of his own narcissistic wounds and sense of injustice, and he presented as a somewhat misunderstood hero figure.

Over time, I began to feel his hurt and need for affirmation. I felt drawn into his need for recognition and after one session wrote 'I am beginning to really love him in a strange sort of way'. As the therapy progressed without absences, I felt like the guiding father as we talked about the possible consequences of his anger and how it avoided his sadness and hurt, which he admitted 'wasn't easy to bear'. Eventually, he realized that bearing these feelings needed more courage than to start a fight, and he began to 'like himself' and his increasing ability to 'walk away' from conflict and alcohol. As therapy progressed, I felt joy when he appeared and greeted me with what I sensed was a shy affectionate smile. Towards the end, he repeatedly reported his peace of mind and how he now 'didn't need drink' and avoided conflict. In the last session, he described therapy as 'one of the best experiences of his life' and was unashamedly recommending it to his friends. I felt a deep respect for him as he blossomed before my eyes and redefined for himself his sense of heroism. I was left with an image of him as 'my hero' as he integrated his hurt and need to avenge. Nevertheless, I was left perplexed by the degree of transformation, which was confirmed by the Clinical Outcomes in Routine Evaluation (CORE) outcome measure. Ready to end therapy, quite confidently he asserted, 'I'll find something to do in this time'.

I still ask myself about the origins of these feelings of joy and fulfilment mixed with confusion and whether they might be adequately expressed using the discourse of the other modalities of relationship. Yet there was a dimension to this relationship that went beyond those demonstrated earlier. The client had transcended his ego inflation with the hero archetype and realized that true heroism lay in the capacity to withstand the hurts of everyday life without having to counterattack. I believed he acquired this from a quality in the relationship that was ineffable and didn't need expression to be manifest. No doubt it aided the working alliance, and yet it was not overtly contracted; it had transferential qualities yet seemed not to require resolution; it was reparative, but it was not intentionally provided; it felt deeply real and yet did not demand definition or disclosure. Gordon (1999) asserts that 'when we reach this stage in therapy, Eros has really begun to come of age and infuse the work and the relationship with enjoyment and stimulus' (p. 57), a position also argued by Worrell in Chapter 1. In alchemical terms, the unspoken erotic *coniunctio* of the therapeutic relationship had resulted in this client developing a love for himself that moderated his need for 'respect' from others that was, in any case, never quite achieved by his aggression.

So what might be the key interventions that suit this modality of relationship? I believe they are the following:

- Normalize sexual attraction as a basic human need and a manifestation of the life force.
- Point out that opposites coexist and that both sexual attraction (Eros) and rejection and anger (Destrudo) are aspects of human nature.
- Explore with clients how they might allow themselves to feel sad, regret and rage, and yet trust that love and the life force will return.

Conclusion

Orbach (1999) argues that 'Over years of practice the therapist develops a confidence about the precise form of her engagement at any moment' (p. 5). Clarkson's framework provides a coherence that guides our understanding of the client–therapist interaction and brings us to the core of what we do as psychotherapists. In looking at sexual attraction using this framework, I have attempted to extract it from the usual prescriptive theories of it representing a developmental problem, psychic defence or transformational symbol. Nevertheless, some argue (Hargaden & Sills, 2002; Lichtenberg, 2008) that there are many variations of the erotic that emerge in the therapeutic relationship, such as the 'relational intrusion' variation discussed by Luca and Soskice in Chapter 10. These may require different interventions and the engagement of different relational modalities, and for a useful exposition of these different perspectives, I refer the reader to Renn (2013). Notwithstanding this, I do not wish to categorize erotic attraction in this way, or suggest that it is a normal event in therapy and the examples I have chosen are where it seems to have played a significant role in the client–therapist dynamic. Whatever the form of Eros evoked, I consider Clarkson's relational framework provides a nondoctrinaire perspective of how to manage and productively work with the relational complexity that sexual attraction brings to the consulting room.

References

Berne, E. (1973). *Sex in human loving*. London: Penguin.

Boorstein, S. (1996). Introduction. In S. Boorstein (Ed.), *Transpersonal psychotherapy*. New York: University of New York Press.

Bugental, J. F. T. (1987). *The art of the psychotherapist*. New York: W.W. Norton.

Clarkson, P. (2003a). No sex please we're counsellors. *Counselling and Psychotherapy Journal*, 14(2), 7–8.

Clarkson, P. (2003b). *The therapeutic relationship* (2nd ed.). London: Whurr.

Clarkson, P., & Nuttall, J. (2000). Working with countertransference. *Psychodynamic Counselling*, 6(3), 359–379.

Fairbairn, W. R. D. (1952). *Psychoanalytic studies of the personality*. London: Routledge.

Ferenczi, S. (1949). Confusion of the tongues between the adults and the child. *International Journal of Psycho-Analysis*, 30, 225–230.

Freud, S. (1905). *Fragments of an analysis of a case of hysteria* (Standard Edition, Vol. 7). London: Hogarth Press. 1953.

Freud, S. (1915). *Observations on transference-love* (Standard Edition, Vol. 12). London: Hogarth Press.

Freud, S., & Breuer, J. (1895). *Studies on hysteria* (Standard Edition, Vol. 2). London: Hogarth Press.

Gelso, C. J., & Carter, J. A. (1985). The relationship in counselling and psychotherapy: Components, consequences and theoretical antecedents. *The Counseling Psychologist*, 13(2), 155–243.

Gerrard, J. (1996). Love in the time of psychotherapy. *British Journal of Psychotherapy*, 13(2), 163–173.

Gordon, S. (1999). Bringing up Eros: A Kohution perspective. In D. Mann (Ed.), *Erotic transference and countertransference* (pp. 42–59). London: Routledge.

Guntrip, H. (1986). My experience of analysis with Fairbairn and Winnicott. In P. Buckley (Ed.), *Essential papers on object relations*. New York and London: NYUP.

Hargaden, H., & Sills, C. (2002). *Transactional analysis: A relational perspective*. Hove: Brunner-Routledge.

Hawke, C. (1996). Book review of the Therapeutic Relationship by Clarkson. *British Journal of Psychotherapy*, 12(4), 405–407.

Hubble, M. A., Duncan, B. L., & Miller, S. D. (1999). *The heart & soul of change: What works in therapy*. Washington, DC: American Psychological Association.

Jacobs, L. (1989). Dialogue in gestalt theory and therapy. *The Gestalt Journal*, 12(1), 42–67.

Joyce, P., & Sills, C. (2001). *Skills in gestalt counselling and psychotherapy*. London: Sage.

Jung, C. G. (1969). *The psychology of the transference*. London: Routledge.

Jung, C. G. (1995). *Memories, dreams, reflections*. London: Fontana Press Ltd.

Kernberg, O. F. (1992). *Aggression in personality disorders and perversions*. London: Yale University Press.

Klein, M. (1997). The origins of transference. In *Envy and gratitude and other works 1946–1963*. London: Vintage.

Laplanche, J. (1995). Seduction, persecution, revelation. *International Journal of Psycho-Analysis*, 76(4), 663–682.

Lichtenberg, J. D. (2008). *Sensuality and sexuality across the divide of shame*. New York: Analytic Press.

McDougall, J. (1995). *The many faces of Eros*. London: Free Association Books.

Mann, D. (1997). *Psychotherapy: An erotic relationship*. London: Routledge.

Moore, T. (1992). *Care of the soul*. London: Piatkus.

Nuttall, J. (1998). Fairbairnian object relations: The challenge to the moral defence in gay men with HIV. *Psychodynamic Counselling*, 4(4), 445–461.

Orbach, S. (1999). *The impossibility of sex*. London: Penguin Press.

Pope, K. S., & Tabachnick, B. G. (1993). Therapists' anger, hate, fear, and sexual feelings: National survey of therapists' responses, client, characteristics, critical events, formal complaints, and training. *Professional Psychology, Research and Practice*, 24(2), 142–152.

Renn, P. (2013). Moments of meeting: The relational challenge of sexuality in the consulting room. *British Journal of Psychotherapy*, 29(2), 135–153.

Rogers, C. (1951). *Client centred therapy*. Bury St Edmunds: St Edmundsbury Press.

Rumi, J. (1994). *Say I am you*. J. Mourne & C. Barks (trans). Athens, GA: Maypop.

Scharff, D. E., & Scharff, J. S. (1998). *Object relations therapy*. London: Karnac.

Stuart, I. (2010). The 'three ways out': Escape hatches. In R. G. Erskine (Ed.), *Life scripts: A transactional analysis of unconscious relational patterns* (pp. 127–150). London: Karnac.

Target, M. (2007). Is our sexuality our own: A developmental model of sexuality based o early affect mirroring. *British Journal of Psychotherapy*, 23(4), 517–530.

Walsh, R., & Vaughan, F. E. (1996). Comparative models of the person and psychotherapy. In S. Boorstein (Ed.), *Transpersonal psychotherapy*. New York: University of New York Press.

Widdowson, M. (2010). *Transactional analysis: 100 key points and techniques*. London: Routledge.

Winnicott, D. W. (1988). *Babies and their mothers*. London: Free Association Books.

Yalom, I. (1980). *Existential psychotherapy*. New York: Basic Books.

3

Existential Psychotherapy and Sexual Attraction

Meaning and Authenticity in the Therapeutic Encounter

Michael D. Berry

The simultaneous uniqueness and universality of human experience is encapsulated in the experience of sexuality and sexual attraction in the therapeutic encounter. While sexuality, as a matter of psychobiological fact, is inevitably – if uncomfortably – present in the consulting room, the experience of sexual psychodynamics between the therapist and the client is idiosyncratic. Where sexual attraction emerges in a significant way (for it cannot be argued that sexual attraction is always a dominant factor in the client–therapist interaction), the therapist requires a coherent and measured strategy for dealing with the experience (Pope, 2000, 2001). Such a strategy requires an effective theoretical foundation, which can account for the ethical and pragmatic aspects of sexual attraction. Existentialism, as an applicable theoretical model for psychotherapeutic practice, provides a means for assessing and negotiating the challenges presented by sexuality in the consulting room, which acknowledges the universal elements of human experience that confront the participants in the clinical encounter, and helps to identify the unique aspects of the encounter and its participants.

Existentialism is a lot of things. While it is, in the first instance, a philosophical movement, it has close links with visual and literary art such that Sartre, the existentialist philosopher and litterateur par excellence, was offered the 1964 Nobel Prize for literature (though he refused it on the basis of artistic principle). Against this backdrop, existentialism can be

Sexual Attraction in Therapy: Clinical Perspectives on Moving Beyond the Taboo – A Guide for Training and Practice, First Edition. Edited by Maria Luca.
© 2014 John Wiley & Sons, Ltd. Published 2014 by John Wiley & Sons, Ltd.

understood as an essentially humanist philosophy, offering a phenomenology of lived experience that situates the individual, and her/his unique human experience, within the context of universal existential struggles. Sartre's work, for instance, is no less than an attempt to account for the human individual's place in the universe – perhaps the most fundamental of questions. This rather ambitious pursuit leads to a distinction, in the pivotal work *Being and Nothingness* – arguably the preeminent text of existentialist ethics – between beings-in-themselves and beings-for-themselves, effectively a distinction between conscious (nonhuman) and *self*-conscious (human) creatures (Sartre, 1943). Whereas beings-in-themselves are subject to binding and inalienable laws, which predict their behaviour and define their essential qualities, humans are different. Human beings are 'without essential natures' and are defined by choice rather than ontological predetermination. In simpler terms: you are fundamentally the product of your own choices.

My focus in this chapter is on the philosophy of existentialism and on the phenomenological commitments of this philosophical model as they pertain to the difficulties associated with sexual desire in the consulting room. Existentialism can offer a profound and meaningful conceptualization of ethical choice, grounded in the concepts of meaning and authenticity – themes that I will elaborate as the basis for determining ethical action in the consulting room. Of particular interest are existentialism's integration with psychotherapy (Van Deurzen, 1998; Yalom, 1980) and the way existentialism's foundational principles and underlying ethical commitments may inform the taboo central to this book: the fraught issue of sexual attraction in the psychotherapeutic encounter. In the next discussion, I will outline some of existentialism's core themes in order to illustrate how this philosophical framework might account for the practical and ethical challenges of therapist–client sexual attraction.

I begin by outlining the *theoretical framework* of existential psychotherapy, highlighting how the key concepts of this dynamic psychotherapy model may account for the initial, taboo experience of sexual attraction between the therapist and the client. After outlining the core existentialist principles that are considered most significant in the psychotherapeutic field, generally, I elaborate the concept of personal meaning, an essential existentialist concept that has particular bearing on the sexual dimensions of the client–therapist encounter. I then use two case examples to outline the clinical approach an existentialist psychotherapist may use to address an apparent sexual attraction between her/himself and the client. A *discussion* of the integration of theory and clinical practice follows. Here, I address the notion of ethical action, vis-à-vis sexual attraction in the consulting room, as it relates to the fundamental principles of existential psychotherapy. Building on the concepts of authenticity and meaning, I outline how psychotherapists may develop a set of existential clinical strategies for addressing sexuality in the client–therapist relationship. I advise that the therapist introduce the intersubjective client–therapist relationship as a topic for clinical discussion, from the outset of the therapy process. This critical acknowledgement of the therapy relationship can provide a way forward, enabling a reflective discussion of the possible meanings and nature of the attraction, grounded in an explicit discussion of core existential themes. I conclude the chapter by emphasizing how existential psychotherapy principles underscore the consequentialist importance of the ethics of the clinical profession (Watter, 2012). Here, I re-emphasize that, from an existentialist ethical framework, the clinician must maintain authenticity by addressing sexual attraction where it becomes relevant to the clinical process, using sensitively attuned language to avoid alienating the client, an idea central to the book, particularly in Chapters 2, 5, 13 and 15. The existential therapist, I conclude, simply cannot bite her/his tongue.

Theoretical Framework

The fundament of existentialism is conveyed in Sartre's succinct quote: 'existence precedes essence' (Sartre, 1945, p. 20). This notion underlies the 'first principle' of existentialism: 'man is nothing else but what he makes of himself' (Sartre, 1945, p. 22). This principle is the cornerstone of existentialist subjectivity: the individual's essential self (essence) is determined by her/his choices in the material world (existence). Consequently, human existence is a state of being in which we are both *free*, with respect to self-determination, and *responsible*, by virtue of our choices and the powerful ethical implications that they have. The latter notion – that humans' unique capacity to choose implies a profound personal responsibility – is a central existentialist concern, which lies at the core of existentialist ethics. Sartre, in fact, went so far as to argue that each action we choose 'involve[s] all humanity' and that, by implication, 'I am responsible for myself and for everyone else. I am creating a certain image of man [sic] of my own choosing. In choosing myself, I choose man' (Sartre, 1945, p. 23). Thus, a psychotherapist confronted by a powerful sexual attraction towards a client – and/or the perception of the client's sexual desire for the therapist – inevitably faces the burden of choice, as, according to Sartre, inaction or avoidance itself, insofar as the refusal to choose, paradoxically, constitutes a choice in itself. This choice invariably carries a profound ethical responsibility that exceeds the parameters of the specific relationship in question (Sartre, 1945). In this regard, existentialism is deeply focused on the ethics of experience, within a humanistic framework that situates the human individual's choices and struggles at the centre of its concerns (Daigle, 2006; Warnock, 1967).

Existentialism is, at first glance, focused on rather bleak humanistic themes. Five core themes, drawn from existentialist philosophy and entrenched within the field of existentialist psychotherapy can be identified (Yalom, 1980). These are freedom, responsibility, death/nothingness, isolation and meaning/meaninglessness. The first two concepts, freedom and responsibility, are inherently linked. While 'freedom' holds a positive common-sense meaning of being exempt from unwanted restraint, existentialism perceives it somewhat differently; we are free by virtue of a fundamental lack of external structure. 'The human being', Yalom (1980) writes, 'does not enter (and leave) a well-structured universe that has an inherent design. Rather, the individual is entirely responsible for – that is, the author of – his or her own world, life design [and] choices' (Yalom, 1980, p. 9). Thus, we are not only *free* to choose but we are also *responsible* for choosing – choice is inevitable and marked by our core ethical responsibilities.

The existential conceptualization of death implies an elemental anxiety – anxiety grounded in the fear of nonexistence/nothingness – that is a root of much psychopathology (Van Deurzen, 2002). Similarly, isolation and meaning/meaninglessness imply an inherent psychological tension. Isolation, existentially, is no less than the knowledge that there is a fundamental gap between ourselves and the universe we occupy – implicating a deep desire for an ultimately impossible fundamental connectedness (Warnock, 1970).

Meaning/meaninglessness, likewise, implies anxiety and an essential desire: in the absence of a fundamental 'meaning of life' – which Yalom (1980) designates 'cosmic meaning' – we are left searching for personal meaning, meaning *in* life. The latter quest can help us understand how the client and therapist affiliate with particular events or behaviours, as sources of apparent meaning. In the psychotherapy setting, specifically, the concepts of freedom/responsibility and choice help us conceptualize the psychotherapist's possible responses to a client–therapist sexual attraction, while the notions of isolation and meaning offer a conceptual framework for interpreting the experience of sexual attraction itself.

Viewed existentially, sexuality is a particular instance of the simultaneously unique and universal aspects of human existence. Sexuality is construed as an 'embodied perceptual experience in our relations with others . . . an embodied intersubjective response to alterity [otherness]' (Smith-Pickard & Swynnerton, 2005, p. 48). While this embodied experience is subjectively and experientially unique, the existential themes that underlie it are universal. As such, the experience of sexual attraction can be interpreted in light of the fundamental aspects of human existence, including the aforementioned experience of mortal awareness, freedom, isolation, and meaninglessness. We may conceive of sexuality and sexual attraction as driven by an attempt to assuage our core existential anxieties and as imbued with a desire to overcome existential isolation and to derive a sense of meaning from life (Van Deurzen, 2002; Yalom, 1980, 1991). This desire for solace, interconnectedness and meaning can naturally evolve into a strong experience of sexual attraction, even between the therapist and the client.

Thus, sexual attraction between the patient and the psychotherapist may be assessed vis-à-vis the universal desire for meaning in life, and the sense of meaning and connectedness that may be at the root of the sexual attraction. The existential psychotherapist may be compelled to ask: what does this sexual attraction really *mean* (i.e., what does it reflect about how the patient and the therapist are negotiating the core existential challenges)? Exploring this line of questioning, in consultation with the patient, may serve as a pragmatic clinical technique, as I outline in the following section.

Considerations of Technique/Clinical Approach

A recent interview with a clinical supervisor, an expert in psychosexual therapy, indicates that sexuality in the consulting room is inevitably situated within a psychologically and emotionally complex intersubjective experience (Openshaw, 2013). While the ethics of the psychotherapy profession avow an objective detachment, the reality of the psychotherapy encounter, as understood within the existential framework, implies a kind of intellectual and emotional closeness between two individuals whose shared (though still unchangeably individual and singular) search for meaning and connectedness may evolve into a sense of intimacy and sexual attraction. The premise of this chapter and, I believe, the importance of this volume on clinical practice are predicated on the fact that simply ignoring sexual attraction in the consulting room may often be an unviable clinical strategy. Not always, but perhaps more frequently than we care to admit, it is clearly necessary to acknowledge, examine and deal with the elephant in the room. This, however, can hardly be a process of identifying unambiguous thoughts and feelings and tidily bracketing them out of the clinical equation. As most therapists can attest, sexual desire is often unwanted or inconvenient, but it rarely disappears simply because we wish, or will, it away.

Consequently, the therapist must address the dilemma of whether to deal explicitly with the sexual dimensions of the client–therapist relationship. This challenge, which may be fundamental for all psychotherapists, is uniquely impacted by a core value of existentialist therapy: authenticity (Sartre, 1945). The therapist who refuses to address sexual attraction in the consulting room may be acting in 'bad faith', a refusal to choose, which, again, is itself a choice. This bad faith is no less than an attempt to evade the responsibility that comes with being-for-itself (Sartre, 1943). The mores of the psychotherapeutic profession make this type of bad faith all the more probable by creating a social pressure for the therapist to conform to a predetermined value set (i.e., to discuss sexual attraction would be a breach of professional boundaries) and disavow her/his freedom to act authentically. From this vantage point, a therapist's refusal to discuss sexual attraction with the client may undermine the therapeutic encounter by leaving unresolved a potentially distracting, or destructive, interpersonal dynamic, and perhaps engendering in the patient questions about the therapist's thoughts and intentions and indeed competence.

The consequences that the therapist's reticence may have for the client, and for the therapeutic process, are the preeminent concern for existential ethics. Existentialism is less concerned with the moral question of 'right' and 'wrong', since a universe defined by freedom in the existential sense can be seen as lacking a fundamental moral imperative (Warnock, 1967). In fact, to assert that an external moral absolute governs our behaviour is an act of bad faith, insofar as it serves to deny personal responsibility for ourselves and our actions (Sartre, 1943). Once again, the important message here is that choice is inevitable. Considering the issue from within the psychotherapeutic framework, Van Deurzen (1998) writes, 'I do not believe that we can make judgements about what is right and wrong, but we can have some sense of what effects might be beneficial or harmful and what we want or are able to live with in the long run' (p. 69). Two brief case studies, one from my own counselling practice and one shared with me by a clinical colleague, help illustrate how a therapist or counsellor may act, with a view to the consequent outcomes for the client, in bad faith, or authentically.

Jennifer, a female undergraduate I saw in my capacity as a counsellor and instructor in a university setting, came in for support with respect to educational stress. During the course of our brief counselling relationship, Jennifer shared her feelings of anxiety and depression, which related to her troubled personal life, challenges that were significantly affecting her academic performance. Objectively, Jennifer was a very attractive woman in her early 20s—beautiful, smart and insightful—and in conjunction with the sympathy I felt for her personal difficulties, I found myself powerfully attracted to her on a sexual level, a feeling that I came to believe was mutual. Though I perceived this attraction as a significant obstacle in our therapeutic relationship, I was reluctant to broach the topic, as I believed it would be a breach of appropriate professional boundaries. Since the counselling format was focused on academic life, sexuality, in general, seemed like a taboo topic, perhaps even out of bounds, and as a fairly novice counsellor, I was very anxious about maintaining a professionally appropriate therapeutic stance. While I engaged her in some degree of exploration of how her ostensive academic anxieties may have been rooted in deeper and more fundamental existential concerns, with, I believe, positive therapeutic effect, I maintained (perhaps forced) a focus on her academic life. However, my attempts to focus on Jennifer's academic work proved unviable, as she drew the sessions towards increasingly intimate topics from her personal life (which I interpreted as both honest and seductive). After a few frustratingly unproductive sessions, I referred Jennifer to one of my more experienced colleagues, for more in-depth psychotherapeutic work.

In my retrospective reflections, I have come to believe that we were psychotherapeutically stuck and that our unspoken mutual attraction fundamentally impeded the clinical process. I have also come to believe that I felt uncomfortable broaching the topic of sexual attraction for personal, rather than professional, reasons. This discomfort undermined my authenticity in the counselling encounter and left me acting in bad faith, refusing personal choice.

Jack, a clinical colleague, offers an alternative model of dealing with sexual attraction in the consulting room, one that better conforms to the ethical precepts of existentialism. An experienced counsellor, working largely with gay male clients, Jack outlines his experience with an adult male client.

The client, Frank, presented for help dealing with social adjustment after relocating to a new area for work. A gay man in his early 40s, Frank expressed concerns about being overworked, having a limited amount of free time and lacking a social network in his new city. Frank had left a partner behind when he moved, and negotiating a long distance relationship was taking a major toll. Increasing feelings of isolation and loneliness were becoming a significant concern. The clinical discussion, grounded in the concrete aspects of Frank's lifestyle, and the way they were affecting his outlook, began to turn towards Frank's sense of sexual frustration at trying to maintain his sexual commitment to a partner who lived in another city. After a few sessions, the conversation turned towards sexual behaviours, thoughts and fantasies, and the atmosphere in the consulting room was increasingly sexually charged. Jack found himself getting aroused in the sessions, as the content of the discussion became increasingly sexual, and believed this arousal was mutual. After a few sessions, he broached the topic, acknowledged his own sense of arousal at hearing about Frank's sexual thoughts and enquired about what Frank was experiencing in the room. Frank readily acknowledged that he too was aroused, and that Jack had become a part of his sexual fantasy life. This acknowledgement of the mutual attraction and mutual experience of arousal served as a point of departure for discussing what the sexual attraction might mean for Frank, who stated that it was likely a product of his sense of loneliness, isolation and sexual frustration.

In this case, my clinical colleague took a difficult tack, addressing the sexual aspect of the clinical encounter head-on, acknowledging his own sexual feelings and enquiring about his client's. Rather than compromise the professionalism of the encounter, however, this line of discussion served to help them move through a threatened impasse and make meaningful clinical progress. In particular, my colleague (who does not self-identify as an existential therapist) used an existentially oriented discussion of *meaning* to access the underlying existential concerns about loneliness and isolation that may have been driving Frank's seductive in-session behaviour and sexual focus.

Discussion

Existentialism – as a philosophical movement and as a psychotherapy paradigm – is widely concerned with ethics, adhering to a humanist framework. This interest in ethics, however, does not lead directly into approbation, or condemnation, of a particular behaviour. Existentialist humanism is a concern with human beings that emphasizes 'the fluidity of human existence – that is, those aspects which allow all members of our species continually to develop, change and become' (Spinelli, 1989, p. 105). Ethics are, ultimately, a choice to be made by the free and existentially isolated individual. Absolute and universal 'rules' have limited value since ethical action can only be determined within the context of unique circumstances. Ethical 'rules' that purport to determine ethical action a priori have a tendency to obscure the inevitability of personal choice and draw us into bad faith (Spinelli, 2007). This ethical framework has significant implications for the psychotherapist attempting to negotiate client–therapist attraction. It cannot be known in advance whether an acknowledgement or discussion of sexual attraction is ethical or unethical – in Van Deurzen's terms, 'beneficial' or 'harmful'. In fact, it cannot certainly be known in advance whether sexual *contact* between the therapist and the client is ethically acceptable. The appropriate course of action can only be determined *in vivo*, in the context of real-life choices.

The latter instance, therapist–client sexual contact is the more titillating issue, though one that is much more difficult to justify, even within the nonabsolute ethical framework of existentialism. Is it *necessarily* or *inevitably* wrong to engage in a sexual relationship with a client? According to existentialism, no. However, a crucial moral concept – which Sartre draws from the German idealist philosopher, Immanuel Kant – provides a strong foundation for interpreting this type of contact. The Kantian *categorical imperative* states, 'act in such a way that you treat humanity, whether in your own person or in the person of any other, never merely as a means to an end, but always at the same time as an end' (Kant, 1964/1785, p. 95). This ethical imperative requires that the therapist treat the client only as an 'end' – a full and complete being with importance and worth equal to our own – rather than as a 'means' in service of our own self-interest. Simply put, we must not use others for our own selfish reasons.

It is difficult to imagine how an existentialist therapist, guided by this ethical imperative, could justify sexual contact with a client. The therapist is duty-bound to acknowledge her/his own self-interest and recognizes that, no matter what the justification for sexual contact is, the therapist may very well be rationalizing a choice that unacceptably imperils the client. As such, Yalom (1980) emphasizes that 'the most flagrant excess is the therapist who, as a 'real person' becomes sexually involved with a patient' (p. 414). He draws from clinical observation, writing, 'I have seen many patients who have had some prior sexual involvement with a therapist. My impression is that the experience is always destructive for the patient' (p. 414). Thus, condemnation of sexual involvement between client and therapist is derived from observation of clinical practice and from a rational assessment of the likelihood that sexual contact will be damaging for the client. This is to say that whether the therapist recognizes it or not, in choosing to engage in a sexual relationship with the client, the therapist is likely to be treating the client as a means rather than an end.

Sexual contact with the therapist simply cannot alleviate the patient's existential anxiety (her/his longing for connectedness and meaning). This exceeds the wider notion of transference. The patient, in this case, desires more than simple physical contact, or proximate acceptance from a transferential figure. The patient may desire fundamental connectedness – an impossible level of intimacy that the therapist by definition cannot provide. In this case, the choice to engage physically with the client veers perilously toward (in fact, is likely defined by) bad faith. Understanding that the client truly desires something that a physical encounter with the therapist cannot possibly provide, a choice to engage physically with the client is duplicitous and inauthentic – an act of bad faith. Existential psychotherapy is grounded in the principle that mortality, freedom, isolation and meaninglessness are existential facts, which the therapy process must acknowledge and address. Likewise, sexual attraction between client and therapist may – in certain cases – be a fact that must be addressed. Acting on a mutual sexual attraction, however, is a matter of choice that must be guided by the principles of respect for the other's being, authenticity and a commitment to the existential themes of meaninglessness (and the quest for meaning), isolation (and the desire for interconnectedness) and anxiety (and the yearning for relief).

Whereas the existentialist ethos is bound to deem sexual *contact* between the therapist and client unethical, basically without exception (though, again, this can only meaningfully be judged from within the clinical encounter), in many cases, acknowledgement of the sexual attraction may be ethically necessary. It is widely noted that, in the consulting room, psychotherapists are broadly reluctant to address sexual matters in general and are even more reluctant to address sexual attraction between themselves and their clients (Openshaw, 2013; Stevenson, 2010). From an existential vantage point, the likely *reasons* for this avoidance are of particular importance. While there is an implicit and explicit rhetoric of professional boundaries that helps justify therapists' refusal to address sexual dynamics between themselves and their clients, this avoidance is ethically dubious. My own research strongly suggests that therapists often avoid discussing sexual issues not out of interest for the client's well-being, or the effectiveness of the therapy, but rather due to the therapist's own discomfort, or fear of embarrassment. Seen in this light, the type of self-deception that permits some therapists to justify

sexual contact is not dissimilar to the self-deception that allows therapists to *avoid* discussing the sexual dimensions of the psychotherapeutic
encounter. The client, in the therapist's view, ceases to be an end and
becomes a means for maintaining the therapist's own sense of balance,
comfort and surety. The rhetoric of professionalism is applied as an ex
post facto gloss, substantiating an anxiety-driven avoidance of clinically
relevant material.

Barker, a key figure working at the intersection of existentialism, psychotherapy, and sexuality, stresses a set of core clinical priorities that
include a holistic view of patients and their sexuality, a problematizing
approach to conventional assumptions about sexuality and an emphasis
on the individual meaning of sexual issues (Barker, 2011). The use of
such a holistic model, which emphasizes individual meaning, is an invaluable means for approaching the therapist–client attraction (Aanstoos,
2012). Within this framework, the therapist can address the attraction as
a matter of fact (rather than as a perversion of the 'natural'/'appropriate'
professional course of the psychotherapeutic encounter), with a specific,
unique meaning. This approach is foundational to the clinical strategies
addressed next.

Strategies for Working with Sexual Attraction

It takes significant courage to acknowledge and discuss therapist–client
sexual attraction with the client. The underlying ideals of professional
ethics and the looming taboo of a sexual encounter are compounded by
fundamental existential anxieties about the potential consequences of
sexual involvement between two people. Is this attraction motivated by a
desire for fundamental meaning? Is it rooted in a desire to be relieved
of existential anxieties, like the prospect of death, the stark reality of
existential freedom or a yearning for connectedness? An existential orientation towards the psychotherapy encounter, and particularly an ongoing
exploration of the core existential themes, provides a prospectively invaluable avenue for addressing client–therapist sexual attraction. Herein the
sexual attraction itself is much less significant than the underlying meaning
of the sexual attraction and the existential themes it may reflect. Existential strategies for negotiating this sexual attraction are, therefore, based
in an exploration of how the attraction may relate to the core existential
anxieties and drives. Effective existential strategies for dealing with client–
therapist sexual attraction begin at the very outset of the therapeutic
encounter and are discussed further.

Existential Strategies for Managing Sexual Attraction

- The therapist should consider the importance of situating the patient's sexuality as a significant issue, and as a topic of relevant and appropriate clinical concern, from the outset of the therapy process. It is hard to imagine that a patient's existential journey would not, in most cases, significantly implicate his or her sexuality. In fact, the way a patient experiences sexual thoughts and feelings can be a powerful avenue for examining her/his underlying existential quest for meaningfulness and connectedness in life (Berry & Barker, 2013). In addition to being a valuable point of discussion in its own right, introducing sexuality – in relation to existential themes – early on in the therapy process serves to normalize sexuality as a topic of clinical discussion, setting the groundwork for later discussions of sexuality, including the psycho-sexual dynamics of the client–therapist relationship.

- Another straightforward strategy for addressing sexual attraction between the client and the therapist consists in establishing the patient–client relationship as a valid topic for conversation, from the outset of the counselling, and as a recurrent consideration. This clinical consideration – the client–therapist relationship – has been identified as a prototypical element of psychodynamic practice in general (Ablon & Jones, 1998; Ablon, Levy, & Katzenstein, 2006) and as an important element of recently emerging clinical methodologies rooted in the psychodynamic tradition (Bateman & Fonagy, 2012). The existential psychotherapist may be well advised to include the psychotherapist–client relationship as a topic of clinical discussion, early on, and ongoingly throughout the process. Unique to the existentialist approach, the therapist will tend to orient this clinical discussion around the ways in which this relationship may be implicated in the core existential struggles around meaning, isolation and the desire for connectedness, and so on.

- The existential concept of meaning provides a means for negotiating the potentially treacherous landscape of therapist–client sexual attraction. By introducing both sexuality, in general, and the client–therapist relationship as topics for discussion,[1] at the outset of therapy, the therapist establishes a foundation for later discussing sexual attraction, should it emerge. Rather than a daunting transferential obstacle, the

---

[1] In fact, focus on the therapy relationship has been identified as a core principle in dynamic therapy more broadly (Shedler, 2010).

sexual attraction is then re-framed as a unique interpersonal reality that holds a specific meaning for both client and therapist in the context of the therapy relationship. Herein, the patient's desire for meaningfulness and relief from anxiety is a vital topic of discussion and may be used to address the possibility that the patient's sexual attraction could represent an attempt to use the psychotherapist as an anchor against the core existential issues (death, freedom, meaninglessness and isolation). After identifying a reciprocal, or unilateral, sexual attraction, the therapist can draw the clinical discussion towards a critical examination of core existential themes: how does the sexual attraction fits in relation to the fundamental human experience of isolation? Is this desire for sexual attraction an attempt to defend against the anxieties associated with existential solitude? Similarly, the desire for existential meaning may be implicated in the sexual attraction. Could the possible sexual connection be seen as a source of existential meaning for one or both parties? This process of questioning both acknowledges the sexual attraction and its contextual situatedness, maintains the methodological focus on existentialism's core themes and examines the possible meanings of the sexual attraction, in a way that, ideally, will overcome the clinical roadblock of an unspoken psychosexual element in the client–therapist relationship.

• This discussion is situated within the nonpathologizing ethos of existential sex therapy: rather than a 'problem', sexual attraction in the consulting room can be treated as a nonpathological given, to be discussed and explored like the other givens of existential reality. By making explicit this sexual attraction, the therapist may use it as a means to help advance the client's understanding of his/her experience of sexual attraction, in ways that may have previously been misunderstood. Moreover, the therapist's acknowledgement of his/her own attraction towards the client, and a shared discussion of what it may mean, further serves to illustrate the universal nature of the existential challenges we all face and the anxiety associated with them.

Conclusion

Within the existential framework, the psychotherapeutic encounter is governed by an inherently consequentialist ethic, which assesses the nature and implications of client–therapist sexual attraction in light of universal existential themes, and within the context of the unique clinical encounter. This is to say that, while fundamental existential principles – meaning/

meaninglessness, isolation, freedom, responsibility, death/nothingness – guide the therapy process, the specific meaning and nature of the sexual attraction can only be reasonably assessed in light of the unique encounter between two individuals. The underlying ethical imperative to respect the being of the other – to respect the other as an 'end' (rather than a means) (Kant, 1964/1785; Sartre, 1943, 1945; Yalom, 1980) – will, in many circumstances, compel the therapist to acknowledge the sexual attraction and discuss this sexual attraction with the client. Here, the possible existential motivations and implications of the sexual attraction become a key point of clinical focus. By introducing both sexuality, in general, and the client–therapist relationship as legitimate and important topics for discussion, at the early stages in therapy, the therapist sets the stage for a prospective return to these considerations, which may become necessary as the therapy process unfolds. Simply put, the existential therapist must be prepared to address and discuss the meanings of a sexual attraction, insofar as her/his clinical practice is bound by genuine commitment to the other and marked by authenticity.

References

Aanstoos, C. M. (2012). A phenomenology of sexual experience. In P. Kleinplatz (Ed.), *New directions in sex therapy: Innovations and alternatives* (2nd ed., pp. 51–68). New York: Routledge.

Ablon, J. S., & Jones, E. E. (1998). How expert clinicians' prototypes of ideal treatment correlate with outcome in psychodynamic and cognitive-behavioral therapy. *Psychotherapy Research*, 8(1), 71–83.

Ablon, J. S., Levy, R. A., & Katzenstein, T. (2006). Beyond brand names of psychotherapy: Identifying empirically supported changes processes. *Psychotherapy: Theory, Research, Practice, Training*, 43(2), 216–231.

Barker, M. (2011). Existential sex therapy. *Sexual and Relationship Therapy*, 26(1), 33–47.

Bateman, A. W., & Fonagy, P. (Eds.) (2012). *Handbook of mentalizing in mental health practice*. Washington, DC: American Psychiatric Publishing, Inc.

Berry, M., & Barker, M. (2013, in press). Extraordinary interventions for extraordinary clients: Existential sex therapy and open non-monogamy. *Sexual and Relationship Therapy*.

Daigle, C. (Ed.) (2006). *Existentialist thinkers and ethics*. Montreal: McGill University Press.

Kant, I. (1964/1785). *Groundwork for the metaphysics of morals*. H. J. Paton (trans.). New York: Harper and Row.

Openshaw, S. (2013/02/26). Interview by M. Berry [web based recording].

Pope, K. (2000). Therapists' sexual feelings and behaviors: Research, trends, and quandaries. In L. Szuchman & F. Muscarella (Eds.), *Psychological perspectives on human sexuality* (pp. 603–658). New York: John Wiley and Sons.

Pope, K. (2001). Sex between therapists and clients. In J. Worrell (Ed.), *Encyclopedia of women and gender: Sex similarities and differences and the impact of society on gender* (Vol. 2, pp. 955–962). San Diego: Academic Press.

Sartre, J.-P. (1943 [2005]). *Being and nothingness* H. E. Barnes (trans.). London: Verso.

Sartre, J.-P. (1945 [2002]). *Existentialism and human emotions*. B. Frecthman (trans.). New York: Citadel Press.

Shedler, J. (2010). The efficacy of psychodynamic psychotherapy. *The American Psychologist*, 65(2), 98–109.

Smith-Pickard, P., & Swynnerton, R. (2005). The body and sexuality. In E. Van Deurzen & C. Arnold-Baker (Eds.), *Existential perspectives on human issues* (pp. 48–57). New York: Palgrave Macmillan.

Spinelli, E. (1989). *The interpreted world: An introduction to phenomenological.* London: Sage.

Spinelli, E. (2007). *Practicing existential therapy: The relational world*. London: Sage.

Stevenson, C. (2010). Talking about sex. In C. Butler, A. O'Donovan, & E. Shaw (Eds.), *Sex, sexuality and therapeutic practice: A manual for therapists and trainers* (pp. 31–54). New York: Routledge.

Van Deurzen, E. (1998). *Paradox and passion in psychotherapy: An existential approach to therapy and counselling*. New York: Wiley.

Van Deurzen, E. (2002). *Existential counselling and psychotherapy in practice* (2nd ed.). London: Sage.

Warnock, M. (1967). *Existentialist ethics*. London: Macmillan.

Warnock, M. (1970). *Existentialism*. London: Oxford University Press.

Watter, D. N. (2012). Ethics and sex therapy: A neglected dimension. In P. Kleinplatz (Ed.), *New directions in sex therapy: Innovations and alternatives* (2nd ed., pp. 85–100). New York: Routledge.

Yalom, I. D. (1980). *Existential psychotherapy*. New York: Basicbooks.

Yalom, I. D. (1991). *Love's executioner and other tales of psychotherapy*. London: Penguin.

4

Knowing but Not Showing

*Achieving Reflective Encounter
with Desire – A Relational
Psychoanalytic Perspective*

Doris McIlwain

In handling sexual desire that arises in the course of psychotherapy, Freud (1915/1957) notes that one must neither gratify nor suppress desire, suggesting that 'the course the analyst must pursue . . . is one for which there is no model in real life' (p. 164). The pursuit is perhaps like the petals in Pound's (1911) poem, 'and as the petals of flowers in falling, waver and seem not drawn to earth' (p. 22), hovering, seemingly resisting something as powerful as gravity, as sexuality. In sustaining an intimate, honest and safe relationship between psychotherapist and client, delicate, courageous art is entailed. The challenge posed by sexual desire in psychotherapy is, firstly, an epistemic one: is it me or is it them; or, more likely is it in-me-out-there? One has to entertain the feelings long enough to get the message, to locate the source(s). So, forms of avoidance promoted by fearful ignorance, shame or guilt are unhelpful. Fearful ignorance, like feeling that attraction is synonymous with a boundary violation or that it should not be happening if one is a good therapist, can produce shame and attempts 'not to know' that desire is present. The perils of cognitive and affective avoidance are considerable, including the enhanced possibility of acting out those desires. Where barriers prevent recognition of desire, we can try to discern telltale signs of its presence, can try to snoop on our own unconscious, or be alert to signs in colleagues and friends that they may not be picking up themselves. In the course of this paper, I use quotations from interviews of therapists from Sydney, Australia, by my former

Sexual Attraction in Therapy: Clinical Perspectives on Moving Beyond the Taboo – A Guide for Training and Practice, First Edition. Edited by Maria Luca.
© 2014 John Wiley & Sons, Ltd. Published 2014 by John Wiley & Sons, Ltd.

doctoral student and now colleague, Dr Anthony Arcuri. I am indebted to Anthony for permitting me to use his interviews in this way. The candour and ease of the interviews addressing a very difficult topic are testimony to his skill and warmth. Any errors in the use of quotations are my own.

In handling desire, one first has to permit it to unfold, rather than distort or detour therapy in defensive directions to shore up one's own peace of mind. This courage is necessary to avoid taking a stance that someone else in the client's life may have taken in the past: bystander (Rachman, Kennedy, & Yard, 2005), frightened abandoner, seduced authority who indulges in fantasies, smiling exploiter, briskly businesslike overcompensator or intrusive policer of desire. One has to be open to what the arrival of sexual desire in therapy means for the client, and this requires being open to signs within oneself. This is part of the epistemic problem, since some forms of therapy suggest that certain feelings and impulses within oneself may be due to a client's communicating by impact – making one come to know how he/she feels by inducing that feeling in the therapist. So just because the sensation comes from within one's own bodily economy is not a sure-fire sign that it is 'all one's own'. Sorting out such instances of projective identification (Ogden, 1979; Person, 1985) from mutual attraction, or from one's own unfinished business, is intensely problematic.

If one regularly experiences attraction to clients, chances are there is some unfinished business of one's own requiring supervisory input or further therapy. If it is an unusual occurrence, it could be that this client has brought feelings to the fore that have long lain dormant, or it may be that on the part of the client, some scripting into a role, enactment of experiences that escape language so far or acting out of conflicts is occurring, in which case their impact on the therapist still implicates the therapist in some way if an answering desire is promoted. I am reminded of Person's (1985) reference to erotic transference (where transference is the reproduction in the present of templates of loving established in past relationships), where there is 'some mixture of tender, erotic and sexual feelings a patient experiences towards the analyst' as being both 'goldmine and minefield' (p. 162). The same is certainly true of erotic countertransference.

Sexual longings arising in therapy may have diverse sources. Many writers have spoken about their possible origin with some seeing them as a recreation of past trauma by the client (Rachman et al., 2005), as a sign of a perverse client's early relations which 'the patient recreated with myself, filling me with excitement and titillation whilst rendering me powerless' (Luca, 2003, p. 660; see also Dujovne, 2002), as a co-created impact of client on therapist, as analyst's unfinished business, or as real love where one must refer on and wait 2 years.

Desire in the Therapy Room

When a client reproduces in the present old templates of what was required in the past to sustain love (transference), therapists may feel scripted into feelings and longings, drawn into relationships and actions (countertransference) that they do not recognize as arising from unconscious 'unfinished business' within themselves. Sexual attraction may arise in just such a way. When sexual attraction enters the therapy room, it is not at all transparent as to what that means. As one therapist said of sexual attraction to clients (in an interview with Dr Anthony Arcuri), 'sexual attraction could mean a whole lot of different things besides just the sex, like, if you look at it, it's not just sex. Like, is sex just sex anyway?'

Sexual desire might be an enactment by the client in recreating dissociated elements from the past. As Giesbrecht, Lynn, Lilienfled, and Merckelbach (2008) note in their meta-analytic review of dissociation, there are two forms of dissociation: detachment (incomplete information processing, preventing connections between component emotional processes) and compartmentalization (discernible empirically by performance fluctuations across states). Kohut (1971) distinguished the horizontal split of repression from the vertical split of dissociation. In the horizontal split, there is a divide between conscious and unconscious, while in the vertical split, consciousness is divided. In describing the form of dissociation closest to the vertical split, Prince (1914) suggests that due to past trauma, a person may have difficulty synthesizing 'sentiments and emotions of a certain character, i.e., those which pertain to certain experiences, to certain systems of remembrances' (p. 499, cited in Berman, 1981, p. 283). This lack of synthesis between 'systems' is a form of psychological partitioning. For Kohut, the split was such that we could not 'look over' partitions within the psyche; for example, in narcissism, vulnerable aspects of the self were separate from the grandiose. Self-states can be quite separate, partitioned-off compartmentalizations of conative, affective bundles, resulting in a fragmented versatility of self – a self like a pack of cards. One cannot 'look over the partitions' between such self-states, because, as Bromberg (1996) notes, within a single dissociated strand of personality, an observing ego is not present, since an observing ego relies on discrepancies and linkages between states or strands. Where desire that arises within a client in a therapeutic situation is split off, and where it is not open to being symbolized, it is likely to be enacted. It is the therapist who might add the ability to reflect in such a moment, to recognize enactment and to discern that scripting is occurring, whereby they feel impelled to respond in particular ways. As one therapist noted, 'And that is part of the training, isn't it? To be able to stand back when the client wants to get you into a certain tango, like, he gets into a victimisation role, and wants you to be the persecutor'. Bromberg (1996) suggests that inter-subjective negotiation is especially vital for those whose personality is dissociatively organized.

The task of the therapist is to allow what may be a client's previously unformulated experience to arise in safety so that the client might find the 'words to say it'. The therapist must be able to reflect on being scripted into impulses to act and on feelings that have an ego-alien quality. The epistemic challenge hinges on the therapist's being able to entertain the possibility that he/she is encountering a client's dissociated material, and/or her or his own unconscious material that has never arisen before. This may be the unique impact of this client on the therapist, or something personal, beyond handling in the therapeutic situation. In the latter case, after seeking supervision, referring on may be the best option. If it is in part how a client is able to get personal needs met, or if he/she bypasses intimacy needs by privileging the sexual aspects of that intimacy, the therapist needs to feel comfortable with him or herself being viewed as sexual, as desired, and be able to reflect on it when an answering personal desire is evoked. There are many barriers to being comfortable with this.

Recognizing the Relevance of Sexual Desire to Psychotherapy

One such barrier is only seeing the occurrence of desire as a problem, but apart from that, as irrelevant to therapy. This is difficult to recognize as a form of avoidance since some systems of therapy do see it as irrelevant. Such a view impedes practitioners within that system of thought in being able to discern possible useful meanings in the occurrence of sexual desire and options to handle it. To avoid the possible significance of its occurrence is, perhaps, the theoretical equivalent of what relationally oriented psychoanalytic clinicians call 'attending away' when describing how processes remain out of awareness. Rather than a forcible removal from conscious awareness, there is a failure to accord meaning and significance to certain events, a failure to link them up to other mental processes, or to find words to express them. Thus, the occurrence of desire for a therapist in a system that accords only problematic significance to it may, like other dissociated processes, remain split off, with the experience of desire remaining unsignified in language and unintegrated into life narratives.

It is common in the pursuit of 'rationality' to assume that one must minimize feelings as early as possible in the process of their unfolding so that they do not taint and disrupt our view of the inner world and external circumstances (McIlwain, 2009). This assumes that they will actually have less effect if ignored. Appraising feelings in advance, pre-emptively, via schemas, does seem to be a less costly way of managing them rather than 'mopping them up' after evocation (Richards & Gross, 2000). However, one has to have come to know feelings and desires rather well to know, in advance, how to appraise them in optimal ways, and to do so pre-emptively. This is not the same thing as avoidance. Pre-existing schemas are helpful; knowing about the many things that sexual desire might signal in advance of its emergence and what to do about it is helpful. Modulating emotional expression, once aroused, is costly: inhibiting memory for incidental details, diminishing emotional vividness in the moment and weakening the narrative structure of recall (McIlwain, 2006) are not conducive to optimal clinical memory or presence.

Desire Doesn't Happen to Good Therapists

Pope, Keith-Spiegel, and Tabachnick (1986) suggest that Freud viewed countertransference (introduced by Freud as a term in a 1909 lecture; Freud, 1910) as an irrational or distorting reaction to the client's transference, which led psychotherapists to believe that their sexual attraction to clients represents a therapeutic error to be hidden or be ashamed of. Freud suggested that the therapist might 'recognize this countertransference in himself and overcome it' (p. 143). Mann (1999) nominated Freud as having a powerful influence on psychotherapists' attitudes towards sexual attraction to clients by his having declared in 1915 that psychotherapists should handle erotic countertransference by means of repression. Freud (1915/1957) declared it to have crucial informational import: 'the phenomenon signifies a valuable piece of enlightenment' (p. 159), seen in context (as having arisen in a particular situation of intimacy and uneven power) and with humility. Yet there is much shame in therapists about the occurrence of desire.

Shame

Handling the emergence of desire via interpersonal forms of coping was rare in the interviews. There was a real reluctance to take it to supervision; it was seen as 'so hard to tell others: everyone says they need to be incredibly strong to do that'. One therapist offers an interesting pair of views on seeking supervision. When viewed as largely the therapist's attraction, the response was one of handling it alone: 'I don't think I would speak with my supervisor'. If it were seen as a client's attraction, the therapist's preferred response is markedly different: 'if it was coming from the opposite side, I would consult immediately with a supervisor'. The decision may be based on perceived manageability of desire; it may be shame about her desire in a therapeutic context. What is evident here is that a tacit distinction is being made between handling desire that arises from oneself and handling desire that arises from the client. Intersubjective exploration of the basis of that distinction would be fruitful. Therapists were very clear about attributes of a supervisor sought: an open-minded, warm, experienced, receptive and uncompetitive person who was able to normalize the experience. These are the kinds of attributes likely to minimize vulnerability and shame in discussion and exploration.

Professionally, the occurrence of sexual desire and its handling need to be recognized, not just as an ethical issue but as requiring skills to handle it which are at the heart of good technique. It is counterproductive for such experiences to be compartmentalized or partitioned off due to shame. At points of challenge and growth as a therapist, such as the occurrence of sexual desire for a client, compartmentalization is diminished by intersubjective reflection such as that provided by supervision, enhancing individual reflective function to permit 'looking over' vertical partitions within the psyche and enhancing integration. Loewald (1988) suggests that the ego is in fact 'held together by libidinal, erotic bonds which in their basic nature are not different from those bonds obtaining in object relations' (p. 24).

In contrast, shame can fragment us, can isolate us from the support of colleagues and supervisors, and also diminish the integration of emotional experience (EE) via producing partitions or vertical splits and via promoting incomplete information processing and, thus, detachment. Responding with shame to felt emotions can undo links between elements of emotion experience or prevent the formation of such links. Working longitudinally with young women [with a verified history of childhood sexual abuse (CSA) who have experienced shame and humiliation], Negrao, Bonanno,

Noll, Putnam, and Trickett (2005) show how normally interlinked emotional processes become separate; they found dissociations between facial expression and verbal avowal with those who do not disclose to a new interviewer their history of CSA, showing more non-Duchene smiles, smiles of appeasement and shame rather than of pleasure (Negrao et al., 2005, p. 97). These specific dissociations may be an adaptive form of coping for those with a history of trauma.

Even without having experienced the full shock of trauma, many people avoid fullness of feeling to cope with emotions that arise that they cannot soothe. Full EE is a multicomponential process. Powerfully influenced by the bodily clout of emotion, EE is shaped by manner of attending (reflective or immersed) to it and of appraising it (as a synthetic whole, or analytically in parts). Taking the emotion of joy as an example, I might experience it as a synthetic whole ('I feel joy') or discern it analytically in parts ('my breath is shallow and I feel light, like running'); I might be reflectively aware of it ('the world seems much brighter when I feel joy') or just immersed in it ('what a gorgeous world!'). With the experience of desire, one's aim is to be reflectively aware of the mingling of present experience and evocation of the past; for example, 'this person is evoking for me that character I found so attractive played by Hugo Weaving in the film *Cloud Atlas*', integrating the meaning of desire in terms of personal history, permitting personal exploration of its significance. Some of the therapists we interviewed seemed to take the experience apart appraising it 'analytically' (in Lambie and Marcel's sense); specifically, they sought to separate thought and feeling as a coping strategy. This disrupts the integration of components of desire. Desire might be felt in a fragmented way: 'what's that clenching in my belly and why is my heart racing?' Uncannily enough, even when the actor has no phenomenological awareness of the bodily signal, it is there for observers to discern. Observers might correctly attribute desire (or anger or anxiety) of which the bearer is entirely unaware (Lambie & Marcel, 2002).

Barriers to recognizing desire may play out differently across genders as Person (1985) notes. She first sets in place Gill's (1979) distinction between 'resistance to the awareness of transference', where it is transference that is resisted and which she suggests commonly occurs in male patients, and 'resistance to the resolution of transference' (Person, 1985, p. 172), where it is the transference that does the resisting and which is commonly found in female patients. This reflects both cultural constructions of femininity and masculinity and also early object relations (p. 173). Person notes that women's embarrassment at 'presuming to be found "sexual" and erotically desirable despite the patient's disclaimers also serves as an impediment to interpreting the resistance to the erotic trans-ference' (p. 172). In short, women may be left holding all the desire as the male patient re-enacts but disavows desire. As one therapist noted, the client may create a 'tango' where he 'gets his needs met by trying to attract people sexually. He may be adept . . . look at what's happening in the relationship. It gives a window into what's happening in the client's psyche'.

Therapist discomfort with and avoidance of awareness of desire can shape therapy in ways that manage (or titillate) the therapist's emotions; one therapist noted that he asked 'questions that I know if I weren't attracted to her I wouldn't be asking'. Avoidance can result in shifting focus from client to self, can cloud judgement or lead to overcompensat-ing. It can change the therapist's role: 'giving them options and answers, and providing advice . . . much as you'd do with friends'. It can leave the therapist vulnerable, caring about how she or he is viewed, or as one therapist noted, 'keeping that client on when it's really time to terminate, or keeping that client on when it's time to refer on'.

In an attempt to overcome motivated avoidance, one can snoop on one's own unconscious by noting behavioural signs that, were one to observe them in another, might indicate attraction. These include noting that one might be looking forward to certain clients' sessions and preparing more, getting dressed up, being more flexible with times and stepping out of role. Ways of avoiding disruption when one notices such signs include maintaining boundaries of a physical nature, like not scheduling as final appointment in the day a client who has inspired a tendency towards getting dressed up, and boundaries of a straightforward psychological nature, such as ensuring that one is being consistent across clients in flex-ibility offered with times and cancellations.

An alternative to taking a slightly behaviourist approach to snooping on one's unconscious and handling desire that is being avoided entails allowing the desire to form so that it has a fully phenomenological char-acter, can be fully experienced, and explored as to its possible contributing causes and meanings. This course of action requires skills that are most likely to form with supervisory input.

Allowing Desire to Form

Courage is required to allow the experience of desire to form, to own it and take responsibility for its co-emergence, as this brings conflict into the picture. Responding with shame avoids this conflict but makes it less likely that an experience will be owned and integrated into one's personality and life narratives (McIlwain, 2003, 2010). Refreshingly, clinicians focused on the 'information that it would give about one's personality. Why am I attracted to this person, what did I find attractive?' Another sought to learn 'about their own vulnerabilities', another owned the experience: 'I am attracted, so it's something about me that has entered the equation'.

Subtle psychological boundaries are required to handle desire which has been allowed to form. They entail having 'a private life' in the presence of another, requiring expressive control. Such privacy has limits since unconscious-to-unconscious communication occurs. In my view, expressive bracketing is a form of neutrality.

Contemporary depth forms of psychotherapy, particularly relational psychoanalysis, have called into question the advantage of therapist 'neutrality', suggesting it creates an atmosphere inimical to empathy by evoking a 'sterile operating theatre' and a certain 'coldness of feeling' (Mitchell, 2000), and may repeat experiences of abandonment and neglect for certain clients. Freud (1915/1957) also noted this in his recommendations regarding handling the countertransference: 'The treatment must be carried out in abstinence. By this I do not mean physical abstinence alone, nor yet the deprivation of everything that the patient desires, for perhaps no sick person could tolerate this' (p. 164). Freud's positive recommendations hover between opposites: neither gratification nor suppression; 'It is . . . just as disastrous for the analysis if the patient's craving for love is gratified as if it is suppressed' (p. 164). He advocates work on the part of the therapist so that the client can experience safety and spaciousness. She should 'feel safe enough to allow all her preconditions for loving, all the phantasies springing from her sexual desires, all the detailed characteristics of her state of being in love, to come to light' (p. 165). Andrea Sabbadini in Chapter 9 of the book illustrates how the Freudian tension of 'neither gratification, nor suppression' appears in analytic work.

Neutrality need not be coldness of feeling, nor a failing to recognize the presence in the room of two people (and two sets of unconscious processes) co-creating a therapeutic relationship. But if there is sexual desire on the part of the therapist, how can we be optimally open to the informational import of such inner signals while managing their intensity? Handling entails recognizing that desire is there in the moment, interrogating its origins and meanings, retaining a receptivity and openness to its significance for self and client, while skilfully modulating its expressive display. Difficult as this may be even in hindsight, it is likely to be most challenging in the ongoing moments of therapy, without considerable skill.

Having a secret desire partitions us, where one part of us knows something another part of us does not know, literally undermining personal integrity. Ironically, the solution I offer is a combination of conscious use of a reflective form of detachment and mindful partitioning called 'facework'. We may achieve this through what Anzieu (1981) calls a reflective encounter with desire rather than an expressive encounter.

The Sublimation of Facework: Knowing but Not Showing

Facework entails the skilful uncoupling of features of emotion. It is a skilful disaggregation. It requires past reflective processes of allowing desire to assemble, a history of having and expressing feelings and desires, accompanied by fully conscious, phenomenal states. In this way, EE is truly mental and does not bypass conscious awareness towards procedural enactment, whereby the expressiveness of the body will give too much away. This history is then followed by an apprenticeship in the disassembly process, where one acquires skills in (with reflective awareness) deflecting full expressive display. The result is a 'resonant neutrality', useful as a means of handling sexual desire. In skilful disaggregation, one might let desire form to get the full message, but once the intensity of the action tendency builds, the body is likely to speak, so modulation is required. Of crucial import is minimizing the expressive burden of one's experience on the other. It is hard work.

Hochschild (1983/2003) studied airline staff coached in 'feeling rules' and 'required to induce or suppress feeling in order to sustain the outward countenance that produces the proper states of mind in others'. Suppression alienates the person from their emotions: 'feeling is thinner, less freighted with consequence'. Facework is not suppression, but sublimation, a form of mindful dissociation that includes the whole bodily economy. If too much has to be controlled, one loses spontaneous warmth and presence, concerns that might be weighed to deciding whether to refer a client on.

With facework, displays of emotion are a spontaneous blend of one's inner experience and therapeutic requirements. Hostage negotiators also require such skill, where successful negotiation entails sensing others' feeling and one's own, yet keeping control of reactions that may harm the process or the other if revealed too soon, or sometimes if revealed at all. Much may hinge on success, from the lives of innocent people in hostage negotiation, to the continuance of therapeutic contact. Straker (2007) describes an agonizing moment of (what I term) facework when doing therapy in apartheid-era South Africa with a young black revolutionary worker who divulges in an instant that he had participated in the neck-lacing of a woman suspected of being a police informer. The demands experienced by Gill Straker were such that she momentarily experienced a disruption in thought itself, but she managed to stay present to the client against all odds. Such skills must be contextually sensitive, requiring moment-to-moment awareness.

Handling Desire in the Moment: Being Prepared to Be Found Wanting

Freud recommended honesty if we do return clients' feelings, but advocates 'not to give up the neutrality towards the patient, which we have acquired through keeping the counter-transference in check' (p. 163).

The therapist must be willing to be found by the client, not cold or absent and denying feelings that will do damage to the intersubjective reality of the client. So facework must be conscious, tailored to the psychoaffective history of the client. If it is achieved skilfully, it can achieve a nuanced accommodation to the client in a breathing, dynamic relationship that captures the client's state on the day, phase of transference and nature of therapeutic alliance. It is less likely to repeat experiences of neglect (for a client) or seem cold if it is achieved with mindfulness and alignment of consciousness, concepts more fully explored by Blonna in Chapter 6. Epstein (1995) suggests bare attention: 'the clear and single-minded awareness of what actually happens to us and in us at successive moments of perception' (p. 110). In bare attention, one may be compartmentalized, focusing only on what is arising now. That may be a conscious alignment in the moment. There can be a loosening of the integration of a sense of self that is adaptive. Loewald (1988) refers to a 'differentiated unity (a manifold) that captures separateness in the act of uniting, and unity in the act of separating' (p. 24). Bromberg (1996) suggests that there is a normal multiplicity of self-states; moving between them with reflective awareness might be part of the skill of a therapist. Goldberg (2007) suggests that what is distinctive about analysts is 'our personal self-reflection'. This 'I' or reflective knower is enhanced by the sublimation of facework that permits a recursive loop on the self.

Part of one's desire goes to the world (or other, or object), and part can loop back to witness oneself as desiring. In this way, one can aspire to reflective containment, a sublimated bracketing of impulses so that one can still reflectively gain information. There is a split between being and seeming; one knows but does not show, and this may have a trade-off for authenticity (Geeves, McIlwain, Sutton, & Christensen, 2013), but authenticity is an ideal that one may approximate only asymptotically if one accepts the reality of unconscious processes and motivations.

Via the resonant neutrality facework offers, the therapist may be alive to primitive desires as a basis for understanding the wishes, impulses and fantasies of those with whom they work, but, says Whitebook (1995), 'he is only analyst to the extent that he has concurrently sublimated those desires . . . into a consistent investment in knowledge and in fostering the patient's autonomy' (p. 240). In the course of therapeutic work, there are fresh encounters for therapists with new material.

Having achieved a certain fullness of desire in the past, one is schematic for conditions of its occurrence and less impelled to act, retaining access to feelings and impulses as sources of information. Therapists' attempts to bracket their own impulses, emotions and values to 'evenly hover' aim to give space to the client's voices and urges in a relationship where he/she is safe and free from interpersonal indebtedness, judgement and exploitation. To conclude the chapter, I summarize some therapeutic qualities necessary in the handling of sexual desire in therapy.

Clinical Strategies

- Forms of avoidance promoted by fearful ignorance, shame or guilt are unhelpful.
- One must permit sexual desire to unfold, rather than distort or detour therapy in defensive directions to shore up one's own peace of mind.
- If too much of oneself has to be controlled, one loses spontaneous warmth and presence, concerns that might be weighed to decide whether one has to refer the client on.
- The aim is recognizing desire, interrogation of its origins and meanings, retaining a receptivity and openness to the information it has about self and client, while skilfully modulating its expressive display.
- Courage is required to allow the experience of desire to form and to be discerned synthetically as a whole, including owning it and taking some responsibility for the co-emergence of desire.
- Modulating intensity of desire requires a conscious partitioning and an alignment of consciousness in the moment.

References

Anzieu, D. (1981). *Le Corps de l'œuvre: essais psychanalytiques sur le travail créateur*. Paris: Gallimard.

Berman, E. (1981). Multiple personality: Psychoanalytic perspectives. *International Journal of Psycho-Analysis, 62*, 283–300.

Bromberg, P. M. (1996). Standing in the spaces: The multiplicity of self and the psychoanalytic relationship. *Contemporary Psychoanalysis, 32*, 509–535.

Cloud Atlas. (2012) Retrieved from http://www.imdb.com/title/tt1371111/

Dujovne, B. (2002). Perverse relatedness. *Psychoanalytic Psychology, 19*(3), 525–539.

Epstein, M. (1995). *Thoughts without a thinker*. New York: Basic Books.

Freud, S. (1910). The future prospects of psycho-analytic therapy. In J. Strachey (Ed.), *The standard edition of the complete psychological works of Sigmund Freud* (Vol. 11, pp. 139–152). London: Hogarth Press.

Freud, S. (1915/1957). Observations on transference love. In J. Strachey (Ed.), *The standard edition of the complete psychological works of Sigmund Freud* (pp. 157–171). London: Hogarth Press and The Institute of Psycho-Analysis.

Geeves, A., McIlwain, D., Sutton, J., & Christensen, W. (2013). To think or not to think: The apparent paradox of expert skill in music performance. *Educational Philosophy and Theory*. doi:10.1080/00131857.2013.779214

Giesbrecht, T., Lynn, S. J., Lilienfled, S. O., & Merckelbach, H. (2008). Cognitive processes in dissociation: An analysis of core theoretical assumptions. *Psychological Bulletin, 134*(5), 607–647.

Gill, M. (1979). Analysis of the transference. *Journal of the American Psychoanalytic Association, 27*(Suppl.), 263–288.

Goldberg, A. (2007). *Moral stealth: How 'correct behavior' insinuates itself into psychotherapeutic practice*. Chicago, IL: University of Chicago Press.

Hochschild, A. (1983/2003). *The managed heart: The commercialisation of human feeling*. Berkley and Los Angeles, CA: University of California Press.

Kohut, H. (1971). *The analysis of the self*. New York: International Universities Press.

Lambie, J., & Marcel, A. (2002). Consciousness and the varieties of emotion experience: A theoretical framework. *Psychological Review, 2*, 210–259.

Loewald, H. (1988). *Sublimation*. New Haven, CT: Yale University Press.

Luca, M. (2003). Containment of the sexualized and eroticized transference. *Journal of Clinical Psychoanalysis, 11*(4), 649–674.

McIlwain, D. (2003). Bypassing empathy: Mapping a Machiavellian theory of mind and sneaky power. In B. Repacholi & V. Slaughter (Eds.), *Individual differences in theory of mind: Implications for typical and atypical development* (Series Macquarie Monographs in Cognitive Science). Sussex: Psychology Press.

McIlwain, D. (2006). Already filtered: Affective immersion and personality differences in accessing present and past. *Philosophical Psychology, 19*(3), 381–399.

McIlwain, D. (2009). Living palely and the rationality of a certain fullness of feeling. *Artlink, 29*(3), 15–24.

McIlwain, D. (2010). Young Machiavellians and the traces of shame: Coping with vulnerability to a toxic affect. In C. Barry, P. Kerig, K. Stellwagen, & T. Barry (Eds.), *Narcissism and Machiavellianism in youth: Implications for the development of adaptive and maladaptive behavior* (pp. 213–232). Washington, DC: APA.

Mann, D. (1999). Erotic narrative in psychoanalytic practice: An introduction. In D. Mann (Ed.), *Erotic transference and countertransference: Clinical practice in psychotherapy*. London: Routledge.

Mitchell, S. (2000). *Relationality: From attachment to intersubjectivity* (Relational Perspectives Book Series). Mahwah, NJ: The Analytic Press.

Negrao, C., II, Bonanno, G. A., Noll, J. G., Putnam, F. W., & Trickett, P. K. (2005). Shame, humiliation, and childhood sexual abuse: Distinct contributions and emotional coherence. *Child Maltreatment, 10*(4), 350–363.

Ogden, T. H. (1979). On projective identification. *International Journal of Psycho-Analysis, 60*, 357–373.

Person, E. S. (1985). The erotic transference in women and in men: Differences and consequences. *Journal of the American Academy of Psychoanalysis, 13*, 159–180.

Pope, K. S., Keith-Spiegel, P., & Tabachnick, B. G. (1986). Sexual attraction to clients: The human therapist and the (sometimes) inhuman training system. *American Psychologist, 41*, 147–158.

Pound, E. (1911). Speech for Psyche in the Golden Book of Apuleius. In *Canzoni*. London: Elkin Mathews.

Prince, M. (1914). *The unconscious*. New York: Macmillan.

Rachman, A. W., Kennedy, R., & Yard, M. (2005). The role of childhood sexual seduction in the development of an erotic transference: Perversion in the psychoanalytic situation. *International Forum of Psychoanalysis, 14*, 183–187.

Richards, J. M., & Gross, J. J. (2000). Emotion regulation and memory: The cognitive costs of keeping one's cool. *Journal of Personality and Social Psychology, 75*, 410–424.

Straker, G. (2007). A crisis in the subjectivity of the analyst: The trauma of morality. *Psychoanalytic Dialogues: The International Journal of Relational Perspectives, 17*(2), 153–164.

Whitebook, J. (1995). *Perversion and utopia: A study in psychoanalysis and critical theory*. Cambridge, MA: MIT Press.

5

The Role of Psychological Proximity and Sexual Feelings in Negotiating Relatedness in the Consulting Room
A Phenomenological Perspective

Paul Smith-Pickard

Introduction

In this chapter, I will argue from my experience as an existential psychotherapist that sexual feelings within therapy are not only unavoidable,
but attempting to deny them can be more problematic than accepting
them. This is particularly so in styles of therapy, such as my own, where
dialogical relatedness and psychological proximity are regarded as central
elements in the work. I describe myself as an existential psychotherapist,
meaning that my work is informed by phenomenology and philosophical
and sociological thought found in continental philosophy.

It seems that sexual feelings between therapist and client are rarely
discussed, except in the context of professional misconduct or as erotic
transference. There is an implicit consensus that sexual feelings in the
consulting room are problematic and are therefore best avoided. This
is by no means an original observation and we might even see it as a
stereotype or cliché of therapy that extends into the public domain. Consequently, we find ourselves living and working in an all-pervasive climate
of opinion that is deeply suspicious and cautious of anything sexual in
the consulting room. I came to the conclusion quite early on in my career
that most therapists find it inappropriate to have sexual feelings towards
their clients, and yet, it is accepted and even possibly expected that clients
will be sexually attracted to their therapist.

Sexual Attraction in Therapy: Clinical Perspectives on Moving Beyond the Taboo – A Guide for Training and Practice, First Edition. Edited by Maria Luca.
© 2014 John Wiley & Sons, Ltd. Published 2014 by John Wiley & Sons, Ltd.

Rather than avoid sexual feelings by attempting to put them out of play, either by a phenomenological bracketing, re-framing them as erotic transference or denying their existence by placing an asexual boundary around the work, I would argue that sexual feelings can be an appropriate and important element in the therapy that can be productively and safely incorporated. However, for this to happen, it is necessary to accept certain existential givens. The first is the primacy of embodiment as a central feature of existence, meaning that we always exist in and through our body. The second is the ever-present phenomenon of existential sexuality, whereby sexual feelings are a constant horizon to our existence.

In this chapter, I will examine the implicit taboo on sexual attraction, before presenting embodiment as a unified system of mind and body, exploring the nature of sexual attraction, and the interpersonal dynamics of existential sexuality. Finally, I will suggest ways to work with psychological proximity and with sexual feelings as a legitimate aspect of the encounter. Then, by using the metaphor of lovers, explore similarities between the intimate narratives of lovers and the dynamics of both verbal and non-verbal dialogue involved in negotiating relatedness in practice.

Theoretical Framework

I will begin by examining the all-pervasive climate of opinion mentioned earlier to try and understand why sexual attraction is seen as unwelcome or threatening to psychotherapists. The implicit taboo surrounding sexual feelings that emerge in therapeutic practice is linked to issues such as professional codes of conduct, institutionalized ethical boundaries, cultural taboos, social perceptions and, of course, the legacy of Freudian psychoanalysis. I remember attending a conference workshop on ethics and being presented with the high incidence of male American psychiatrists accused of sexual misconduct with their clients. At that time, state regulation of the profession was being proposed, and the presenter was attempting to base a whole strategy of ethics for psychotherapy in the United Kingdom on the sexual misconduct of some male psychiatrists in another continent. I am not arguing against sexual misconduct being regarded as a major ethical transgression, simply pointing out that making it the foundational image for an ethical strategy, when there are many ways in which to be unethical, besides sexual exploitation and misconduct, is an overt example of an institutionalized repressive attitude towards anything sexual in psychotherapy.

The findings of my own research (Smith-Pickard, 2006b) supported the view that sexual attraction is potentially present in the majority of therapeutic encounters. Many of my co-researchers, all psychotherapists, experienced sexual feelings as problematic. They reported a sense of shame and failure when they were sexually attracted to their clients, and if a client expressed sexual feelings towards them, they assumed that they had done something wrong and felt responsible for allowing it to happen. They reported a rupture in the focus of the therapy and in their ability to maintain psychological contact, becoming disconnected from their clients. They were also reluctant to take this to supervision for fear of being judged as unethical or inappropriate in their work. Other co-researchers, however, were prepared to accept the inevitability of sexual feelings being present. They spoke enthusiastically about the value of being able to hold and negotiate the feelings between them and their client and to work innovatively at the edge of therapeutic boundaries. None of my co-researchers suggested that working with these issues was either straight-forward or without risk, but some of them did recognize the potential for therapeutic gain.

Generally speaking, however, emotional involvement in therapy is treated with some caution, as Van Deurzen-Smith (1997, p. 219) suggests: 'There is much evidence from a century of psychotherapy that the realities of what is usually referred to as "transference" and "countertransference" can only be neglected at one's peril'. This mention of transference brings us to one of the legacies of Freudian psychoanalysis, namely, the disavowal of the therapist's body by accepting the sexual feelings of the patient while at the same time attempting to deny their impact on the therapist. At its core, the transference hypothesis relies upon a Cartesian split of mind and body, privileging mental processes over embodied experience, where desire becomes a disembodied mental construct. This, according to Mann (1997, p. 16), is an attempt 'to de-erotize the inherently erotic'. From an existential perspective, this attempts the impossible as sexual desire is always incarnate. What I desire is another person, a body brought to life through consciousness, a person who will desire me in return. What I desire is to be desired and existentially validated by existing in someone else's eyes as someone who has sexual significance. Any form of psychotherapy aiming at relational connection and closeness will inevitably open up a non-verbal affective dialogue, and it is within this dialogue of embodied inter-experience and relational proximity that sexual feelings and desire emerge, experienced as a form of self-consciousness and disturbance within our bodily senses.

Although the origins of the taboo on sexual attraction in psychotherapy may in part be traced back to the origins of psychoanalysis, not all of the blame can be attributed to Freud. It is universally acknowledged that sexual activity with a client is an exploitative abuse of power and trust. It is the ultimate ethical misdemeanour. Unfortunately, this ethical taboo extends into the realm of anything sexual, or potentially sexual, including the use of touch and the presence of sexual feelings. While sexual misconduct may be relatively infrequent, sexual attraction between client and therapist, or therapist and client, appears to be a more frequent phenomenon. Indeed, it has been so since the dawn of psychoanalysis when, according to Webster (1996, p. 111), Breuer fled in panic from the bedside of his patient Anna 'O' when she expressed sexual feelings for him, thus providing the inspiration for his colleague Freud's hypothesis of 'transference love' as an attempt to explain sexual attraction in the patient and to absolve the therapist from responsibility.

To be sexually attracted to someone is to recognize his or her sexual significance for us. They emerge as someone we have sexual interest in, as opposed to those whom we do not. Although we can experience this attraction as a longing or a feeling of enchantment, it does not necessarily mean that we have a desire for physical intimate contact or sex with this person, although obviously this could be the case.

In many ways, sexual attraction in the consulting room is probably no different from everyday life, where, as a fundamental aspect of our lives, the desire to be found attractive as well as finding oneself attracted forms the basis of many, if not most, of our interpersonal relationships. We develop a sense of self in the world through our impact on others and their impact on us through acts of mutual reciprocity, where we feel significant in our own and others' lives. The therapeutic encounter differs here from other reciprocal and complementary relationships in as much as the therapist's desire to be found attractive, however subliminally experienced, cannot override the client's needs for existential validation.

There are also other obvious differences between everyday life and therapy, such as the feelings of anticipation that develop out of the ritual of regular appointments, along with the deliberate attempt to engage in a deeply personal way with another human being in the intimate proximity of a private space for a limited time span. Merleau-Ponty (1996, p. 156) proposes that there is an erotic structure to the way in which we perceive the world, so that whatever situation we find ourselves in, we will be looking for the sexual value or meaning in that situation. He describes this as 'the mute and permanent question that constitutes normal sexuality'. While we might take exception to the normative imagery of sexuality, it should not get in the way of seeing that we approach life with sexual interest and anticipation. Consequently, whenever two people meet, there is always the possibility and potential for sexual interest to develop, especially if they are alone. I am certainly not suggesting that every consulting room is a cauldron of desire, anymore than it is a sterile emotional space, but I would suggest that sexual feelings and attraction, at some level, are a likely outcome, and even possibly, an inevitable consequence of the proximity within the relational therapeutic encounter, as Maria Luca intimates in the introduction. So what might we understand by sexual attraction from an existential perspective?

Sexual attraction does not lend itself to precise definitions or logical causality. It is highly subjective and covers a wide range of phenomena, from mild erotic interest to overwhelming sexual desire. Although constructed on a range of cultural, sociological or psychological factors, there is usually another more mysterious element at play in sexual attraction. This is the unexpected element of amorphous randomness exemplified in mythology by Cupid's arrows.

Sexual attraction is an interpersonal phenomenon that we experience as felt sensations within our bodies that requires another embodied being to be the focus of our interest. This silent dialogue of desire is experienced through the body as 'an erotic comprehension not of the order of understanding . . . desire comprehends blindly by linking body to body' (Merleau-Ponty, 1996, p. 157). Our consciousness is drawn down into our body, and if we are unused to recognizing or focusing on bodily felt sensations, then we might not immediately recognize the subtle impact of sexual attraction. Awareness of our sexual interest may only be subliminal so that we may not know why we are attracted, or even why we are attractive to another. Sexual attraction can feel as if it has crept up on us unawares and has taken us by surprise.

Sexual attraction is not necessarily mutual and reciprocal, and there is a whole matrix of possibilities within the dynamics of sexual interest that can get played out in therapy. Attraction may be overtly or covertly expressed and we are not always aware of others' feelings towards us. We may realize that they like us, have warm feelings towards us, or even find us attractive in some way, but we are not always aware of them finding us sexually attractive. In addition, we may recognize that another person has all the attributes of being sexually attractive, but it does not necessarily mean that they are sexually attractive to us, or that we have any sexual interest in them. What creates sexual interest for us in another person can often seem unexpected and confusing, not just to ourselves but also to others around us.

However, if someone expresses a sexual interest in us and demonstrates in some way that they find us sexually attractive, then it can stimulate a response in us, where a person who was hitherto someone who we had no specific sexual interest in may suddenly become someone who we have a sexual attraction for. This induced reciprocity comes about by their existential validation of us as someone significant in their eyes. However, if they realize that they are not sexually attractive in our eyes, our unresponsiveness can invoke a sense of failure in them. It can feel at some level like an annihilation of their existence in their inability to make a difference to us.

This illustrates some of the complexity surrounding sexual feelings in negotiating relatedness in the consulting room. Psychological proximity can become a dance in the tension between proximity and distance, requiring sensitive presence to regulate and maintain therapeutic contact. It also reminds us of the immense power of these feelings and how fragile our sense of self can be around them. One way into understanding this labyrinth of dynamic relational possibilities is through the interpersonal phenomenon that I have described elsewhere as existential sexuality (Smith-Pickard, 2006a, 2009).

Existential sexuality is, first and foremost, an embodied interpersonal phenomenon extending beyond orgasmic or genital focus. It is present throughout the lifespan and describes the primary way in which we project ourselves into the world and seek existential validation from the world by claiming some significance in the lives of others.

Sex and sexuality are clearly related but only in as much as sex is but one aspect of sexuality, 'an imaginary point determined by the deployment of sexuality', says Foucault (1990, p. 155). Using the terminology of existential philosophy, we could describe sex as an ontic manifestation of an ontological sexuality that, according to Merleau-Ponty (1996, p. 168), is 'always present like an atmosphere'. Existential sexuality exists much of the time without sexual intention or genital focus and this is an important link with sexual attraction because it too can also be experienced without the intention of sexual contact. In fact, I would suggest that in the consulting room, it frequently is without sexual intent, although as in everyday life, it can easily become sexualized if the possibility of sex emerges from the ground of existential sexuality and social encounter.

In existential sexuality, there is an attempt to focus the other's consciousness within their body, to make them aware of bodily sensations as self-consciousness while at the same time offering one's own body/ self to be impressed upon by receiving the resemblance and otherness of the other. What we have is a relational system that aims at a mutual reciprocity by attempting to capture or appropriate the embodied con-sciousness of the other. It is reciprocal or intersubjective because the body I have/am is the site of my perception, and because I can see, I am aware that I can also be seen, sense and be sensed. I am in the world and the world is in me and I cannot step outside of this reversible relationship with the world to become a detached observer or an isolated subject. My awareness of my own visibility means that I am always self-conscious and conscious of the potential gaze of the other. In other words, subjectivity is always intersubjectivity.

What I am describing as existential sexuality is a system of reciprocity whereby we fascinate and are fascinated by the other, appropriate and are appropriated by the other, and desire the other's desire for us. Existential sexuality and embodiment are irreducible elements of existence that carry the possibility of sexual attraction into all our relationships. This can create an edge of ambiguity in negotiating relatedness in therapy that I will attempt to illustrate in the next section, with some reflections on sexual attraction and the use of supervision.

Considerations of Clinical Approach

The first time that I took an experience of a female client expressing sexual attraction towards me to supervision, I was told that it was inappropriate to continue working with her and needed to refer her to another therapist. When reluctantly I tried to refer her, she understandably accused me of betrayal and abandonment. A few years later, with another client and another supervisor, I was offered explanations for my client's professed attraction such as erotic transference and projective identification. I was told not to take any of it personally as it was simply unconscious material from the client's past, re-emerging in the therapy and was not about me. What suffered here was the supervision, because it did not match my sense of what was taking place in the therapy and I lost some faith in the super-vision process. However, it also made me question what I needed from supervision, so that in the long term, it proved a valuable experience.

The advances from these two clients were completely unexpected because I had not regarded myself as a sexual being in the consulting room. I was not aware of any sexual interest on my part towards either of these clients and felt safe playing a role as an asexual therapist. However, it did still feel that something had gone wrong, and I had to ask myself, what was I doing that might encourage these feelings of desire in my clients? In my attempt to engage in psychological proximity, was I becoming too close, too intense? Did my denial of the possibility of sexual feelings leave both my clients and myself vulnerable to the impact of sexual attraction?

I continued working with the second client from a phenomenological perspective, acknowledging and exploring the feelings in the room as real, whereby she accepted that I was of much more use to her as a therapist than as a lover, albeit a therapist she had certain feelings towards. It is only with hindsight that I can see another dynamic of sexual attraction being played out here, that was between the two female supervisors and me. The first supervisor, an older woman, treated me as a protégé and attempted to have a social relationship. The second was a younger woman who I saw for both individual and group supervision. I found her sexually attractive, and there was always a slight frisson in the room between us when we met for individual supervision that evaporated in the group setting.

These experiences took place in the early part of my career, when I was relatively inexperienced and, in all fairness, so were my supervisors. I have chosen to mention these particular experiences because they illustrate some of the points I have raised earlier about responses to the implicit taboo, expectations of an asexual encounter and the problems of not engaging with sexual feelings.

By contrast, some years later, I worked with a female client I felt very sexually attracted towards. Fortunately, I had a male supervisor who I trusted enough to explore this with and he helped me to focus on the client's needs within the work while still acknowledging my feelings. I am certain this woman was aware of the mild erotic charge in the room, but through the understanding and support I received from my supervisor, I was able to negotiate a high level of psychological proximity without engaging in any seductive erotic intrigue. It was enough for me to recognize my own feelings of sexual attraction and to not be caught up in sexual fantasy. I have no idea at all what she thought about me, other than she appeared to find in me a trusted and warm professional, and was appreciative of the work we did together.

I recall another client, a very successful and creative woman who was trying to unravel some very complex family issues and trying to come to terms with them. I have to confess that I was somewhat overawed by her intelligence and sophisticated vocabulary. Slowly, a connection developed between us that did not feel sexually charged but was certainly intimate. I still find it difficult to find words that describe much of what took place between us because so much was said between us without being verbalized. It was as if there was another silent narrative taking place. I had never felt such understanding for another person or felt so understood. This was probably the closest I have ever been to another person without experiencing sexual feelings or being a lover. And yet, I did not know how to speak about it to my supervisor. I certainly tried very hard, but the words that came out did not seem to adequately match the experience. My supervisor also tried very hard to grasp my experience, but my lack of clarity in attempting to describe an experience that was for the most part non-verbal made it impossibly difficult for him. When I was with this client, there was something about us being in each other's presence, a sort of joy and flow, and at some level, almost a sense of guilt that we could be so close. We never spoke about it to each other, perhaps because it was so palpable that we didn't need to, or perhaps it felt too dangerous to try. I think we both liked the person we found in ourselves when we were working together, and this seemed to enrich the work rather than detract from it.

Some years later, I found an insight into some of these and other experiences with clients in the work of Adrianna Cavarero (2006). The insight is that we are all narratable, and our unique life stories require the presence of another to be told and heard, and that certain stories require the presence of a lover. I was struck by the similarity between the stories lovers tell each other and the stories told in therapy. Reading about the narratable self also reminded me again of this last client.

Discussion

The vulnerable naked space of lovers is a psychological container in which we might invite our lover to see 'who' rather than 'what' we are. This 'who' emerges in an act of reciprocal storytelling and caresses where we both tell our life story and hear it told to us by ourselves. We hear ourselves narrate ourselves in new ways, not as rehearsed information but spontaneously through involuntary acts of memory. They are often stories in free fall, told in reverie where we meet and witness ourselves in a new light. In the lover's acceptance of who we are in our bare humanity, there is a tender redemption and an existential validation.

The reciprocal act of listening and storytelling reveals us to each other in an embodied narrative of existential sexuality, interwoven with a spoken narrative that emerges from the involuntary recall of our life stories. It is like a dance of possibilities where we become something or someone we never could have become by ourselves. Who we meet in this dance may not be who we thought we were, or who we thought that we could be, or even who we wanted to be. The metaphor of dancing here represents the dynamic flow of tension and the regulation of proximity and distance in maintaining psychological contact. It also points to the difference between the formal protocols of social dancing and dancing with a lover, and how this might reflect the difference between a therapeutic stance that protects against the effect of sexual attraction and one that embraces it.

While it is tempting to see the therapeutic dyad through the metaphor of lovers, it can only ever be as unconsummated lovers. A lover is only a would-be lover without the presence of a beloved to invoke their spontaneous self-narration. The absence of sex does not devalue the metaphor but rather encourages us to wonder in what ways we might be like lovers in the therapy, so that clients can hear themselves narrate themselves in new ways.

I have thought for a long time that a large part of my task as a therapist is to try and create a space for clients to hear and meet themselves, in other words, to reveal 'who' they are, not just to me but also to themselves. This phenomenological 'who' that I am describing here should not be confused with a fixed identity or a true self. We are all different with different people in different contexts. Who someone is with me is not the same as he or she would be with another therapist. The stories they tell me are the stories that they tell me alone. They would tell their stories differently to another therapist and even differently to me in another context. However, within the stories, there always remains something relatively constant that we feel as a centre of gravity, and that we can see and read in the look of recognition in a friend's eyes; otherwise, we would be without any identity at all. It is within the telling of the stories that self-reflection takes place, and in the listening and acceptance that existential validation occurs, and shifts in identity are forged. Sexual attraction may occur because the validation makes clients feel significant in our eyes, or perhaps more significantly, when there is a level of sexual attraction, there is a greater possibility for a narrative in free fall, for self-meeting and for potential optimal relational proximity and depth. There may also be a higher level of emotional investment in the therapy when sexual attraction is present.

Open and honest supervision is an imperative here, as there is a real danger that attempts by the therapist to engage at any significant depth with clients may be interpreted as seduction or an expression of sexual interest towards them. However, it is even more dangerous for the therapist to succumb to the temptation to elicit existential validation from the client by being the focus of the client's sexual interest. Such is the reciprocal nature of existential sexuality, that the dynamics of sexual attraction make us all vulnerable and yet more human in the therapy.

In my own practice, I have been looking at ways in which I can work with an awareness of sexual attraction and develop strategies from the insights I have gained from my clients about the fluid nature of psychological contact, and from using the metaphor of lovers, to invoke an atmosphere for unrehearsed self-narration.

Strategies for Working with Sexual Attraction

- Reflecting on the metaphor of lovers to negotiate relatedness through psychological proximity and sexual feelings in the consulting room, I developed the idea of the *lovers' gaze*. This gaze is not an objective view but one that seeks the uniqueness, the immeasurable 'who' of the beloved.
- The therapist's gaze is not simply a visual perception but a whole body perception that requires *an opening out of oneself to receive the unique otherness* that makes the beloved this person and not any other. It is necessary that the therapist's listening body is both responsive and expressive, and is able to regulate the depth of contact with another, much in the way we are able to bring our visual perception into sharp or soft focus.
- The therapist's body can invite response and dialogue by connecting to the other's body in an attempt to reach beyond the verbal narrative into the non-verbal realm of embodied inter-experience and construction of meaning. The therapist's attentiveness invites narration as a response to her/his listening body.

We know that we exist because of our impact on others and their impact on us. In the therapeutic encounter, client and therapist become the necessary other for each other in creating an identity that complements and distinguishes their respective roles in the encounter. They have the potential to bring each other into existence, to create genuine proximity and relatedness, or equally to deny and negate each other.

Conclusion

I have offered the metaphor of therapy as a space where therapist and client are unconsummated lovers bound to each other by the desire to make a difference to each other. The metaphor of lovers in this paradox is a potent one, as it always has a possibility of becoming an actuality if we stray beyond the edge of therapy. If the image of lovers is a metaphor, then sexual attraction is an actuality, and both provide us with therapeutic capital if we are willing to work with them.

Despite the implicit taboo on sexual attraction in therapy, it is a phenomenon to be openly explored with curiosity and respect and not with intrigue and fantasy in order to feed an inappropriate need for validation. We carry our histories in our bodies, and exploring sexual attraction and feelings can provide insights into habitual patterns and structures of relating unmet needs and desires, as well as the manner in which someone projects himself or herself into the world. This may sound like transference under another name, but that is not the case. What we are exploring is an actual person-to-person, body-to-body encounter, occurring in the present moment that is impacting on both therapist and client. The encounter is always co-constructed out of a mutual reciprocity, as is sexual attraction. In order to monitor my awareness of sexual interest and the dynamics of existential sexuality in the room, I find myself asking questions such as to what degree is Merleau-Ponty's 'mute and permanent question' present here? Do I have sexual interest in this person? Do I detect any sexual interest towards me? Do I have feelings of warmth or dislike for this person? These and similar questions help me position myself with my client to find appropriate levels of proximity or distance so as to listen like a lover to their self-narration. These questions help me negotiate relatedness and maintain a responsive ethical stance grounded in the immediacy of the relational ebb and flow of contact between my client and me in the present moment.

If we step out beyond the taboo of sexual attraction and allow ourselves to invest a level of emotional involvement in the therapy, of course, there will be risks involved as there are in any form of therapy. Part of my own internal compass for working safely in what can feel like a relational free fall is asking myself how easy it is to bring this to supervision. If it is difficult, I am either outside the boundary of therapy or too close to the edge.

Finally, we have to acknowledge that there is a risk in using all of these sexual elements, as I have suggested, in negotiating relatedness with clients at an intimate and meaningful level. The risk is that, like lovers, we will find it hard to leave each other, and so it is extremely important that we ask ourselves: how, when the time comes, do we disengage therapeutically with our clients without it feeling like a denial of their innermost self?

References

Cavarero, A. (2006). *Relating narratives: Storytelling and selfhood*. P. Kottman (trans.). Oxon: Routledge.

Foucault, M. (1990). *The history of sexuality: Vol. 1, an introduction*. R. Hurley (trans.). London: Penguin.

Mann, D. (1997). *Psychotherapy: An erotic relationship*. London: Routledge.

Merleau-Ponty, M. (1996). *Phenomenology of perception*. C. Smith (trans.). London: Routledge & Kegan Paul.

Smith-Pickard, P. (2006a). Transference as existential sexuality. *Journal of the Society for Existential Analysis*, 17(2), 224–237.

Smith-Pickard, P. (2006b). *The body of encounter. A phenomenology of embodied inter-experience* (unpublished doctoral thesis). Metanoia, Middlesex University.

Smith-Pickard, P. (2009). Existential sexuality and the body in supervision. In E. Van Deurzen & S. Young (Eds.), *Existential perspectives on supervision* (pp. 68–78). Basingstoke: Palgrave Macmillan.

Van Deurzen-Smith, E. (1997). *Everyday mysteries*. London: Routledge.

Webster, R. (1996). *Why Freud was wrong*. London: Fontana.

6

An Acceptance Commitment Therapy Approach to Sexual Attraction

Richard Blonna

This chapter will highlight how the principles and practices of acceptance and commitment therapy (ACT) can help therapists be mindful of, and manage their sexual attraction towards, clients. Instead of trying to control, avoid or eliminate sexual attraction, therapists can learn how to be mindful of it, accept it and coexist with it as they continue to serve their clients according to their professional codes of ethics.

Introduction

It is very common for sex therapists, coaches or educators to routinely encounter clients and students to whom they are sexually attracted. While it is clearly a breach of professional ethics for therapists, coaches and educators to *have sex with* their clients and students, being *sexually attracted to* them is not. Having sex with someone is a physical act, a behaviour that one can control. Being sexually attracted to someone is not. It is a type of mental activity that cannot be controlled, avoided or eliminated. In fact, ACT research regarding managing unwanted cognitive activity (troubling thoughts, painful emotions, etc.) shows that the *worst* way to deal with it is to try to control, avoid or eliminate it. This approach actually *increases* the troubling thoughts and painful emotions (Hayes, Barnes-Holmes, & Roche, 2001). Human sexual attraction is unique in

Sexual Attraction in Therapy: Clinical Perspectives on Moving Beyond the Taboo – A Guide for Training and Practice, First Edition. Edited by Maria Luca.
© 2014 John Wiley & Sons, Ltd. Published 2014 by John Wiley & Sons, Ltd.

that it is not regulated by fertility cycles or other factors inherent in other species. Human sexual attraction originates in the mind and can occur countless times a day, 365 days a year, until death. Therefore, sexual attraction towards clients and students cannot be regulated by professional boards and ethical codes of conduct. The responsibility for managing sexual attraction rests squarely on the shoulders of professionals entrusted with the care and nurturing of clients and students.

What Is ACT?

ACT is a form of psychotherapy based on cognitive behavioural therapy (CBT) and relational frame theory (RFT) (Hayes et al., 2001). An underlying premise of ACT is that clients' mental distress and problematic behaviour is due to psychological inflexibility caused by unhelpful cognitions that are inconsistent with their values and goals. In addition, these unhelpful cognitions cause clients to get 'stuck' in a psychological rut. ACT helps clients become more psychologically flexible, get unstuck and behave in ways that support their goals and values. Getting unstuck and developing greater psychological flexibility starts with understanding the relationship between unhelpful self-talk, emotions and behaviour.

ACT helps clients examine the helpfulness of their thoughts, personal scripts, emotions and mental images in meeting their values-congruent goals. To help determine what is helpful and what isn't, clients are taught to answer this basic question: 'Are these thoughts, personal scripts, emotions, mental images helping me behave in ways that are consistent with my values and values-congruent goals?' If the answer is yes, the thoughts, personal scripts, emotions and mental images are accepted as being helpful and the clients continue to behave in ways that move them closer to meeting their values-congruent goals. If the answer is no, the thoughts, personal scripts, emotions and mental images are rejected and attention on them is redirected to engaging in purposeful behaviour. Shifting attention off unhelpful thoughts, personal scripts, emotions and mental images and onto purposeful behaviour (particularly physical activity) results in the unhelpful cognitions dissipating on their own (Luoma, Hayes, & Walser, 2007).

ACT refers to the mind as a 24/7 thinking and feeling machine that works nonstop, churning out cognitions (Eifert & Heffner, 2003; Hayes, Strosahl, & Wilson, 1999). Many of those thoughts, feelings, personal scripts and mental images the mind churns out are related to sex. Like a computer that's always on, the mind constantly processes information and is capable of running multiple programmes at the same time. Instead of running word processing, spreadsheets or other computer software, the mind's programmes are thoughts, emotions, mental images and personal scripts.

Thoughts are the basic building blocks of your cognitive functioning. Some are rational and logical, while others couldn't be more irrational or illogical. Some thoughts originate from a conscious effort to create them, while others come and go like the wind. Some thoughts are related to sexual attraction to clients and students.

Emotions are essentially impulses to act. They're the result of an evolutionary process that forces people to stop, pay attention, analyze a threatening situation and act, all within a split second. Some of the stronger emotions like fear and anger are linked to the mobilization of energy that occurs during the fight-or-flight stress response. Sexual emotions including love, lust and passion are among the most powerful feelings there are.

Thoughts and emotions combine to form personal scripts about specific aspects of life. These scripts are the little internal story lines that accompany learning experiences. Clients and therapists have personal scripts related to childhood, work, school, relationships, politics and the world at large, just to name a few. In addition to these themes, many personal scripts relate to sexual scenes. Like thoughts, these scripts can be helpful or unhelpful, logical or illogical, factual or inaccurate, neutral or emotionally charged, and real or imagined. Often, sexual and other scripts become outdated when they are no longer helpful in meeting values-congruent goals.

Mental images are the internal pictures people see when they close their eyes and observe what their mind conjures up. Mental images can be neutral or linked to emotions. Some mental images are accompanied by pleasant emotions like hope, love and satisfaction. Others are linked to painful or negative emotions like jealousy, fear, worry and anxiety. Some sexual mental images are quite graphic and can be arousing or unsettling. For a variety of reasons, people often don't want to view themselves as sexual beings. This is often the case when therapists', coaches' and educators' minds conjure up images related to being sexually attracted to their clients and students.

Like the operating system and other programmes on a computer's hard drive, many of the mind's programmes run in the background without people even realizing they are on. For example, one can read this page while also listening to sounds in the environment, processing sensory inputs (changes in lighting, temperature and smell) and even daydreaming.

The mind never stops working; you couldn't even turn it off even if you wanted to.

Like viruses that invade a computer and cause it to freeze, unhelpful thoughts and feelings, along with the negative self-talk that often accompanies them, can invade the mind's programmes, slow its processing and cause it to freeze. When this happens, the mind, like the hard drive on a computer, gets stuck and can't function properly. When this happens to people, they feel stuck and can't move forward. To get unstuck, the mind, like a computer needs to be rebooted and cleared. ACT uses helpful exercises, activities and metaphors to help clients do this.

Research related to relational frame theory, the learning theory that underlies ACT, has found that past learning (sexual and otherwise) plays a major role in processing troubling thoughts and painful emotions in the present moment. According to this research, when people learn something new, they learn it in relation to other things that are specific to that time and place. This is called *the relational frame* for that learning experience. It is the *context* for the learning. RFT research has found that the context of learning is as important as the content of what is actually learned (Hayes et al., 2001).

For example, therapists', coaches' and educators' sexual learning all took place at specific times, with specific people, in a variety of different places, and was linked to specific thoughts, feelings, personal scripts and mental images. The actual content of what occurred during the sexual learning experiences was forever linked to the context in which the learning occurred. These *initial* relational frames may be helpful or unhelpful in managing *present moment* sexual attraction and encounters. When people recall these learning frames of reference or describe them to someone else, they are actually referring to their mind's *version* of the experience. This is a version of the event – not the actual event. ACT and RFT teach clients that they can get into trouble when they believe that their *thoughts about* past or imagined sexual encounters are the same thing as actual experience in the present moment. Every time people recount past sexual experiences, they are always subject to embellishment or distortion, because they are based on memories of the events. This is important for people to understand because it can help them shift their focus off their outdated, unhelpful sexual cognitions when necessary. Unhelpful sexual thoughts, emotions, personal scripts and mental images about past events do not have to dictate present moment or future behaviour. Acceptance training teaches people that they do not have to control, avoid or eliminate troubling sexual thoughts, emotions, mental images and personal scripts in order to behave purposefully in the present moment and to move forward in the future in a values-congruent way.

Accepting What Can't Be Controlled

The acceptance part of ACT has four dimensions: (1) becoming more mindful of sexual thoughts, emotions and actions; (2) understanding how sexual thoughts, emotions and actions support or oppose personal values and goals; (3) accepting what can't be controlled (sexual thoughts, emotions, personal scripts and mental images); and (4) accepting what can be controlled (sexual behaviour and physical environment) (Blonna, 2010).

1. Mindfulness is a thread that runs through every aspect of ACT. Mindfulness means paying attention to each moment and being more aware of internal (thoughts, feelings, body sensations) and external (immediate physical environment) events that occur in the present moment. Becoming more mindful of internal and external sexual issues is a key first step in accepting them.
2. Values clarification is crucial to understanding how sexual thoughts, emotions and actions either support or oppose your values and goals. Therapists, coaches and educators have sexual values that relate to gender roles about masculinity or femininity, body image, relationships, childbearing, intimacy and a host of other sexual issues. ACT does not set any standards for what the sexual values should be. ACT takes a values-neutral approach based on helping people live lives that are consistent with *what they value* about their sexuality. The goal of ACT is to help people behave in a more values-congruent way. For most therapists, coaches and educators, having sex with clients or students is not consistent with their professional values. It can derail these careers in an instant. Being *sexually attracted to* clients or students, however, may or may not be inconsistent to the values associated with these professions. ACT training could help therapists, coaches and educators understand the difference.
3.&4. Accepting what can and can't be controlled is a key element of ACT. While people *can't control* the sexual thoughts, feelings, personal scripts and mental images that occur in their minds almost nonstop, they *can control* their behaviour, how they act *in relation* to them. For example, just because a therapist is feeling very attracted to a client doesn't mean he/she has to try to have

sex with him/her. In reverse, just because a client is coming on to a therapist does not mean the therapist is obligated to accept the offer and have sex with him/her.

Committing to Values-Congruent Action

The commitment part of ACT revolves around committing to actions that are consistent with personal and professional values and goals. A big part of commitment training is learning how to set values-congruent goals and objectives and to stick to them. Acceptance and commitment work together by using personal and professional values and goals as the starting point in setting the direction of one's life. Acceptance and commitment work together with all types of goals, sexual and otherwise. Commitment training shows people how to coexist with troubling thoughts and painful emotions while taking values-congruent action in meeting their goals. Commitment training shows people that they don't have to control, avoid or eliminate painful sexual thoughts and feelings in order to act in ways that are more consistent with their personal and professional sexual values and goals. For example, therapists do not need to control, avoid or eliminate their troubling thoughts and painful emotions related to being attracted to their clients. They can accept that these cognitions exist, admit that they are troubling and painful and then commit to coexisting with them as they continue to work with the very clients they are attracted to. In addition, they shift their focus off of the attraction and onto what needs to be done to help the clients. This shift in focus helps the attraction dissipate on its own.

The Importance of Words and Thoughts in ACT

Sexual memories are often filled with words and self-talk that undermine present thinking and contribute to getting stuck. ACT operates from the premise that all words and thoughts don't have equal weight. From an ACT perspective, three kinds of words and thoughts exist: (1) helpful; (2) minimally important or silly; and (3) illogical, negative and self-destructive.

Helpful words and thoughts support people's values and help them meet their goals. For example, imagine you are a therapist working with a client you are attracted to or who is very seductive. You might find yourself thinking, 'Boy, this is very distracting. Staying focused on her story is much harder because of this attraction. I need to take a deep breath and get centred again'. This kind of thinking and the words used to express it help the therapist stay focused and accept the hard work involved in working with this client.

Thoughts that are of minimal importance or silly usually don't play a role in getting stuck. For example, imagine you're a therapist working with the same client and you find yourself thinking about what he might look like with his clothes off. You say to yourself, 'I bet he has a great body under those clothes'. You realize your thoughts have drifted away from listening to his story and onto your fantasies about what he might look like with his clothes off. To manage this type of thinking, you simply acknowledge what happened and tell yourself, 'That was interesting. I'd better get my mind back on my work or I'll never be able to help him'.

The third category of thoughts (illogical, negative and self-destructive) makes it difficult for therapists to meet their values-congruent professional goals. For example, imagine you're a therapist working with the same client and you find yourself thinking, 'Wow, this woman is really coming on to me. She is practically asking for it. I can cancel my next appointment and ask her if she wants a drink. I could probably have sex with her right in the office. She looks like she really wants me. I'm a jerk if I do not take advantage of this situation'. This kind of unhelpful thinking is inconsistent with your values as a therapist and is contrary to your goals of helping clients and fostering your career and discipline. ACT therapists help people become more mindful of their thinking and of the words they use and to assess their helpfulness or unhelpfulness.

Sexual Fantasy and ACT

Sexual fantasies are a special form of words, thoughts and personal scripts that can be useful in helping clients and therapists manage sexual attraction toward each other. Sexual fantasy can be used to help clients and therapists explore their sexual attraction in healthy ways. Coupled with masturbation, fantasies provide a safe, exciting release of sexual tension and a way to coexist with sexual scripts that are unhelpful to the therapeutic relationship and the values system that supports it. Clients and therapists view sexual fantasies as part of the 'minimally important or silly' category of thoughts that their minds churn out endlessly. Rather than take them overly seriously or feel threatened by them, they can be used as erotica to play with and enjoy. There is no need for therapists and clients to discuss the content of their fantasies, only to view them as another category of cognitions whose helpfulness can be assessed and accepted or rejected.

The ACT Model of Psychopathology

Almost all therapists have unhelpful sexual thoughts, feelings, personal scripts and mental images associated with sexual attraction. When they don't see these for what they are, unhelpful mental traps, they get stuck in them (or 'hooked' by them as ACT practitioners like to say) and are unable to move forward. ACT proposes that people (therapists included) get hooked and stuck because they lack the psychological flexibility required to think through and manage threatening sexual information and situations (Hayes, 2005), a subject discussed in Chapter 4, from a psychoanalytic perspective, by Doris McIlwain. The model used to explain this is called the ACT model of psychopathology (Hayes et al., 1999; Luoma et al., 2007). While sexual attraction to clients is not a clinically diagnosed sexual disorder such as erectile dysfunction, the model can still be used to describe getting stuck on cognitions related to sexual attraction.

The ACT model of psychopathology identifies six core processes that contribute to being psychologically inflexible and getting stuck: (1) lack of clarity of values; (2) dominance of outmoded scripts and learning; (3) cognitive fusion; (4) attachment to the conceptualized self; (5) experiential avoidance; and (6) inaction, impulsivity and rigidity. The six processes work independently and combine synergistically when getting stuck. They are used to explain getting stuck in any aspect of life including sexual attraction to clients and students (Hayes, 2005; Hayes et al., 1999).

Lack of clarity of values

As previously mentioned, ACT is a values-based form of therapy. Values are the guiding principles for how people want to live their lives. They represent the different directions people take in exploring goals that contribute to living a meaningful life. Therapists, coaches and educators have values related to helping and nurturing that are consistent with their chosen professions. They also have values that relate to sex. Sometimes the two sets of values can conflict with each other, as in the case of sexual attraction to clients and students. One misconception most people have regarding values is that they are fixed and do not change. In fact, values are fluid and usually change over the course of people's lives. This can be very confusing and threatening, especially if the values that are changing are tied to strongly help moral and ethical beliefs. Sexual values fall squarely in this category and because of these ties.

Some therapists have never actually spent time examining what they value as adults. They accept the values instilled in them over time by their parents and their culture and don't really question them until they are in situations where the values no longer work for them in meeting their goals. In a sense, they've outgrown certain values and are not sure what to replace them with.

Sometimes, they find that the sexual values that guided them for the first 40 or 50 years of their lives no longer provide them with the direction they need as they make midlife transitions related to new relationships and careers. Women in their 40s and 50s who, up to this point in their lives, have viewed themselves as someone's 'mum' or 'wife' find that the values associated with these roles change as they reenter the workforce or return to graduate school after their children are grown and leave the nest. Many male and female therapists who are divorced or widowed struggle with evaluating whether the sexual values they have that are related to being married will guide them in forming new relationships or in some version of celibacy.

These examples illustrate how changing social situations can lead to a lack of clarity regarding sexual and other values. When people are not clear about their values, they can feel like sailboats without rudders. They are at the mercy of the prevailing winds and currents and will go wherever they push them. There are strong social and cultural sexual winds that constantly try to push people around. You see them expressed every day in all forms of media and from every area in society (politics, entertainment, religion, etc.). They can move people in all kinds of sexual directions. Being unclear about sexual values can be a major reason related to getting stuck on how to manage the issue of sexual attraction to clients.

Attachment to the conceptualized self

The conceptualized self is the picture the mind creates of the self. ACT refers to the conceptualized self-viewpoint as a *self-as-content* view. The conceptualized sexual self represents the sum total of all of the things contained within someone's mind up until any given point in their life. In many instances, this is an accurate representation of the objective reality of the person's sexual life. In other cases, it is not. The mind can distort, embellish, forget and attach labels to pieces of the conceptualized sexual self that create stereotypes and limitations for understanding and explaining things. It can also embellish the allure of 'forbidden fruit', sexual relationships and activities that have been off-limits to someone for a host of moral, ethical, legal and values-based reasons.

A self-as-content view can be of past events or events that have not occurred yet. It is the view the mind creates by thinking about something as opposed to directly experiencing it in the present moment. Sometimes, the mind's perception of something that happened in the past is very different from what actually happened. The same holds true for events that have not yet occurred. When people become attached to the view created by their conceptualized self, they mistakenly believe that their thoughts about something are the same as directly experiencing it. Often, one's beliefs about how something will turn out are very different from how they actually turn out (Hayes et al., 1999). A perfect example of this is a therapist's misreading a client's sexual cues and acting on these beliefs. If this happens, the effects can be deleterious to clients' and therapists' professional careers. This is why it is sometimes best to leave certain sexual cognitions at the fantasy level and not try to make them a reality.

Cognitive fusion

Cognitive fusion is the over-attachment to certain aspects of the conceptualized self. The mind can fuse with all kinds of unhelpful sexual thoughts, personal scripts, feelings and images. People often fuse with some aspect of their sexuality that keeps them stuck. One example for men relates to being 'tough'. Traditionally, American men are raised to be tough. Being tough means being more action oriented than introspective. It also means handling problems yourself, not admitting weakness and not asking for help. Most American men do not spend a lot of time discussing their needs, wants and feelings. To do so is viewed as not being very manly. Men are supposed to 'tough things out' by themselves. Opening up to another person and sharing their feelings and insecurities is the antithesis of being tough. Not only are most American men raised this way, but they also identify with it. In ACT terminology, they fuse with the tough aspect of their conceptualized self. They become 'tough guys' and avoid acting in ways that undermine this toughness. This can lead to getting sexually stuck. If you are a male therapist and you are stuck on being unable to manage your sexual attraction to clients, toughing it out might not be the best solution for getting unstuck.

Dominance of outmoded scripts

Often, the mind fuses with what ACT calls outmoded scripts. As previously discussed, a personal script is really a story that the mind creates about some facet of one's sex life that is related to experience and prior learning. A sexual script becomes outmoded when it is no longer helpful to someone in meeting their goals and staying true to what they value. People often get stuck when they feel trapped and controlled by outmoded personal or relationship scripts that no longer represent who they really are as individuals or a couple. For example, imagine that you are a male therapist and one of the sexual scripts you have is related to feeling foolish for not taking advantage of all sexual opportunities when they present themselves. It might have developed when you were younger and less sexually experienced or during college and young adulthood when sexual experimentation was a bigger part of your life and your friends' lives. Whenever it developed, it is still there, lurking beneath the surface waiting to reappear at the most inopportune time. One such time would be when, as a therapist, you are now faced with a seductive client who comes on to you sexually. Part of how your mind interprets this is through the filter of the outdated script from your young adulthood.

Experiential avoidance

A common response to dealing with uncomfortable thoughts and painful feelings related to sexual attraction to clients is to try to control, eliminate or avoid them. The problem with this approach is that you cannot shut your mind off and when you try to control, eliminate or avoid troubling sexual thoughts and feelings, it only makes them worse and will continue to keep you stuck (Eifert & Heffner, 2003; Hayes et al., 1999).

People also try to avoid troubling thoughts and feelings about issues, such as sexual attraction, by drinking excessively and using psychoactive drugs to keep their minds off troubling thoughts and painful emotions. While these distraction strategies can be effective in the short term, they can often create new sources of distress because they create new risks that may not be very helpful in meeting personal and professional goals and values as a therapist (Ciarrochi & Bailey, 2008). The best way to deal with internal sexual factors is to accept them and shift one's attention off of them.

Inaction, impulsivity or rigidity

Inaction, impulsivity and rigidity are closely related to the other five components of psychological inflexibility but are slightly different. Inaction means taking no action. It is a subtle form of avoidance. It means not addressing the problem of sexual attraction in any way. Impulsivity means acting on impulse rather than in a way that is consistent with values and goals. Clients (and therapists) who impulsively act on their sexual attraction do so because it is consistent with outdated values and sexual roles. Therapists should discuss these outdated values with clients. Therapists can explain to clients that cognitions and behaviour associated with sexual attraction to each other are not wrong, they just are. Rather than try to control, avoid or eliminate them, they can be accepted and viewed as something to coexist with, until they are replaced by more helpful ones.

It could result in reacting to being stuck by taking action that will be regretted later. Rigidity means being rigid or inflexible. It relies on outdated scripts about the way things 'should be' and does not allow any room for looking at issues like sexual attraction from a different perspective. Once again, therapists can discuss this with clients and explain that becoming more mindful of rigidly adhered to outdated and unhelpful sexual cognitions and behaviour is a valuable step in learning how to get unstuck. When people are rigid, they only see one possible way to view a situation or behave in relation to it.

Getting Unstuck

Since the ACT model of psychopathology is founded on the belief that people get stuck because of psychological inflexibility, it is logical to assume that the way to get unstuck is to develop greater psychological flexibility. The more flexible people are psychologically, the less likely they are to get stuck and hooked by unhelpful thinking traps related to sexual attraction to clients.

ACT identifies six core therapeutic processes for developing greater psychological flexibility: (1) being present (developing mindfulness), (2) defining valued directions, (3) acceptance training, (4) commitment (taking action), (5) cognitive defusion and (6) self as context (Luoma et al., 2007). While each one is not directly targeted to offset one of the six contributing factors to psychological inflexibility, in some cases it does work out that way. For example, defining valued directions is specifically designed to offset lack of clarity of values and cognitive defusion is designed to over-come cognitive fusion.

Mindfulness

Mindfulness is best described as moment-by-moment awareness. Mindful-ness can be developed through informal and formal training. Informal mindfulness training revolves around developing attention-building skills. Informal training involves using short activities to help people become more aware of internal (thoughts, scripts, etc.) and external (environment) sexual stimuli. Formal mindfulness training involves learning and practis-ing mindful meditation (Germer, 2005).

Becoming more aware of what is going on in one's mind and your im-mediate environment can help make people more aware of when they are falling into the thinking traps related to sexual attraction that cause them to get stuck. For example, when one experiences cognitive fusion and attachment to an unhelpful part of the conceptualized self that limits options and contributes to getting stuck, being mindful that this is happening is the first step in correcting the problem and shifting to a different mindset. When one is experiencing a values conflict or is not clear about what one's values are related to a specific sexual issue, the starting point to managing this is being mindful that this lack of clarity exists in the first place.

Internal mindfulness training involves helping therapists become aware of their sexual thoughts, personal scripts, emotions and mental images and how they contribute to sexual attraction issues. Most people either do not pay attention to these things or try to dismiss them if they cause emotional distress. They are not aware that they are experiencing things such as values conflicts, cognitive fusion and rigid adherence to outmoded sexual personal scripts that keep them stuck.

It is important to realize that becoming more mindful of sexual thoughts, feelings, personal scripts and mental images is not the same thing as trying to figure out 'why' people think and feel the way they do. It is not about judging or evaluating sexual cognitions for their inherent 'goodness' or 'correctness' or seeing how they measure up to some societal standards. It is really a heightened awareness of 'what' people are thinking and feeling, not 'why' they are doing so. The only 'analysis' that goes on is examining how the sexual thoughts, feelings, personal scripts and mental images help or hinder meeting the person's values-congruent goals. The intent is not to feel guilty about what one is thinking or feeling, but to help that person become more aware of their helpfulness or unhelpfulness (Ciarrochi & Bailey, 2008; Hayes, 2005).

Defining valued directions

Defining valued directions is another way of saying clarifying values. There are four steps to defining valued directions: (1) exploring values, (2) choosing and ranking values, (3) publicly affirming values and (4) acting on values (Blonna, 2010). Exploring sexual values means helping people become more mindful of what they value by taking the time to formally list and organize their values. Choosing and ranking values involves identifying core and satellite values. Core values are the ones people are not willing to compromise on. Satellite values are things that give life meaning and direction but are open to negotiation and compromise. For example, a core value might be honesty, something that guides someone's life and interactions with others. It would be difficult or impossible for someone with this value to be in a relationship with someone who viewed honesty as something situational, only to be used when they felt it was necessary. Political engagement might be an example of a satellite value. While it is important for someone to vote and be a member of a political party, they could tolerate being in a relationship with someone of a different party who does not value politics as much.

Publicly affirming your values means letting others know about them. This can range from being willing to talk about them with partner(s), friends and associates to expressing them in public forums and in writing. Acting on your values means not just talking about them but living them.

Acceptance training

As mentioned previously, the best way for people to deal with troubling thoughts and painful emotions is to accept them and continue to take the values-congruent action steps that will help them live the life they want and deserve.

Acceptance training revolves around three things: (1) understanding that people cannot control internal sexual factors (thoughts, personal scripts, emotions, mental images) that are keeping them stuck; (2) understanding that they cannot work everything out in their heads, that taking action and experiencing something directly is the only way to understand what it really means; and (3) learning how to coexist with the pain and suffering that accompanies taking values-congruent sexual action. Acceptance training goes hand in hand with commitment training. Acceptance is a mindset and commitment involves taking action. Accepting the pain and suffering of taking values-congruent action doesn't necessarily mean that the actions taken will always work out or that it is the right thing to do. A big part of acceptance is realizing that sometimes people will make the wrong decision and will need to chart a new course of action. Acceptance is understanding that the only way to find this out is to take a risk and to endure the troubling thoughts and painful emotions that come with trying something new.

Let's use sexual attraction to a client as an example. Imagine that you have a seductive client whom you are attracted to and who you feel is making sexual advances towards you. You can accept that the attraction exists and that it makes you uncomfortable. Rather than try to control the thoughts, feelings, personal scripts and mental images associated with your attraction, you shift your focus off of them. Your mindfulness training will help you be more aware of the presence of these unhelpful cognitions and how they interfere with serving your client to the best of your ability. When you accept the unhelpful thoughts, feelings, personal scripts and mental images and shift your attention off of them and onto something else, they naturally begin to fade as you focus your attention elsewhere. When doing this, it is important to not judge or evaluate your unhelpful cognitions. You are not on trial. You are not immoral or unethical for having these thoughts and feelings; you are just human and are experiencing unhelpful cognitions.

Commitment (taking action)

The most effective way to commit to behaviour, whether it relates to sexual attraction or anything else, is to set clear goals related to what one wants to accomplish. Clear values-based goals and measurable objectives help reduce ambiguity and provide you with a clear structure and framework for taking action. Taking action is easier if it is based on clear goals and measurable objectives. For example,

Goal: to not act on my sexual attraction to clients
Measurable objective #1: By the end of next week, I will begin my mindfulness training by meditating at least once for 10 minutes.
Measureable objective #2: By the end of next week, I will begin to redirect my focus off of my troubling thoughts.

Cognitive defusion and self as context

Cognitive defusion and adopting a self-as-context view go hand in hand. Cognitive defusion revolves around learning how to defuse from unhelpful aspects of the conceptualized self that relate to sexual attraction to clients. Cognitive defusion activities help people learn how to distance themselves from the unhelpful thoughts, feelings, personal scripts and mental images that are keeping them stuck on the issue of being sexually attracted to clients. Creating distance literally means stepping back from unhelpful thoughts, personal scripts, mental images and emotions and seeing them as just parts of the self. This kind of view allows one to acknowledge and accept these unhelpful parts for what they are, just *parts* of the person. One is more than the content of his/her thoughts at any point in time.

The following activity, The Whiteboard, is an example of a strategy that can help therapists defuse from unhelpful sexual thoughts, feelings, personal scripts and mental images and take a more self-as-context view of life.

Clinical Strategy for Managing Sexual Attraction

The white board

Instructions: In order to do this activity, you'll need a whiteboard or flip chart with markers.

- The next time you have unhelpful thoughts, personal scripts, mental images and emotions related to sexual attraction to clients that are contributing to you feeling stuck, stand in front of a whiteboard with markers.
- Write down the following heading: Unhelpful sexual thoughts my mind is telling me about my sexual attraction to my clients.
- List all of the thoughts your mind is telling you about the sexual situation. Be sure to list all of your thoughts, no matter how crazy, silly or inconsequential they might seem.
- Now repeat steps 1–4 using the following additional headings: Personal Scripts, Mental Images and Emotions.
- When you are done, put down the marker and step back a few feet from the board.
- Tell yourself: 'These are merely unhelpful thoughts, personal scripts, mental images and emotions, they are not me. I am much more than these individual parts of my mind. They do not have to influence how I behave towards my client'.
- Feel the distance you have between you and these unhelpful thoughts, personal scripts, mental images and emotions.

- Now step back even further to put more distance between you and these unhelpful thoughts, personal scripts, mental images and emotions.
- Compare the power of these unhelpful sexual thoughts, emotions, personal scripts and mental images as you further distance yourself from them and repeat the statement 'These are merely unhelpful thoughts, personal scripts, mental images and emotions, they are not me. I am much more than these individual parts of my mind. They do not have to influence how I behave towards my client'.

Give yourself enough time to let the distancing sink in. Learning how to distance yourself from the workings of your mind takes time, but you can do it.

References

Blonna, R. (2010). *Stress less, live more: How acceptance and commitment therapy can help you live a busy yet balanced life.* Oakland, CA: New Harbinger Publications.

Ciarrochi, J. V., & Bailey, A. (2008). *A CBT practitioner's guide to ACT: How to bridge the gap between CBT and ACT.* Oakland, CA: New Harbinger Publications.

Eifert, G. H., & Heffner, M. (2003). The effects of acceptance versus control contexts on avoidance of panic-related symptoms. *Journal of Behavior Therapy and Experimental Psychiatry, 34*(3–4), 293–312.

Germer, C. (2005). Mindfulness: What is it? Does it matter? In C. Germer, R. Siegel, & P. Fulton (Eds.), *Mindfulness and psychotherapy.* New York: Guilford Press.

Hayes, S. (2005). *Get out of your mind and into your life: The new acceptance and commitment therapy* (with S. Smith). Oakland, CA: New Harbinger Publications.

Hayes, S. C., Barnes-Holmes, D., & Roche, B. (Eds.) (2001). *Relational frame theory: A post-Skinnerian account of human language and cognition.* New York: Plenum Publishers.

Hayes, S. C., Strosahl, K. D., & Wilson, K. G. (1999). *Acceptance and commitment therapy: An experiential approach to behavior change.* New York: The Guilford Press.

Luoma, J. B., Hayes, S. C., & Walser, R. D. (2007). *Learning ACT: An acceptance and commitment therapy skills-training manual for therapists.* Oakland, CA: New Harbinger Publications.

7

Addressing Sexual Attraction in Supervision

Kirsten W. Murray and John Sommers-Flanagan

Ethical models predictably involve consultation and supervision as necessary steps in the ethical decision-making process. As a consequence, it is no surprise that when feelings of sexual attraction emerge in clinical and professional relationships, reaching out to colleagues and mentors is recommended. However, researchers have noted that exploring sexual attraction during supervision is all too often avoided (Ladany, Hill, Corbett, & Nutt, 1996; Ladany et al., 1997). For example, in a review of quantitative and qualitative research, Ladany (2004) reflected on the puzzling fact that supervisors appeared to rarely bring up the possibility of sexual attraction, '. . . even when there were clear signs that sexual attraction was present' (p. 13).

Herein lies the gap: although interpersonal and sexual attraction is acknowledged as common in counselling and psychotherapy, there is also evidence that training and supervision norms make direct discussion of sexual attraction taboo (Ladany, Klinger, & Kulp, 2011; Pope, Sonne, & Greene, 2006; Rodolfa, Kitzrow, Vohra, & Wilson, 1990). As an illustration, some supervision texts in the helping professions do not even include references to sex, sexuality or attraction. In contrast, in this chapter, we deal with the issue directly and offer suggestions on how to address sexual attraction in training and supervision. It should be noted that many layers of relationships are encountered in supervision (examples include relationships between supervisor and supervisee, supervisee and client, and even

Sexual Attraction in Therapy: Clinical Perspectives on Moving Beyond the Taboo – A Guide for Training and Practice, First Edition. Edited by Maria Luca.
© 2014 John Wiley & Sons, Ltd. Published 2014 by John Wiley & Sons, Ltd.

supervisor and client). For the purposes of this chapter, our primary focus is on supervising the attraction that occurs in the supervisee–client relationship. As most other chapters highlight, effective supervision is fundamental to the management of sexual attraction. In addition, sexual attraction is examined as a common and natural response that can inform a continuum of action, from nonaction to boundary transgressions and multiple relationships. Finally, practical models and strategies for addressing sexual attraction in supervision are introduced and applied to case examples.

Sexual Attraction in the Supervisee–Client Relationship

In their writings on ethics, Pope and Vasquez (2007) have referred to sexual attraction in the supervisee–client relationship as 'very common' (p. 209). More specifically, in a survey of 585 psychotherapists, Pope, Keith-Spiegel, and Tabachnick (2006) reported that 95% of men and 76% of women reported feeling sexually attracted to a client on at least one occasion. They further reported that a minority of therapists acted on their sexual attraction (9.4% of men, 2.5% of women), but that a majority of therapists (63%) indicated they felt distress over their feelings of sexual attraction. Interestingly, only 9% of respondents believed their training had been adequate enough to help them deal effectively with feelings of sexual attraction towards clients.

It appears that supervisee sexual attraction can develop immediately during an initial therapeutic encounter or follow a slower trajectory based on repeated personal contacts during longer-term therapy. Either way, sexual attraction has been reported as having the potential to influence therapy in both positive and negative ways. For example, based on quantitative and qualitative research, Ladany et al. (1997) noted that some therapists 'believed that they were more invested, caring, and attentive than usual because of the sexual attraction' (p. 418). Although this positive influence was possible, more often therapists considered sexual attraction as a source of tension, distance, distraction and bias in the therapeutic relationship.

Although the whole concept of sexual attraction is both idiosyncratic and a culturally constructed biopsychosocial phenomenon, there appear to be common client factors that therapists tend to find attractive. Specifically, Pope and his colleagues (2006) reported, based on their survey data, the top five attractive client qualities:

• Physical attractiveness
• Positive mental/cognitive traits or abilities

- Sexual
- Vulnerabilities (e.g., childlike, needy)
- Positive overall character/personality (Pope, Keith-Spiegel, & Tabachnick, 2006, p. 105).

These results are generally consistent with Ladany et al.'s (1997) findings that therapists primarily described themselves as either physically or interpersonally attracted to clients. Generally, male and female therapists used similar terms to describe the qualities they found attractive; exceptions included males identifying 'physical attractiveness' and females identifying 'successful' much more frequently.

Strategies for Training and Supervision

The potential for sexual attraction within clinical relationships is both natural and ordinary. Nevertheless, specific methods for addressing these attractions remain on the periphery of professional training and supervision. Instructions on how to move forward when attraction develops remain broad. When attraction surfaces, therapists report several strategies: (1) seeking consultation, (2) obtaining supervision, (3) client referral and (4) obtaining therapy (Ladany et al., 1997). Although not incorrect and potentially helpful, these strategies are descriptively simplistic, and the nuances and details necessary for them to be successful tend to be ignored.

This section focuses on how to facilitate exploration, *reduction and management* of sexual attraction. Our focus is on reduction and management, primarily because completely eliminating sexual attraction is unrealistic and unattainable. In fact, therapists typically report that sexual attraction is never completely resolved (Ladany et al., 1997). Consequently, we endorse and describe processes where greater understanding and insight is used to reduce sexual thoughts and feelings (Bridges, 1994). The strategies described next focus on managing sexual attraction in ways likely to reduce or eliminate inappropriate or unethical therapist behaviours.

Training

Ethical principles related to sexual attraction and strategies for dealing effectively with attraction should be integrated into graduate training programs and workshops or continuing education sessions. Three primary goals of group trainings on clinician sexual attraction include (1) creating a safe environment for discussion and normalizing sexual attraction, (2) exploring appropriate behavioural responses and (3) establishing professional relationships for future consultation. The teaching methods are as important (if not more so) as curriculum goals and content. Experiential learning using role play, coaching and application to case vignettes is recommended across helping professional contexts (Ladany et al., 1997; Rodolfa et al., 1990). Specifically, Downs (2003) reported that when counsellor educators had experienced prior role playing or coaching in response to sexual attraction dilemmas, they 'were significantly more comfortable bringing up the topic of sexuality in the clinic or classroom' (p. 9). Facilitating trainings of this nature often become more about the experience created than reciting of academic content and recommendations. Concrete opportunities to try out different words when broaching sexual attraction while remaining open and accepting to disclosures are invaluable and, we would argue, more effective in preparing therapists, supervisors and educators to respond to such dilemmas in real-world settings.

Creating a safe environment for discussing and exploring sexual attraction is challenging and complex. Just as we have set the tone and context for this chapter (e.g., that attraction is normative and the aim of interventions is to manage sexual attraction), the same contextualization must occur to develop a safe learning environment. In a recent study, Ladany and colleagues reported that two qualities of the 'best supervisors' were being open and skilful in facilitating discussions (Ladany, Mori, & Mehr, 2013, p. 28). As a consequence, it is strongly recommended that professionals who facilitate supervision trainings set a tone that is open, accepting and explorative regarding sexual attraction. This is especially important in group situations where 'trust may be wanting' (Rodolfa et al., 1990, p. 315). When contextualizing trainings that include content about sexual attraction, statements of focus might include the following:

- Let's all try to remember that thoughts and feelings related to attraction are common in clinical settings and that having sexual thoughts and feelings is much different from acting on sexual impulses.
- During this training, I hope you will all openly reflect on your feelings, behaviours and values. I recognize this sort of open exploration involves risk and courage.
- As a group, we will work to be open and accepting of all disclosures, including those focusing on sexual attraction; at the same time, our

goal is to support each other in achieving ethical and therapeutic responses.

- The confidentiality of what you say in here is limited. I encourage all of you to respect each other's confidentiality. But in the end, you all need to judge for yourselves how open you want to be during our time together.
- When faced with sexual attraction dilemmas, we will work to think flexibly and develop a multitude of options that comply with ethical standards and practical realities.
- If a performance evaluation is connected to this experience for you, your evaluation will not be based on the depth or frequency of disclosure but rather on active engagement in the learning process.
- (In cases where participation is not voluntary) This training is mandatory, but I still hope we can explore how this training can best meet your needs for a useful learning experience (Pope et al., 1993; Rodolfa et al., 1990).

After laying the groundwork for safety and openness, instructors are responsible for these words not becoming empty; that is, instructors must be prepared to enforce these ideals when challenged. For example, judgemental responses to disclosures or vignettes of attraction must be stopped and explored (What values and feelings are provoking the judgemental response? How is the group affected when sexual attractions are met with judgement?). Although these ground rules and ideals can form a clean and concrete list, enacting them is a complex effort of responding flexibly in the moment and attending to group process and group needs rather than the next item on the lesson plan. Demonstrating leadership that is not afraid to attend to deeper processes, relationships in the room and sustaining the concrete expectations of the group instils trust in the leadership; the instructor is backing up his or her expectations in the immediate lived experience – even when content and process become difficult. Being able to trust in leadership is especially critical when exploring topics like sexual attraction.

Because sexual attraction is often accompanied by shame and guilt (Ladany et al., 1997; Pope et al., 1993), a safe training environment for exploring dilemmas that trigger these feelings requires that participants be responsive and accepting. Pope et al. (1993) further delineated this as an acceptance-of-content process. It needs to be clear that being responsive to participant disclosures does not imply agreement or support for specific behaviours. Instead, the emphasis is on carefully attending to participants and peers and on exploring and understanding meanings of specific disclosures. With this in mind, instructors model norms where group participants take on roles that are supportive, encouraging and direct. When facilitating ethics trainings that include discussions of sexual attraction, it is critical that leaders model and maintain honest and direct communication, as the risks for a benign group and learning experience are high when participants fulfil *only* supportive, empathetic and open roles. Engineering this balance can be as simple as asking participants about what is not being said or acknowledged by themselves and other group members (Pope et al., 1993).

Once a safe environment is established, exploring appropriate behavioural responses to sexual attraction can ensue. Specifically, it is especially important for facilitators to move beyond general solution statements like 'refer' or 'seek supervision' and to engage participants in rich and specific responses to case vignettes, role plays or even personal disclosures (Ladany et al., 2013). When exploring behavioural responses to sexual attraction, instructors or facilitators can integrate behaviourally specific solutions guided by literature, ethical codes, research and self-disclosure. These may include the following:

- Practising the language one might use when disclosing an experience of sexual attraction during therapy to a supervisor or trusted colleague
- Role-playing responses that minimize shame and embarrassment when peers seek out consultation to disclose issues of sexual attraction
- Exploring methods for identifying attraction that may lie outside of awareness
- Brainstorming and practising specific coping and containing skills to use in sessions where attraction is present
- Supporting the general practice of nondisclosure to the client/supervisee when the clinician/supervisor experiences sexual attraction in the relationship to prevent harm and exploitation (Bridges, 1994; Ladany et al., 1996; Pope et al., 1993).

Additional recommendations for experiential training design include using (1) gender neutral vignettes, (2) small groups for reflection using structured question prompts to facilitate a safe and guided discussion, and (3) employing recorded critical incident vignettes that have the power to evoke and stimulate more challenging clinical realities than written cases (Bridges, 1994; Rodolfa et al., 1990). Although our endorsement of experiential learning and its effects is clear, professional resources and references also remain an important component of professional and pre-professional trainings. Connecting participants with detailed bibliographies, educational material, professional contacts and consultants from professional and licensing boards are vital resources.

When providing trainings that include a focus on sexual attraction, an important goal is to build trusting relationships among participants. This is because after graduate school, participants may rely heavily on peer consultation when addressing sensitive issues like sexual attraction. As an example, in their 1996 study, Ladany and colleagues found peer supervision to be a prominent alternative to disclosing critical issues to supervisors, or as they concluded, 'people with the least amount of supervision and counselling experience may be offering the most supervision' (p. 21). In light of these findings, it is critical that trainings address not only personal responses to attraction in professional contexts but also how one may respond as a supervisor or consultant in these situations.

Supervision

For a variety of reasons, talking directly about sex and sexuality is often a socially constructed taboo. This may be because when it comes to sexual attraction between clinicians and clients, there is a deep paradox that inhibits open discussion. On the one side, as Pope and Vasquez (2007, p. 209) noted, it is 'very common' for therapists to feel sexually attracted to clients. Yet, in bold contrast, acting on sexual feelings with clients has been uniformly prohibited since at least Freud. As a consequence, it can be challenging for both supervisee and supervisor to talk directly about thoughts, feelings and impulses that are so closely linked to highly unethical behaviour that risks professional and financial ruin.

Two additional and unique factors in the supervisory relationship influence the disclosure and discussion of vulnerable and taboo topics: supervision is evaluative and is often involuntary. As you might imagine, evaluative and involuntary properties influence everything from rapport building to disclosure and power structures. Because of unique double binds in supervision (e.g., expectations to disclose and be vulnerable about personal and professional challenges directly to someone who is evaluating you), we will outline considerations for addressing sexual attraction across supervision domains, including (1) considerations within the supervisory relationship, (2) the value of role induction and establishing norms,

(3) facilitating supervisee disclosure and the art of broaching, and (4) employing specific models and strategies.

Considerations within the Supervisory Relationship

Supervision is a safety net for quality client care and the foundation for clinical skill development. At the crux of supervision is the rapport built between supervisee and supervisor. This relationship facilitates (or impedes) supervisee self-disclosure and open inquiries for help; and let us be clear that the courage it takes to reach out and make needs known, especially when topics evoke shame and embarrassment, is no small task for a supervisee under evaluation. The consequences of supervisees not making their struggles and needs known are great, and can ultimately compromise client care and supervisee clinical development. In cases where sexual attraction arises, a trusting supervisory relationship is the cornerstone for exploration and intervention. Without trust, there will be little genuine openness.

Consideration of supervisee developmental needs and attention to power differentials in the relationship is critical to developing helpful supervisory relationships. When engaging in supervision, it is paramount that supervisors conceptualize supervisees from a developmental lens and contextualize their needs accordingly (Stoltenberg & McNeill, 2010). Supervision is not a 'one size fits all' endeavour, and if treated as such, supervisors miss opportunities to be responsive to diverse supervisee needs. For example, with many beginning therapists, the initial developmental step involves cultivating the therapists' awareness and then acknowledging the possibility that sexual attraction exists.

In addition, the role of power in supervisory relationships cannot go unacknowledged. While it is impossible to remove the power differential completely, movement can be made towards a more collaborative relationship in supervision. Supervisees cite many reasons for nondisclosure in supervision, and many are a product of how power unveils itself. Supervisees will avoid risking disclosure because of 'deference to the supervisor, impression management, and fear of political suicide' (Ladany et al., 1996, p. 18). If the supervisor uses an evaluative role to bolster a one-up power position, the supervisory relationship is at significant risk and supervisee needs may go undetected. Consequently, we recommend being transparent about a supervisor's evaluative role and how this influences supervision at the outset. We recommend that supervisors acknowledge and work to diffuse the power differential by setting norms for supervision as a place for support, growth, interpersonal sensitivity and mutual trust.

Role Induction and Establishing Norms

Similar to counselling and psychotherapy, role induction in supervision is essential (Sommers-Flanagan & Sommers-Flanagan, 2012). Role inductions clarify expectations and begin to set norms of what is talked about in supervision and how these topics are discussed. Depending on supervisee developmental level, it becomes the supervisor's responsibility to both co-construct supervision expectations and teach the supervisee about supervision (e.g., helping a supervisee decide what content and process variables to review in supervision) (Ladany et al., 1996). Role induction can include how sessions are reviewed, supervisee and supervisor responsibilities, the supervision model(s) employed and a review of a supervisor's professional disclosure statement (Bernard & Goodyear, 2009). In some cases, the supervisor's professional disclosure statement may include specific statements regarding supervisee and supervisor responsibilities. These responsibilities could include emphasizing the supervisee's responsibility to discuss all issues possibly affecting treatment process and outcome and the supervisor's responsibility to broach sensitive topics, such as potential sexual attraction. A more direct norm setting about sexual attraction may also be necessary. Describing sexual attraction as a common experience and potential topic for supervision lays the groundwork for later communication about sexual attraction.

Beyond a formal professional disclosure statement, it is vital to give permission and set the norm that personal issues can and often should be explored. This can be done with a statement such as 'In supervision I will usually ask you how it feels to be in the room with a particular client'. Additionally, supervisor self-disclosure or immediacy may be employed to further set a norm of openness. Establishing this as a behavioural norm in supervision may be especially crucial, as it appears that about 60% of nondisclosures in supervision may be related to supervisee personal issues (Ladany et al., 1996). When exploring personal issues, carefully distinguishing the role of supervisor from therapist is critical. The supervisor must be clear that personal issues will be viewed from a lens of how these issues impact the supervisee as a therapist/supervisor.

Facilitating Supervisee Disclosure and the Art of Broaching

Although infrequent, when discussed in supervision, topics related to sexual attraction are most often initiated by supervisees (Ladany et al., 1997). This evidence, however, does not indicate there is a high frequency of supervisee disclosures of sexual attraction. In fact, in one study, 97.2% of supervisees reported withholding information from their supervisors and 83% of supervisees passively hid their sexual attraction. This pattern is likely to leave important topics unexplored in supervision (Ladany et al., 1996). Given the evaluative, and sometimes involuntary, nature of supervision and its inherent power dynamics, supervisees may find themselves in the throes of strategic self-preservation, seeking to minimize negative impressions and to maximize positive impressions with supervisors (Bernard & Goodyear, 2009; Ward, Friedlander, Schoen, & Klein, 1985). The fact is that supervisors often write letters of recommendation to licensing boards about supervisee competence and readiness to become a professional. Given this direct example of supervisor evaluative power, it is easy to see why supervisees might be reluctant to disclose that they sometimes feel sexually attracted to a client. Nevertheless (and somewhat surprisingly), supervisees have reported feeling 'relieved and welcomed the opportunity to process the issue' when their supervisors broach a sexual attraction dilemma (Ladany et al., 1997, p. 422). Due to inherent power differentials and burden of risk for supervisees, we view supervisors as the primary responsible party for initiating discussions of sexual attraction in supervision.

This brings us to the art of broaching, or bringing up sexual attraction in supervision. Broaching sexual attraction in supervision braids together a number of factors such as timing, a present focus, attention to the supervisory relationship, and facilitating curiosity, collaboration and acceptance. We define broaching as taking a curious and exploratory stance to examine possibilities of sexual attraction in clinical relationships. In supervision, sexual attraction should not be approached as an absolute, unless it begins with a supervisee's self-disclosure. Instead, supervisors can 'wonder' along with the supervisee, floating and exploring possibilities based on concrete observations. Because broaching should be grounded in concrete observations, it is recommended that supervisors utilize audiotaping, videotaping and live supervision to observe counselling sessions rather than relying on supervisee self-reports or case notes (Ladany et al.,

1996, p. 22). When broaching, supervisors can use a concrete recorded or live example and engage the supervisee from a curious stance. Examples include the following:

- 'I'm noticing some drifting in the session where you guide the client to exploring sex in his intimate relationships. Yet, I'm not sure how this fits with his presenting problem. What is drawing you to exploring his sexuality?'
- 'I could be totally wrong, but it seems to me like there's just a little bit of flirting going on in this session. What do you think?'
- 'I notice you and your client sometimes engage in what seems like longer than usual mutual eye contact'.
- 'It seems harder for you to make eye contact with this client than it has been for you to make eye contact with other clients. Have you noticed that too?'

Extending invitations like these can result in a variety of supervisee responses; each time sexual attraction is broached, unique responses are sure to follow. Frequent reactions to sexual attraction can include surprise, startle, shock, guilt, fear of being criticized, frustration, confusion and discomfort (Pope et al., 1993). The effectiveness of a supervisor's response rests on his or her ability to attend to supervisee reactions in the moment, normalize the attraction and clearly separate attraction from sexual action. Comments that are critical or deprecatory can inhibit openness (Ladany et al., 2013). For example, saying something like 'You're not feeling sexually attracted to this client, are you?' could easily shut down an opportunity for open exploration and discussion.

Bringing the supervisory relationship to the here and now can be incredibly effective when acknowledging and moving forward with sexual attraction dilemmas. In fact, addressing the impact of sexual attraction often strengthens supervisory rapport (Ladany et al., 1997). Ignoring supervisee reactions or possible struggles with sexual attraction creates a negative loop in supervision, whereby overlooking the issue contributes to more distance and confirms an already struggling supervision relationship (Ladany et al., 1996).

Given these recommendations for *how* to broach, a remaining question is *when* to broach. In other words, what are the clues that sexual attraction dilemmas may be occurring in clinical relationships? Pope and his colleagues (1993) noted that sexual attraction frequently lingers outside of a therapist's awareness and identified several clues to unacknowledged sexual attraction. Patterns of behaviour include such things as dehumanization of the client or the therapist, avoidance, obsession, isolation of the client or the therapist, undue special treatment of a client, sexual fantasies, boredom and interesting slips. Again, this is not an inclusive list nor does it mean that these behaviours are unequivocal signs of sexual attraction. Rather, these are clues that it may be appropriate to broach sexual attraction issues and to link the behaviours as a rationale for exploration. If the attraction is occurring outside of the therapist's awareness, be aware that discovering this blind spot in the presence of a supervisor is accompanied by significant vulnerability and should be approached with sensitivity and emotional support.

Conceptual Framework

The foundations of establishing the supervisory alliance, role induction, setting norms and employing broaching techniques are critical components for addressing sexual attraction in supervision. A larger conceptual framework to organize these actions can rest in a number of supervision theories and models. While many are effective, one of the most flexible and responsive is the discrimination model (Bernard, 1979). Research suggests that supervision utilizing 'didactic, supportive, and collaborative components' results in supervisees perceiving supervisors as more open and, in return, making more disclosures in supervision (Ladany et al., 1996, p. 22). As such, the discrimination model presents a similar flexibility in both the role of the supervisor (that of a teacher, counsellor or consultant) and where the supervision focus is directed (personalization, intervention or conceptualization).

The flexibility included in the discrimination model can allow shifts from didactic (teaching) responses to counsellor and/or consultant, as needed. The beauty of this model is that supervisors have the flexibility to respond to supervisees' immediate needs in a variety of ways. For example, a supervisor may notice a supervisee attending more to the wife in a couples counselling session and stating, 'You are clearly beautiful, and your husband is having difficulty seeing you as a sexual being'. The supervisor takes note of this behaviour as a possible clue of sexual attraction and can lay the foundation for broaching with a teaching role. In the teaching role, the supervisor reminds the supervisee that attraction can surface in clinical situations often, and without warning or awareness. Next, the supervisor may choose a consultant role to facilitate broaching the cues of sexual attraction in the session, stating, 'When I watch you interact with her in session, I notice you attend to her more and compliment when applying interventions. I'm curious if there is a part of you that is attracted to her?' Next, the supervisor may shift to a counsellor driven response that attends to the impact of broaching in the here and now, empathizes with the supervisee's reaction and checks in about the status of the supervisory alliance. The fluidity of this model is an excellent match for difficult topics like sexual attraction, as it allows movement that is responsive to immediate supervisee needs.

The model's fluidity continues beyond supervisor chosen roles, moving from the *how* to focus and into the *where*. There are three places where supervisors can focus: conceptualization, intervention and personalization. There is no doubt that personalization (personal reactions to a client, session content, etc.) will be an element of focus when sexual attractions arise. When addressing sexual attraction from a personalization lens, helpful explorations may include supervisees' beliefs and reactions when someone is attracted to them, and how their attraction to others may manifest (Ladany et al., 1997). Keep in mind, it is easy to narrow the scope of supervision and *only* focus on attraction as a personalization issue. While it is essential to recognize this personalization and to explore it fully with supervisees (Pope et al., 1993), attending to case conceptualization and intervention needs is equally critical. For example, when considering interventions for the session, supervisees should be made aware that disclosing attraction to a client is likely more harmful and exploitive than advantageous, and, in most cases, using immediacy or self-disclosure should be avoided as an intervention (Goodyear & Shumate, 1996; Ladany et al., 1997; Pope et al., 2006). When using an intervention focus, the supervisor can focus on interventions to help manage and reduce sexual attraction and also help the supervisee refocus therapy interventions on the client's presenting issue. Last, conceptualization must also be explored; how we think about clients and cases is not immune to sexual attraction dilemmas. In fact, conceptualization skills may be particularly vulnerable, as supervisees have found issues of sexual attraction to be particularly 'intrusive and distracting' (Ladany et al., 1997, p. 418). Taking a conceptualization focus in supervision can redirect the supervisees to the primary client issue and help them remain grounded in these conceptualizations.

A final note about the discrimination model's flexibility is that it can be integrated with a variety of theoretical orientations. It becomes the supervisor's role to collaborate and explore sessions from the supervisee's theoretical lens, be it psychoanalytic, person-centred, narrative, and so on.

This fluidity allows supervisees to learn and employ *their* theoretical orientation with a supervisor, grounded in a supervision model, rather than a specific clinical model that may narrow the focus of supervision and not fit with the supervisee's theoretical framework.

In the following case example, a developmental approach to supervision is emphasized. The supervisor establishes a strong supervision relationship and uses that relationship to help the clinician in training focus initially on values-based discomfort and later on sexual attraction. Dimensions of Bernard's (1979) discrimination model are articulated in the case.

Case Example: Therapist Discomfort and Sexual Attraction

Julie, a 26-year-old student in a clinical training program, is enrolled in professor Suzanne's practicum course. To fulfil the requirements of the course, Julie meets with Suzanne weekly for supervision, reviewing recordings of her counselling sessions at the university's counselling centre. Julie's skill development is on target and Suzanne has come to see her as one of the stronger students in the course. Two months into the semester, a solid supervisory relationship is present. During a preceding supervision session, Suzanne successfully broached a lurking personalization issue. Julie had been counselling a female student athlete in her first year at the university who identified herself as lesbian. After Suzanne witnessed discomfort in Julie when addressing her client's sexual orientation, she broached the issue, asking, 'In session, you looked a bit nervous when talking about her girlfriend. I'm wondering if this was a risk for you?' Julie agreed that it was and disclosed that she was a member of a local conservative church, something that she had felt pressure to hide during her time in the program. Suzanne learned more about Julie during this supervision, including her personal values for committed heterosexual relationships (especially her own marriage) and her struggle honouring both her own personal values and those of her clients. Supervision continued with a primary focus of helping Julie resolve this struggle and maintaining an open, empathic and validating rapport with clients who might have or be exploring sexual behaviours inconsistent with Julie's personal values.

Then came Dan. Julie began counselling with Dan, an attractive senior at the university seeking career counselling. When reviewing session recordings, Suzanne noticed that Julie blushes more in session, touches Dan's shoulder or knee for emphasis and often portrays herself in a flirtatious, self-deprecating light (all behaviours that have not been witnessed in previous sessions or supervision). Suzanne senses another personalization issue, one of attraction, may be playing out for Julie. Given the success of Suzanne's last intervention, she pushed ahead, stating, 'You seem to be blushing more in session, and touch him a bit more frequently. I'm wondering if you might be attracted to Dan?' Julie withdrew, horrified, stating, 'No. I mean, I would never. I'm married. I can't believe you would think I would go after a client!'

In this case, the supervisor's broaching of sexual attraction elicits supervisee defensiveness. As a consequence, the following supervision plan, including specific supervisor responses and goals, is pursued:

- Repair the supervisory rapport utilizing the counsellor role, attending to the here and now of the supervisory relationship and showing empathy for Julie's embarrassment.
- Clarify the difference between sexual attraction and sexual actions while normalizing attraction as a common experience.
- Bring awareness of Julie's assumptions of supervisor judgement to the here and now while exploring shame or guilt she may hold and how her value system has been affected.
- Address attraction and its potential to play out in multiple ways in counselling sessions, even when counsellors are in committed relationships.
- Using the teacher role, develop interventions that Julie can use in session to reduce responses like blushing, self-deprecating remarks and touching.
- Explore the potential for Dan's attraction to Julie using a consultant role.
- Set a norm for supervision as a place to explore and address attraction dilemmas, facilitating awareness on how sexual attraction impacts the counselling relationship and client outcomes.

This case illustrates the competence and sensitivity needed for supervisors to effectively address supervisee sexual attraction. The extent to which the preceding plan succeeds depends upon a myriad of factors, including, but not limited to, how well the supervisor has established a foundation of trust and mutual exploration, supervisee commitment to personal and professional development, supervisee openness to expanding personal awareness, and supervisor skill at shifting among different roles within the supervision relationship.

Parallel Process and Concluding Comments

Sexual attraction is a ubiquitous human phenomenon that can appear in a variety of relationship contexts. Additionally, human relationship patterns are frequently repetitive. This universal potential for sexual attraction and repeating processes in interpersonal relationships reminds us that sexual attraction may also develop, quickly or over time, in supervisor–supervisee relationships. These attractions may emerge independent of dynamics within the supervisee–client relationship, but parallel process also implies that sexual attraction in the supervisor–supervisee relationship can sometimes mysteriously mimic dynamics within the supervisee–client relationship.

Searles (1955) originally described the parallel process: '. . . processes at work currently in the relationship between patient and therapist are often reflected in the relationship between therapist and supervisor' (p. 135). The parallel process is an intriguing and often mysterious phenomenon. Although its roots are in psychoanalytic theory, there are no clear explanations for how and why it sometimes occurs. Nevertheless, its presence and potential is a clinical reality and serves as a reminder that we are all vulnerable to sexual attractions that may be both surprising and predictable.

In closing, we want to re-emphasize that supervisors should develop collaborative and open relationships with supervisees. Consistent with the discrimination model, these relationships can and should be multidimensional. When it comes to addressing sexual attraction that arises within the supervisor–supervisee relationship, we recommend following the guidelines we have offered in this chapter. Rather than exploring sexual attraction in the here and now with the individual towards whom the feelings are directed, we strongly recommend managing your impulses and possibly seeking outside consultation as a means of minimizing professional risk.

References

Bernard, J. M. (1979). Supervisor training: A discrimination model. *Counselor Education and Supervision*, 19(1), 60–68.

Bernard, J. M., & Goodyear, R. K. (2009). *Fundamentals of clinical supervision* (4th ed.). Upper Saddle River, NJ: Pearson Education.

Bridges, N. A. (1994). Meaning and management of attraction: Neglected areas of psychotherapy training and practice. *Psychotherapy: Theory, Research, Practice, Training, 31*(3), 424–433.

Downs, L. (2003). A preliminary survey of relationships between counselor educators' ethics education and ensuing pedagogy and responses to attractions with counseling students. *Counseling and Values, 48*(1), 2–13.

Goodyear, R. K., & Shumate, J. L. (1996). Perceived effects of therapist self-disclosure of attraction to clients. *Professional Psychology, Research and Practice, 27*(6), 613–616.

Ladany, N. (2004). Psychotherapy supervision: What lies beneath. *Psychotherapy Research, 14*(1), 1–19.

Ladany, N., Hill, C. E., Corbett, M. M., & Nutt, E. A. (1996). Nature, extent, and importance of what psychotherapy trainees do not disclose to their supervisors. *Journal of Counseling Psychology, 43*(1), 10–24.

Ladany, N., Klinger, R., & Kulp, L. (2011). Therapist shame: Implications for therapy and supervision. In R. L. Dearing & J. P. Tangney (Eds.), *Shame in the therapy hour* (pp. 307–322). Washington, DC: American Psychological Association.

Ladany, N., Mori, Y., & Mehr, K. E. (2013). Effective and ineffective supervision. *The Counseling Psychologist, 41*(1), 28–47.

Ladany, N., O'Brien, K. M., Hill, C. E., Melincoff, D. S., Knox, S., & Petersen, D. A. (1997). Sexual attraction toward clients, use of supervision, and prior training: A qualitative study of predoctoral psychology interns. *Journal of Counseling Psychology, 44*(4), 413–424.

Pope, K. S., Sonne, J. L., & Holroyd, J. (1993). *Sexual feelings in psychotherapy: Explorations for therapists and therapists-in-training.* Washington, DC: American Psychological Association.

Pope, K. S., Keith-Spiegel, P., & Tabachnick, B. G. (2006). Sexual attraction to clients: The human therapist and the (sometimes) inhuman training system. *Training and Education in Professional Psychology, 5*(2), 96–111.

Pope, K. S., Sonne, J. L., & Greene, B. (2006). Therapists' sexual arousals, attractions, and fantasies: An example of a topic that isn't there. In K. Pope, J. Sonne, & B. Greene (Ed.), *What therapists don't talk about and why: Understanding taboos that hurt us and our clients* (pp. 27–41). Washington, DC: American Psychological Association.

Pope, K. S., & Vasquez, M. J. T. (2007). *Ethics in psychotherapy and counseling: A practical guide* (3rd ed.). San Francisco, CA: Jossey-Bass.

Rodolfa, E. R., Kitzrow, M., Vohra, S., & Wilson, B. (1990). Training interns to respond to sexual dilemmas. *Professional Psychology, Research and Practice, 21*(4), 313–315.

Searles, H. F. (1955). The informational value of the supervisor's emotional experiences. *Psychiatry, 18*, 135–146.

Sommers-Flanagan, J., & Sommers-Flanagan, R. (2012). *Clinical interviewing* (4th ed., update ed.). Hoboken, NJ: John Wiley & Sons.

Stoltenberg, C. D., & McNeill, B. W. (2010). *IDM supervision: An integrative developmental model for supervising counselors and therapists* (3rd ed.). New York: Routledge/Taylor & Francis Group.

Ward, L. G., Friedlander, M. L., Schoen, L. G., & Klein, J. G. (1985). Strategic self-presentation in supervision. *Journal of Counseling Psychology, 32*(1), 111–118.

8

Sexual Attraction in Conjoint Couple Therapy

Steven M. Harris and Tina M. Timm

Our clients, in their vulnerability, divulge the most personal and private details about their lives with the hope that we will be accepting and understanding of the experiences they have had. Further, they put immense trust in us that we will offer sound counsel to assist them. In so doing, they become close to us and we to them. In this relationship, the therapist bears the responsibility to 'first do no harm' to the clients because of the inherent power inequity in the therapeutic relationship. One area of potential harm in the practice of psychotherapy occurs when the intimate nature of the therapeutic relationship becomes confused or blended with sexual feelings. This chapter focuses on feelings of sexual attraction that occur when the treatment modality is conjoint couple therapy, where the unit of treatment is a couple.

It has been well established that sexual attraction is something that happens in both individual psychotherapy (Pope, Sonne, & Holroyd, 1993) and in couple therapy (Harris, 2001; Harris & Harriger, 2009; Nickell, Hecker, Ray, & Bercik, 1995). For many of us, it is easy to understand how an attraction between therapist and client could develop in the private therapeutic relationship when two people engage in a process that includes deep self-disclosure with high emotional content. This is especially the case when there are only two players in the therapeutic relationship. The very secretive nature of the meeting, the protections afforded the relationship, the content discussed and the unconditional positive

Sexual Attraction in Therapy: Clinical Perspectives on Moving Beyond the Taboo – A Guide for Training and Practice, First Edition. Edited by Maria Luca.
© 2014 John Wiley & Sons, Ltd. Published 2014 by John Wiley & Sons, Ltd.

regard can all contribute to the development of an intense bond between the players in the therapeutic relationship.

Harris and Harriger (2009), in their article on sexual attraction in conjoint therapy, conducted a review of the mate selection literature and discovered that the therapeutic relationship contains many of the key elements that are present in our most intimate relationships. For example, proximity, shared values and goals, physical attraction and social/cultural expectations that facilitate bonding in committed/intimate relationships (all a part of what is present when two individuals develop into a 'couple') could also be a part of the therapeutic relationship. They contend that some of the elements that contribute to successful therapy seem to parallel those in intimate couple relationships. However, it may be more difficult to see how an attraction between therapist and client, or client and therapist, could develop when the unit of treatment is a couple who present to therapy together to work on improving *their* relationship. In calling attention to this topic, we echo the words of Young (2010), who suggested, 'Couple and family therapists are likely to face a broad range of sexual ethical dilemmas as comes with the territory of the intimate nature of their work' (p. 90).

Sexual attraction in conjoint therapy takes on additional levels of complexity because of the triad of relationships present in the room. A therapeutic alliance must be maintained with each partner while simultaneously monitoring the relationship of the partners with each other. A change within any of these relationships affects the others. As the relationship gets closer (whether real or perceived) between the therapist and one of the partners, the relationship with the other partner may be jeopardized. The intensity of this can be heightened when it is fuelled by sexual attraction. Knowing that your partner is attracted to someone else can elicit feelings of vulnerability, insecurity, jealousy or anger. Feeling attracted to someone other than your partner can evoke curiosity, confusion, excitement or perhaps embarrassment. It is imperative that the therapist addresses these dynamics directly to avoid the work stalling, deteriorating or terminating prematurely. While therapists know this theoretically, even the most seasoned therapist may struggle to know how to handle it appropriately. There are a number of factors that can impact a therapist's ability or willingness to address attraction in conjoint therapy.

Lack of Training

First of all, many clinical training programmes do not require training in conjoint therapy specifically. For those that do, they may never address how to recognize and negotiate what to do when sexual attraction presents itself. Accredited couple and family therapy programmes are the most likely places to address it because they require both courses and specific practical experiences in working with couples and, in some instances, may even require a course on sex therapy. However, this is no guarantee that sexual attraction within conjoint therapy would get covered. Another barrier is that there are few opportunities to add to this knowledge base after the degree completion. Consequently, it is feasible that couple therapists could go their entire professional career without learning how to handle this complex, and yet very common, clinical dilemma.

Self of the Therapist Issues

Not all therapists feel confident or comfortable in addressing human sexuality topics in therapy (Harris & Hays, 2008). In some cases, a therapist may have blind spots around the interpersonal dynamics associated with attraction, or may have outright denial of the possibility of this happening. Luca and Boyden's study (Chapter 13) found that denial and avoidance, in particular, were prominent in experienced therapists' handling of sexual attraction. In these cases, it would be wise for the supervisors of these therapists to encourage some self-exploration.

Anecdotally speaking, there are a number of therapists who select a mental health career because they have had some significant emotional struggles in their own personal development. Many students' interest in the field is piqued because, through their studies, they begin to get answers to the questions they have had for years about their own family life. As supervisors and trainers of clinicians, we can testify that the metaphor of the 'wounded' healer is far too common to disregard as merely cliché. When the search for these answers is related to sexuality (e.g., a history of sexual abuse or an over-sexualized emotional climate in the therapist's family of origin), there may be an increased intensity for the therapist who is in a situation where attraction is occurring. It is imperative that these therapists do their own healing around these issues so as not to use the therapy setting for this purpose. Once therapists have 'done their own work', they may be even more adept at handling these situations (Timm & Blow, 1999).

More Difficult because the Partner Is There Too

While some therapists may feel fine addressing sexual attraction with an individual, it is harder to do so when the client's partner is also in the room. The thoughts and feelings of both parties need to be considered. Therapists may be 'protective' of their partners. They may worry about making their partner feel insecure about the stability of their relationship or their confidence in their level of attractiveness to their partner. Therapists may worry that bringing this up may cause further distance within an already struggling relationship or may elicit feelings of competition. On the other side of the equation, therapists might worry about embarrassing the partner who is having the attraction. Still, another barrier to bringing up the issue of a client's possible attraction to the therapist is the whole 'deniability' of the attraction.

Consider the therapist who has been getting cues that a client in conjoint therapy is attracted to her. It takes significant courage to tactfully address it, and the therapist becomes vulnerable when she suggests that an attraction may be influencing their work in therapy. A client can easily deny that an attraction exists, and there might be some increased incentive to do so because their partner is present. In cases where the client denies the attraction, the therapist could end up looking arrogant, self-absorbed, narcissistic or even unethical for suggesting such a thing. Negotiating the tension between all these competing forces may ultimately conspire to keep a therapist from addressing it.

Ambiguous Presentation

This is when the therapist questions himself or herself, 'Is this really what's going on?' 'Who am I to think this person is attracted to me?' 'Is the partner just being insecure and jealous for no reason?' and one of the most common, 'What if I'm wrong about it?' 'What happens if I try to address it and it doesn't go well? I might be left sitting here feeling embarrassed and incompetent'.

Many times, sexual attraction shows up in conjoint therapy in subtle ways. A husband says things that sound slightly flirtatious, a wife wears a shorter skirt, phone calls, emails or texts start being sent in between sessions, a partner requests an individual session to talk to you about something they do not want their partner to know about, a small gift is given, and so on. Any one of these does not mean there is sexual attraction. However, if it begins to be a pattern, it should not be ignored. In areas that are highly ambiguous, the therapist may not be able to cite a specific behaviour or comment, it is just 'a feeling' they get. When this is the case, therapists are even less likely to address it for fear they are just imagining it. This underscores the important role that supervision can play when the dynamics of sexual attraction are involved in conjoint therapy.

How Attraction Can Happen in Conjoint Therapy

This section provides a variety of case vignettes informed by practice experiences that illustrate how sexual attraction between clients and therapists can present itself in conjoint therapy. Some are written from a narrative perspective, like a story one could read about that occurred to a set of people the reader would not know. Other vignettes are written from a more first-person perspective, as if the things depicted in the vignette were occurring to the reader. This allows the reader a couple of different ways to experience this phenomenon and how it can play out across different situations. In all cases, we provide follow-up questions to facilitate discussion for either a classroom or a clinical supervision setting.

Attraction from the client to the therapist

Clients become attracted to their therapist for a variety of reasons. Markovic's study in Chapter 15 suggests that it is more difficult to handle in couple therapy. It is important to remember that clients do not typically think about the rules of ethical therapeutic engagement the way therapists do. While many clients will have an innate sense of propriety and don't initiate therapy with the intention of developing an attraction to their therapist, becoming attracted to their therapist may be interpreted as a sign that they should nurture that attraction. It may be that their personal model for connecting with people leads them to believe that when they feel an attraction to another person, they should nurture that relationship to deepen the connection. Other people acknowledge that while an attraction may be present, it is not necessary to read more into it than it being an unintentional and fleeting by-product of interacting with another person. The following vignettes illustrate attraction from the client towards the therapist.

Why can't you be him?

Patti and Jim began couples therapy 6 months after Patti had a miscarriage. Married for about 6 years, they had been trying to conceive for over a year. Both reported being excited when Patti became pregnant. However, in week 12, Patti lost the baby. Jim was out of town for work when it happened and didn't return home for three days because 'there was nothing he could do to change it'. Patti was devastated by the loss and deeply hurt that Jim did not come home as soon as he found out. In the wake of the loss, Patti's symptoms of depression were moderate and persistent; as a result, she and Jim became increasingly distant. Jim began encouraging her to get pregnant as soon as possible, but Patti feels this isn't the answer. She feels as though Jim doesn't understand the depths of her grief. In their first session, Patti stated that she is thinking about divorce because 'clearly Jim doesn't care about me'.

Their therapist, Bob, was a seasoned couple therapist and noticed around the fourth session that Patti came in looking much brighter and was wearing make-up and nicer clothing. He initially took this as a sign that her depression was lifting. In the next couple of sessions, she wore increasingly revealing clothes and began finding ways to make physical contact with Bob (requesting a hug at the end of sessions). Her interactions took on a flirtatious tone. In the eighth session, Jim came in highly agitated and started the session by saying he was sick and tired of hearing about Bob all the time at home. He stated, 'day in and day out it's Bob this and Bob that'. Last night we got in a big fight and I said, 'Why don't you just marry Bob then!'

Initially, Patti was defensive but finally admitted to thinking about Bob outside of their sessions and finally broke down in tears and said, 'You listen to me. You care about me. You say exactly what I want Jim to say. There are times I wonder what it would be like to be your wife'.

- How would you feel in this situation if you were Bob?
- Would you be interested in meeting with either member of this couple individually? If yes, for what purpose?
- What are your main concerns with this situation?
- If you were supervising Bob's clinical work, what is the most important thing you'd want him to know about your understanding of his work and the situation with this client?
- What advice would you give to Bob in moving forward with this client?

What is something I said?

Andrew and Sylvia had been married for 16 years when they began sex therapy to help them restore health to their sexual relationship. Sexual contact had waned to about once a month, and on those occasions, Andrew reported that Sylvia 'just laid there like she couldn't wait for it to be over'.

Sylvia stated that she was uninterested in sex and just did it because she knew she 'should', not because she enjoyed it.

During the first session, perhaps out of his anxiety about being there, Andrew made several odd statements, including 'So, do you watch us have sex?' and 'I bet it's fun to sit around all day and talk about sex with people'. The therapist, Sally, who wore her wedding ring and had a picture of her husband on her desk, began receiving comments from Andrew that made her uneasy, such as 'Your husband is pretty lucky to be married to a sex therapist. I bet he gets it all the time'. Andrew's comments were typically downplayed by him saying he was 'just kidding'. However, the comments began to be increasingly sexualized and more personal. While processing a sensate focus homework assignment, he talked about being aroused and how there was 'no way that she couldn't notice because he was "much bigger than most"'. At one point in the therapy, he suggested that they could solve their problem by inviting someone else to join them and asked Sally, 'Do you make house calls?'

Between sessions Sally received an email from Sylvia asking her to stop 'dressing up' on the day they came in. She expressed concern that an attraction her husband had toward Sally was making it difficult to make progress in therapy and that being a guy, 'he gets too "distracted" by your clothes to focus on our work together'. She also inquired about whether they should get a referral to a male therapist.

- If you were Sally, what would be your biggest concern with this case?
- As Sally's supervisor, what would be your biggest concern with this case?
- How do the personal effects that decorate our offices invite clients into our intimate world?
- How much responsibility should a therapist take to control the experience that other people may have towards him or her (i.e., manner of dress, physical appearance and office decorations)?
- If you were Sally, how would you respond to the email enquiry from Sylvia?

Your Facebook friend

Maria and Jackie had been dating for about 2 years and living together for 6 months. They came in to therapy because Maria had just found out that Jackie had sex with an ex-girlfriend at a party. Jackie had been dating this same woman at the time that they met. Now, Maria is not sure if she wants to stay with Jackie. She had been cheated on repeatedly while in a heterosexual relationship in the past and she swore she would never again stay with anyone who could do this to her. They came to therapy wondering if there was hope for their relationship.

The therapist, Emily, was a recent graduate working in a Community Mental Health Agency. She wasn't sure how to handle some of the more personal questions that Maria began to ask her, like 'What are you doing over the weekend?' and 'Do you live in the area?' She began to be suspicious of Maria when she started running into her at places in the community. While these meetings were, most likely, coincidental, each time, Maria wanted to engage in a lengthy conversation that Emily started to feel were 'too friendly'. It was during one of these conversations that Maria asked her a question that referenced something Emily had posted on Facebook the previous day. This realization caused her a great deal of anxiety and she had trouble sleeping that night. She realized that Maria had been checking out her Facebook page despite not being included in her list of 'friends'.

During supervision, she requested to transfer the case to another therapist, the supervisor helped her to process how to move forward without jumping to solve the situation with a transfer. The next session, Emily began by asking Maria directly if she ever thought about what it would be like to have a relationship with her outside the therapeutic context.

- Do you agree that not transferring was the right 'next step' with this client?
- How do Maria's actions towards the therapist parallel the couple's presenting problem?
- Have you ever had a client ask you to be friends on Facebook or other social media? How have you responded? How is this related to the dynamic of attraction?
- What potential danger do you see with the therapist asking Maria if she's ever thought about having a relationship with her outside of therapy?
- Are there times when it is appropriate to transfer a case? If so, when?

Attraction from the therapist to the client

In many schools of psychotherapy, the term we use to describe the process of a therapist becoming attracted to a client is countertransference. This term, in traditional psychoanalysis, describes a subconscious process that occurs within the psyche of the therapist but lies outside the therapist's awareness. Countertransference can become an initial rationale for a host of unethical behaviours and may be the main reason that many therapists engage in personal psychotherapy to resolve their own 'issues'. A different way of conceptualizing how sexual attraction occurs in therapy is to consider the elements needed (or the essential ingredients necessary) for two people to become attracted to one another (i.e., shared time and space, common goals, understanding and intimacy). This explanation for how attraction develops places more emphasis on natural occurring phenomena within the therapeutic relationship. Regardless of how the attraction may develop in the experience of the therapist, the therapist is still held to ethical standards that demand that professional boundaries remain intact. The following vignettes illustrate the therapist's attraction to the client.

Too Hot to Handle

Tyler initiated couple therapy by setting up an appointment for himself and his wife, Madison. He reported wanting to 'save his marriage' as the reason for therapy. Over the phone you find out that Madison has recently told Tyler that she loves him, she's just not 'in love' with him. He is distraught and asks for the soonest appointment they can get. When you first meet the couple, you are struck with what a strikingly handsome couple they are. Both seem to be in great physical shape and are well groomed. They are articulate and seem to be emotionally and mentally well adjusted. As far as the content of the session goes, there is nothing that stands out to you as major red flags, no drugs, alcohol, affairs, no personality disorders, and so on. You assess that this is a couple that has not made a lot of investment in the relationship and are now feeling disconnected from one another. At the same time, you cannot shake a very strong sexual attraction you feel toward Madison. She is attractive, articulate, engaging, and you find yourself staring at her body throughout the session when you believe neither she nor Tyler can see you do it. When you are in session with the couple, you are aware of her beauty and your sexual attraction toward her, but you carefully balance the time you spend talking with each member of the couple so you don't come across as being overly interested in her and risk offending Tyler. During one of the sessions, Tyler is venting on how much attention people, and men in particular, give to Madison and how he has struggled with feeling like he is in constant competition with other men for her attention (despite her disagreement with and downplaying his concern). He asks you, 'Admit it, you think she's hot too, don't you?' You immediately blush and feel put on the spot by his accusation.

- What are your thoughts about responding truthfully to Tyler's question?
- What possible impact may that have on the therapeutic relationship?
- Does this scenario change much in your mind if Madison is the one who expresses concern about competing with other women for Tyler's attention and then asks you the same question about Tyler? How?
- If you have become attracted to a client, when is the best time to begin talking about it? With whom should you speak?
- Is it necessary to refer a couple to another therapist when you feel attracted to a member of that couple?

Can't get you outta my head

You are out to dinner with your partner and thoughts of a client couple you met with earlier continue to enter into your mind. These thoughts come to you as images of this couple's sexual relationship that you create based on the content discussed in your session. You find yourself dwelling on sexual acts the clients described in session. At first, you don't give these thoughts much attention or concern. However, as the evening progresses, you find that these thoughts are beginning to become more frequent and intrusive. Later that night, in the middle of a sexual encounter with your partner, you find yourself fantasizing that you are with one of the members of this couple and you initiate sexual acts you heard described earlier in session. As the fantasy develops in your mind, you realize it has raised the level of sexual intensity for both you and your partner. At the conclusion of your sexual encounter, your partner says, 'That was awesome! Our lovemaking hasn't been this intense in years. What's gotten into you?'

- What do you say to your partner in response to this question?
- How do you think these fantasies might affect the therapeutic relationship?
- How do you think you'll act in the next session with the couple?
- When is the best time to get supervision for your work with this client?
- How much of your 'self' will you share with your supervisor (supervision/case consultation group) about this situation?

Wrong number

You have been practising couple therapy for over 10 years and you stay in contact with your colleagues from your graduate training. On occasion, you consult with them and share information with them about your clients. On a particularly busy day, you have been texting a former classmate between sessions to talk about one of her cases. Just before going into a session with a client that you find very sexually attractive, you jokingly text your friend that you've got to go because you're about to 'spend an hour talking sex with one of the hottest people on earth ☺'. Unknown to you, you accidentally sent the text to the couple with whom you're meeting. They receive the text as you all enter the session.

- What are the dangers associated with focusing on a client's attractiveness?
- What steps could have been taken to prevent this situation?
- Is this something that you're likely to bring up in supervision?
- Can you see any scenario in which this turns out to be positive?
- If you are the supervisor and you hear about this situation, what are your main concerns?

How to Handle Sexual Attraction in Conjoint Therapy

In wrapping up a chapter like this, we want to offer some practical advice to those who may be experiencing an attraction dynamic within the context of conjoint therapy, either from or towards a client. While most of the strategies apply in both situations, we feel a strong need to emphasize that we cannot envision a situation where it would ever be appropriate to initiate a conversation with a client about your attraction towards him/her. The vulnerable state in which our clients present, and the trust they put in us to act professionally, demands that we protect them. Even if you are a therapist who believes that honesty must guide all that you do clinically, we recommend that your honest feelings towards a client be filtered through a collegial consultation or clinical supervision. Asking yourself if what you are about to disclose to your clients will ultimately help them with what they came to therapy for or will it detract from their clinical goals is one way to check the appropriateness of any self-disclosure.

In presenting on this topic to a graduate class on ethics, I (SMH) once had a student who told me that he trusted so much in the power of truthfulness and honesty in therapy that he believed he could disclose an attraction towards a client and that it would be to the client's benefit. I asked if he would do a role play with a classmate, acting as a client, so he could show the class how he might go about his honest and truthful declaration of attraction. After a few awkward moments and stilted conversation, the student broke from the role play, turned to me and said,

'For some reason it just doesn't feel right for me to share that with the client'. I thanked him for his honest response. It is not right for therapists to share their feelings of sexual attraction with their clients. This must be a topic of consultation with capable and trusted colleagues.

In addition to the stern warning and voice of client advocacy we raised in the previous paragraph, we offer some suggestions on how to proceed when sexual attraction becomes part of the conjoint therapy you conduct.

Normalize it

As mentioned earlier, human beings are bound to become attracted to other human beings. Thinking strictly from an evolutionary perspective, we seem to be influenced by biological drives that propel us towards noticing the attractiveness of others, or feeling a sense of 'comfort around' or 'ease with' certain other humans. It is these feelings that help us find a 'mate'. These feelings can be the very early seeds of attraction, and when coupled with discouragement in or disenchantment with a current love relationship (like most of our couple clients who are struggling), it is not hard to see that the comparison of our partner to an idealized other (a therapist or one of our clients) can easily lead to an attraction. Our biological drives do not distinguish between being attracted to a client (or a therapist) or being attracted to any other human being. So, one of the first things we need to admit to ourselves and acknowledge is that as humans, it is normal to become attracted to another human. As discussed above, there are a number of factors specific to the therapeutic context that further intensify the likelihood that sexual attraction will occur. The key thereafter, is to know how to go about addressing it.

Talk openly about it

If a member of a couple you are treating is attracted to you, or you think something like that is happening, we encourage you to talk about it. This is the elephant in the room in many cases. If you don't address it, you run the risk of sending the message that certain things are 'off limits' to discuss in the therapeutic relationship. This is a message no therapist should want to send in conjoint therapy. Healthy relationships (the overarching goal of conjoint therapy) can only develop in an environment where people are open and honest in their communications. To neglect a relationship dynamic that has the potential to adversely affect the couple borders on negligence.

If you are the one attracted to your client, we still say, 'talk openly about it' . . . but do so in supervision. If you've developed an attraction to a client, you must remember that this is something *you* have to deal with. If it becomes problematic (meaning you can't seem to move past your attraction), it is imperative that you do not discuss it with the client. The client did not initiate therapy so you could process your attraction to him/her. Telling a client that you're attracted to him/her immediately changes the agenda for therapy. It takes the focus off of the client's presenting problem(s) and puts it on your relationship with the client. This is something your client did not consent to.

Address the effect on *both* parties

Given that it affects both clients and potentially their relationship, processing the attraction of a client towards you should take place in a conjoint session, not one on one. Having an individual session can potentially do more harm than good. It can intensify the feelings because now there is a 'secret' being shared that the third party is not privy to – hereby creating *more* intimacy. As in any conjoint therapy, the partners are each given a chance to talk about how they feel about the attraction and to reflect on how it is or may continue to affect the work that is being done.

Do not assume that addressing it one time means you'll never have to revisit the issue again. It is the therapist's responsibility to check in again and see how things are going. Many times, having had the initial conversation will shift the dynamic. Because it is no longer the elephant in the room, it does not have the same power. What had previously been distracting is now out of the way and allows for deeper work. Remember, discussing difficult topics models for the couple that this is what healthy communication and effective conflict resolution can look like.

Using supervision and case consultation

We strongly believe that supervision (individual or group) and/or case consultation is essential in the processing of sexual attraction in conjoint therapy – both when it is a client towards the therapist or vice versa. Ideally, the supervisor or colleague will do the very thing that we do for the clients – normalize it. While the thoughts and fantasies may be common, the degree to which they exist needs to be carefully assessed. If supervision was not sought promptly, boundaries may have been subtly or not so subtly crossed. While we would love to be able to go back and have a 'do-over', that is typically not possible. So, appropriate actions must be taken to shore up shaky personal boundaries. In some cases, offering to video or audio record sessions to be reviewed in supervision can re-establish a boundary. Reviewing audio or video data from the sessions can also provide concrete examples of how interactions between client and therapist have strayed from the therapeutic agenda. If a therapeutic rupture has occurred, the therapist must work to repair it. If individual therapy (or conjoint therapy) is needed on the part of the therapist, it should be sought.

Transfer and termination

Oftentimes, due to the lack of comfort with the issue, the reflex is to refer the couple to another therapist. While this may be easier for the therapist, it can cause damage to the couple. They may be left confused or angry about the termination. What, if anything, was said to them about the need for a referral? Was the therapist honest, or did he or she make up another reason for the transfer? How does it help them if the attraction then manifests itself in the next therapeutic situation? Do they keep getting transferred from one therapist to the next until someone is willing to deal with it?

However, having said that, we realize that there may be times when referring to another therapist is necessary. For example, when it is the client who is attracted to the therapist and it has been addressed repeatedly and unfortunately is still a distraction or still seems to jeopardize the therapeutic relationship, it may be advisable. If it comes to this, we recommend that the issue of transferring is processed thoroughly with the clients present and that the decision to terminate and transfer be made as collaboratively as possible.

If it is a therapist's attraction to one of the partners, and even after supervision has been sought the intensity of the attraction does not decrease, or it increases, a transfer may be appropriate. If physical and/or emotional boundaries have been crossed to the point where ethical violations have been made, it will be necessary to terminate the therapeutic relationship. This course of action should also be accompanied by a report to the state ethics board from both the therapist and the supervisor involved.

Self of the therapist

Probably the best preventative work a therapist can do regarding sexual attraction in conjoint therapy is to really know one's self and how that self impacts the therapy you provide. We cannot emphasize enough the important role that self-exploration plays in a therapist's development. Really knowing one's self provides an 'early detection' system for the dynamics of attraction. Asking colleagues and clinical supervisors to help you 'know yourself' and discover how the self acts like a tool in therapy is invaluable. Additionally, we believe that talking about sexual attraction in conjoint therapy should be classified as an advanced skill for therapists. As such, it is often something people do not think of or do effectively until they have logged some significant experiences in therapy (either their own or that of their clients). Before many therapists get to the point where they could effectively address a client's attraction, they first need to become more comfortable discussing the basics of client sexuality (Harris & Hays, 2008). Comfort with one's own sexuality can be increased in a number of ways, including preparing and presenting a sexual genogram or a timeline of significant sexual influences to a supervisor or trusted colleague (Belous, Timm, Chee, & Whitehead, 2012; Timm, 2009).

Conclusion

While conjoint therapy may offer a buffer to the dynamics associated with sexual attraction in therapy, it is in no way an inoculation from it. Being open to the fact that human beings develop attractions for a variety of reasons and in a variety of situations should help normalize the fact that sexual attraction is not something people typically go looking for in therapy. We have never known a client who began therapy with the hope that they would fall for their therapist. Similarly, we've never supervised or taught a therapist in training that entered therapy with a similar hope. Sexual attraction can sidetrack the goals of therapy and leave both members of the client couple feeling embarrassed, confused, hurt and angry. When handled ethically and properly, it can reaffirm boundaries, protect the client, the therapist and the profession, as well as set a course for more effective treatment.

References

Belous, C. K., Timm, T. M., Chee, G., & Whitehead, M. (2012). Revisiting the sexual genogram. *The American Journal of Family Therapy*, 40(4), 281–296.

Harris, S. M. (2001). Teaching therapists about sexual attraction in therapy. *Journal of Marital and Family Therapy, 27*(1), 123–128.

Harris, S. M., & Harriger, D. J. (2009). Sexual attraction in conjoint therapy. *The American Journal of Family Therapy, 37*(3), 209–216.

Harris, S. M., & Hays, K. W. (2008). Family therapist comfort with and willingness to discuss client sexuality. *Journal of Marital and Family Therapy, 34*(2), 239–250.

Nickell, N. J., Hecker, L. L., Ray, R. E., & Bercik, J. (1995). Marriage and family therapists sexual attraction to clients – An exploratory study. *The American Journal of Family Therapy, 23*(4), 315–327.

Pope, K. S., Sonne, J. L., & Holroyd, J. (1993). *Sexual feelings in psychotherapy: Explorations for therapists and therapists-in-training.* Washington DC: APA.

Timm, T. M. (2009). 'Do I really have to talk about sex?' Encouraging beginning therapists to integrate sexuality into couples therapy. *The Journal of Couple and Relationship Therapy, 8,* 15–33.

Timm, T. M., & Blow, A. J. (1999). Self-of-the-therapist work: A balance between removing restraints and identifying resources. *Contemporary Family Therapy: An International Journal, 21*(3), 331–351.

Young, T. L. (2010). Sexuality, boundaries, and ethics. In L. Hecker (Ed.), *Ethics and professional issues in couple and family therapy.* New York: Routledge.

9

Bound to the Mast
Reflections on Analytic Abstinence

Andrea Sabbadini

The subject of erotic transference and countertransference in psychoanalysis[1] is close to our profession's bone, and bringing it up inevitably evokes a certain anxiety even in experienced therapists. It is because of his anxiety in this area, after all, that at the dawn of our profession, Joseph Breuer (Anna O's therapist) abandoned the newborn practice of psychoanalysis to the fatherly cares of his younger and intellectually more progressive colleague.

'You must bind me very tight, standing me up against the step of the mast and lashed to the mast itself so that I cannot stir from the spot', wrote Homer in *The Odyssey* (1991, Book 12, pp. 161–163). Odysseus wanted to hear the Sirens' wonderful music, and he had his crew bind him hand and foot to the mast as his ship approached their island. Others had simply fallen prey to their 'honey-sweet tones' (Homer, 1991, p. 187), or refused to hear it by plugging their ears with beeswax.

Some years ago, I was referred for analysis a young lecturer, Miss A, who was to stay in London only for a few months to complete her

---

[1] Although in this chapter I shall only refer to situations where the psychoanalyst is male and his analysand female, what I will describe could as easily apply, *mutatis mutandis*, to female therapists analyzing male patients, or indeed to the homosexual aspects of any analytic couple.

Sexual Attraction in Therapy: Clinical Perspectives on Moving Beyond the Taboo – A Guide for Training and Practice, First Edition. Edited by Maria Luca.
© 2014 John Wiley & Sons, Ltd. Published 2014 by John Wiley & Sons, Ltd.

academic research. She was a stunningly beautiful woman who quickly developed an intense erotic transference towards me. She would dress provocatively, yet always in good taste, and talk openly about her sexuality and her attraction for me, making flattering remarks about my looks and personality, and clearly indicating that she would have liked to transform our professional relationship into an intimately personal one. At times, I found Miss A's seductive behaviour quite irresistible and almost felt tempted to give in to my feelings for her. However, I managed to retain my relatively neutral analytic attitude consisting of the interpretation of her interest in me and the understanding of my interest in her as aspects of the transference and countertransference dynamics. I was helped in that difficult task by two events.

First of all, one evening, Miss A and I coincidentally saw each other at the theatre. We only exchanged a polite greeting there, but the next day she told me how greatly shocked she had been to realize that I existed also outside my consulting room. This made me more clearly aware that, in fact, contrary to my own illusion, I only existed for her as a psychoanalyst – and she for me as a patient – within the transference and countertransference relationship.

Secondly, she once reported an episode from her past that further strengthened my resolve to consider her infatuation for me as being unrealistic, which in turn helped me to put my own attraction for her in its proper countertransferential perspective. Miss A recounted how one morning, when she was an adolescent, she put her mother's dressing gown on, as she often did, and found in its pocket a passionate letter addressed to her mother from her physician, who was obviously her lover, and who intended to put an end to their affair. Miss A was upset by her discovery and felt deeply betrayed by her mother because of it. This memory involving Miss A's identification with her mother confirmed to me the repetition compulsion quality of her seductive behaviour towards me. I then felt much freer to listen to her without being distracted, as I had previously been, by countertransference interferences.

Around that time, by the way, I also found it helpful to reread Freud's masterly article *Observations on Transference Love* (1915), which in fact also deals with countertransference, and I drew great support from it in my internal struggle, especially reading the beautifully balanced page where he questions the genuineness of love feelings emerging during psychoanalysis. 'Analytic technique', Freud wrote in no ambiguous terms, 'requires of the physician that he should deny the patient who is craving for love the satisfaction she demands. The treatment must be carried out in abstinence' (Freud, 1915, pp. 164–165). And he added: 'It is . . . just as disastrous for the analysis if the patient's craving for love is gratified as if it is suppressed' (Freud, 1915, p. 166).

Before she left to go back to her country, I referred Miss A to a colleague with whom she successfully continued the work she had started with me. She wrote to me a few years later to tell me how helpful our analytic relationship had been for her and to announce that she was now happily married and expecting her first baby. I felt delighted.

In the analytic consulting room, we always find, among other fanciful objects, also two bodies. These bodies – with their appearance, clothes, movements, sounds, warts and all – affect one another. It is true that the use of the couch – whatever the patient's fantasies may be about lying down, concerning issues of sexuality, dependence and loss of control through eye contact – partly removes the most immediate awareness of the bodies from the room; but, *alas*! it does not remove the bodies themselves.

In my countertransference towards Miss B, a patient who had been abused by her father when she was a child, I often felt like a castrated analyst, unable to penetrate her problems with my interpretations. 'I cannot imagine you being real', she once told me, 'because you would then acquire a penis, and I couldn't stand that'. Miss B could only relate to men if they represented the good, understanding, affectionate father she had never had – the man without a penis whom she wanted me to be in the transference. Miss B's dilemma was trying to keep me physically present in her mind in order not to feel abandoned to her own resources as she had felt in childhood, without turning me at the same time into a sexual body, lest she felt again threatened by abuse.

The female analysand lying down in front of a male therapist, seated well out of her sight, allows her sexuality to be exposed to his scrutiny, but has to close her eyes to any transference awareness of the analyst as a man in flesh and blood; while the male analyst could, indeed should, look at (or rather listen to) his patient but could not stand *his own* sexuality being exposed to her gaze. In one of the famous frescoes in the Cappella Brancacci in Florence, we can observe the opposite situation – that could rather apply to a female analyst and a male analysand (detail from Masaccio's *The Expulsion from the Garden of Eden*, ca. 1424–1428). There, Masaccio dramatically represents Adam and Eve at the moment when God chases them away from the Garden of Eden and they suddenly become aware and ashamed of their carnal knowledge. What is remarkable in that painting is that while Eve covers her genitals with a hand and her breasts with the other, Adam is portrayed covering his eyes, as if the painter were trying to tell us that the man would not mind exposing his body but could not tolerate watching Eve's nudity, while she could look at him but could not stand being seen herself.

Some therapists, adhering to the 'beeswax in the ears' stance, claim – as Joseph Breuer did a century ago – that, as the psychoanalytic relationship is a clinical one, there is no room in it for sexual feelings, let alone their expression. It is the mechanism of denial: if something threatens you, pretend it does not exist.

However, the majority of analysts recognize that the therapeutic relationship, insofar as it is an emotional intimate rapport between two people, must be charged with feelings, including erotic ones, which should be openly expressed. Whether this 'expression' should only be verbal (the patient being invited to freely talk about her sexual fantasies to which the analyst will offer, when appropriate, his interpretations) or also involve some physical or even explicitly sexual contact will depend on the therapist's own theoretical, technical and ethical principles.

The view that some amount of bodily contact between analyst and patient (with all sorts of variations on the theme, from a handshake to genital intercourse) is to be allowed, or even encouraged, has been advocated not only in so-called humanistic circles but also among various forms of psychoanalysis, from Ferenczi's 'active therapy' to Alexander's provision of 'corrective emotional experiences'. In my view, these approaches do not take into sufficient account the enormous power that the psychoanalyst – through a setting facilitating regression and specifically through the establishment of the transference – holds in relation to his patients. This power derives not just from the analyst's authoritative professional status but more importantly from his intimate knowledge of his analysand's internal world. I believe that the risk of such power not being used therapeutically, but abused for reasons of exploitation, becomes intolerably high whenever sexual activity is allowed to break through the boundaries of a relationship the very essence of which rests in the trust that the analysand can allow herself to feel for her analyst.

Seven centuries ago, Dante, showing his profound understanding of narcissism, warned us that 'Love absolves no-one beloved from loving' (Amor ch'a nullo amato amar perdona, Alighieri, 1926, p. 103). The psychoanalyst is no exception and has to deal with serious technical as well as ethical problems. Beeswax in his ears is just not good enough. What is he then going to do with his patient's erotic transference if this evokes in him erotic countertransference feelings towards her? Our analytic practice requires us to follow certain rigorous, if not rigid, principles. In this case, I can see no valid alternative to adhering to the Freudian recommendation of analytic abstinence, whereby the wishes of the patient should be interpreted – often, if not always, within the transference situation – and not fulfilled. Odysseus can only survive the Sirens' seduction by remaining bound to the mast. The analytic abstinence, which Fox redefined as 'the guideline for the on-going management of the analytic situation in terms of frustration-gratification' (Fox, 1984, p. 228), is related to the taboo against incest. Person has found that 'therapists who act out with patients are often re-enacting problems in their own analyses, much as the parents who abuse their children were themselves abused as children' (Person, 1983, p. 201). This links the good enough parent to the good enough analyst in the sense that both may have sexual feelings towards their children or patients, but neither can act upon them without causing serious damage.

I find it difficult to conceive of the analyst's erotic feelings for his patient as other than a countertransference reaction to something that the patient is, consciously or more often unconsciously, conveying to him. This 'something' is meaningful (e.g., the patient's seductive behaviour in a session could be the repetition of a pattern established in childhood to obtain his or her father's love) and is often overdetermined (e.g., it could also have a defensive function: 'Look at my legs, not at my problems!'). The boundary violations resulting in acting out of the erotic transference and countertransference are often the result of the analyst's failure, possibly motivated by anxiety and unresolved personal issues (see, among others, Gabbard, 1994; Gabbard & Lester, 1995; Gabbard & Peltz, 2001), to adequately examine and interpret the sexual component of the analytic relationship. In other words, when an analyst, due to his own unacknowledged countertransference, fails to recognize his patient's sexual feelings for him as being a manifestation of her erotic transference, he will be unable to interpret them and will instead end up either ignoring or exploiting them.

We do not know how common the acting out of erotic transference and countertransference feelings between analysts and analysands actually is. I suspect it takes place less frequently than we might imagine, the incest taboo being a major obstacle to its actualization, yet more often than we want to believe. In my opinion, such therapeutic sailors (their crew includes many illustrious names, from Carl Gustav Jung to Masud Khan) are set on a destructive course, often implicating more than just themselves and their patients. The scandal within the Italian Psychoanalytical Society a few decades ago is a good example of the domino effect of sexual acting out on the part of an individual analyst. His lack of self-discipline – the slackening of his superego ties to the mast of safe sailing – had dramatic effects not only on himself and his seduced patient but also on large numbers of Italian colleagues, candidates and analysands, eventually leading to the splitting of that society and to repercussions within the international psychoanalytic community at large. The problem of erotic transference and countertransference, whether or not leading to acting out, is a political one, in as much as issues of power and possible abuses of it are part and parcel of all aspects of the analytic relationship.

It is my opinion that we psychoanalysts have no alternative to keeping our personal life well separate from our professional one. Our analytic integrity must have a priority over our individual needs or wishes, including erotic ones. In other words, it is our responsibility to make sure that the reality principle should ultimately prevail over the pleasure principle, which is one of the reasons why our work is so difficult to appear almost 'impossible' (Freud, 1937, p. 248). We must listen to the Sirens' song, and learn from it, but at the same time, we have to remain bound to the superego mast of our principles if our ship is to take us safely to Ithaca through the perilous waters of the analytic journey.

References

Alighieri, D. (1926). *La Divina Commedia*. Milano: Bietti & Reggiani.

Fox, R. P. (1984). The principle of abstinence reconsidered. *International Review of Psycho-Analysis*, 11(2), 227–236.

Freud, S. (1915). *Observations on transference love* (Vol. 12). Standard Edition, (1958). London: Hogarth Press.

Freud, S. (1937). *Analysis terminable and interminable* (Vol. 23). Standard Edition, (1964). London: Hogarth Press.

Gabbard, G. O. (1994). Sexual excitement and countertransference love in the analyst. *Journal of the American Psychoanalytic Association*, 42(4), 1083–1106.

Gabbard, G. O., & Lester, E. P. (1995). *Boundaries and boundary violations in psychoanalysis* (2nd ed.). Washington, DC: American Psychiatric Publications. 2008.

Gabbard, G. O., & Peltz, M. L. (2001). Speaking the unspeakable: Institutional reactions to boundary violations by training analysts. *Journal of the American Psychoanalytic Association*, 49(2), 659–673.

Homer. (1991). *The Odyssey*. Translated by E. V. Rieu. Harmondsworth: Penguin Books.

Person, E. S. (1983). Women in therapy: Therapist gender as a variable. *International Review of Psycho-Analysis*, 10(2), 193–204.

10

Why Can't We Be Lovers? The Love-Obsessed Clients Who Stalk Their Therapist

Maria Luca and Juliet Soskice

The question in the title of our chapter 'why can't we be lovers?' was borrowed from a paper by Celenza (2010). We chose it because it encapsulates a common clinical dilemma for therapists if a client's sexual attraction is expressed through 'obsessive relational intrusion' (ORI) of the therapist. Clients who come to therapy are looking for validation of their existence. In the words of Alain De Botton (2006): 'Perhaps it is true that we do not really exist until there is someone there to see us existing, we cannot properly speak until there is someone who can understand what we are saying in essence, we are not wholly alive until we are loved'. However, for clients presenting with ORI, the feeling is one of demand to be loved. Spitzberg and Cupach (2003), conceptualizing ORI from a relational and interactional perspective, define it 'as repeated and unwanted pursuit and invasion of one's sense of physical or symbolic privacy by another person, either stranger or acquaintance, who desires and/or presumes an intimate relationship' (p. 351). Stalking, from a psychologically relational perspective, has indeed received little attention in the literature, with some exceptions such as Spitzberg and Cupach, who conducted a comprehensive review of the literature on stalking and developed the idea of client obsessive relationality. It is not within the scope of our chapter to delve into conceptualizations of stalking in clinical settings (see Mullen, Pathé, & Purcell, 2000 typology). Our aim is to place stalking of therapists on the map and highlight its manifestation and impact on therapists

Sexual Attraction in Therapy: Clinical Perspectives on Moving Beyond the Taboo – A Guide for Training and Practice, First Edition. Edited by Maria Luca.
© 2014 John Wiley & Sons, Ltd. Published 2014 by John Wiley & Sons, Ltd.

through clinical examples. By this, we hope to encourage others to investigate the experience of therapists who are increasingly, in an Internet era, becoming the target of stalkers.

All therapists at some point in their career will experience sexual fantasies or sexual attraction towards a client (Giovazolias & Davis, 2001; Pope, Keith-Spiegel, & Tabachnick, 1986) or will be the object of a client's erotic fascination (Mann, 1994, 1999). Our choice of subject arose out of a series of troubling and unanswered questions developed through clinical practice and discussion, and the notably conspicuous absence of any publications on how therapists feel or handle harassment, where this is characterized by obsessive interest, intrusions and expressions of sexual desire from clients. 'Somewhere at the nebulous nexus of privacy and possessiveness, courtship and criminality, intrusion and intimacy, lies the phenomenon of stalking' (Spitzberg & Cupach, 2003, p. 345). If the client who begs for an answer to such a question exhibits behaviours towards the therapist typical of an 'intimacy stalker', (see Mullen et al., 2000) who tirelessly pursues the therapist often by showering her with unwanted gifts, incessant demands for sexual involvement, intrusion into her private life through gathering information about her from the Internet, how does the therapist handle it? We know little of the impact on the therapist when she or he becomes the object of a client's stalking. Whether male or female, all therapists, irrespective of gender or sexual orientation, are vulnerable to stalking by clients due to the nature of the therapy setting. Research is also scarce on other dynamics in therapeutic settings that may make any therapist more vulnerable.

A Dashing Therapist

Sibilla, a 41-year-old wife of a wealthy businessman, was suicidal and unhappy in her marriage when she presented for therapy with Roberto, an Italian, well-respected clinical psychologist who commutes to his clinical practice in Milan 3 days a week while living in the country with his second wife and three children. Working with suicidal patients was one of his specialisms and he had published widely on the subject. The work with Sibilla was open ended and they met once a week. In the fourth session, Sibilla announced that she decided to end therapy, as she felt overwhelmed, but she found working with 'such a dashing therapist rather difficult'.

Roberto was not new to patients developing erotic fantasies about him, and his attempts to interpret and help Sibilla understand seemed ineffective. Sibilla decided to continue therapy. Eighteen months into the work, she arrived for her session to announce that she had visited Roberto's home town on her own, as she had never been there before. She said that her husband had no idea, and in any case, he would not care. Roberto explored what felt like an intrusion into his home life, but Sibilla insisted that this was a coincidence and part of her decision to be more adventurous and get to know the countryside. She then asked what the local guesthouse was like, as she planned to visit on a regular basis. As she put it: 'I have fallen in love with your home town'.

A week later, she announced that she was now staying at Roberto's local guesthouse and 'I was offended that you did not acknowledge me at the local market on Saturday. I saw you with your wife and children'. Roberto said that he had not seen her and focused on interpreting what he understood to be a type of erotomania. Sibilla's fury was evident and Roberto began to feel intruded upon and very angry himself. Sibilla's erotomania during this time intensified. She persistently brought little gifts for Roberto who reminded her that this was a professional relationship and he could not accept any gifts. This did not deter her from continuing to bring gifts, stating: 'my mother always gave gifts to family and they gladly received them with gratitude'. Roberto, feeling exasperated replied: 'Well, I'm not yours or your mother's, family . . . I am your therapist for goodness sake!' Once he calmed himself down, he realized that he had taken the bait and was drawn into a collusive dynamic with Sibilla, who looked pleased that she managed to elicit such a powerful emotional response in Roberto. When a birthday card arrived from Sibilla at Roberto's home town address with lots of kisses, and in the same week, an avalanche of text messages ending with love and kisses, Roberto called his supervisor in a fit of rage. He felt that despite all the exploration and clinical strategies discussed in supervision, he failed to contain Sibilla's erotomania. On the contrary, Roberto said to Laura, his supervisor, it was escalating and he felt besieged, fearful and worried about his family. They discussed the option of ending therapy with Sibilla and agreed that she should be referred to a female therapist, one of Roberto's colleagues at the Therapia Milano clinic.

The following day at her session, Sibilla announced that she was divorcing her husband and was moving to a house a few miles from Roberto's family home. She intended to set up a small business with money she expected from the divorce settlement, she said. For Roberto, this felt like the end of the road. He seized the opportunity to raise termination of the work. Halfway through saying 'I've thought about our work over the last 2 years and feel that there is nothing more I can do to help you and would recommend . . .', Sibilla stormed out. She returned for the next session apologizing profusely and begging Roberto to continue working with her, adding that 'we are meant to be together, why can't you see that?' He explained that, regrettably, he felt that she would benefit from working with a woman colleague and that this was to be their last session. The harassment continued for months until Roberto, in consultation with his supervisor, decided to involve the police. Roberto's first marriage in his student days and subsequent divorce to a famous Italian actress was all over the Internet and this made him feel helpless in protecting his privacy. He suspected that Sibilla had looked him up on the internet and found all the information she needed to feed her erotomania and stalking behaviour. Despite a police warning, Sibilla continued months after therapy ended, with unsolicited calls, texts and cards to Roberto. A meeting between a team of clinicians and the police determined that Sibilla was best placed in a rehabilitation centre programme for stalkers. This eventually helped her contain her stalking behaviour, but she declared to the rehabilitation programme coordinator that Roberto will always remain her 'true love' and if 'not in this life, then in the next I know we will be together'.

Anyone who has experienced love and erotic desire might sympathize with Sibilla in the above example. Sexual attraction is, after all, accompanied with emotions of desire to seek out embodied union with the other. 'The love between two partners brings together the personal, the erotic, and possibly even the sexual attraction and energy of two persons and thus changes both partners' ways of being' (Jeanrond, 2007, p. 254). This implies that love is transformative and lovers become transformed through this shared experience. Indeed, love, as it manifests in erotic desire, is commonly described as a blissful experience where the loved ones feel the spark of aliveness and become creative and admiring of each other. The oceanic feeling dominates, and the lovers lose themselves in a state of bliss. But what happens when romantic love and sexual attraction is unrequited, or psychotic, as discussed in Roberto and Sibilla's professional relationship? Clinical relationships lend themselves to intimacy while prohibiting sexual involvement. As therapists, we are expected to talk about sex, sexuality and erotic desire, among other subjects. But when do we draw the line when the *talking cure* fails and stalking prevails?

It is even more challenging for therapists 'when the affective valence leans erotic, countertransference once again becomes taboo' (Celenza, 2010, p. 176). Yet, we learn from our trainings that clients need to feel desirable to the therapist; hence, we must show willingness and receptivity to sexual feelings from our clients, tolerate our own towards the client and encourage the development of mutuality and reciprocity within the professional boundaries. It is a tall order for therapists to allow the development of erotic mutuality, experience the throws of erotic desire for a client, while simultaneously resisting temptation to act on their desire. We all know that it is not purely the client's seductiveness that creates the erotic in therapy. The therapist's own subjectivity and needs can play a part. This induces guilt in most of us, given that we associate our erotic desires for a client with the professional taboo.

Clients, in their own unique ways and due to their own psychic search for equilibrium and ultimately integration, stir so many passions in us. In this way, we can understand behind the veil of defences what is going on in their subjective world. However, there is a fine line between talking about and interpreting sexual attraction or erotic desire, and handling situations where such feelings manifest in intrusive, harassing client behaviours. The examples which follow are intended to highlight clinical issues in relation to stalking situations.

Intimacy Stalkers

I wasn't expecting to see you here

Paul, a 52-year-old male therapist had been the target of stalking by a female client both during the therapy and for years after therapy ended. He recalled that he had seen Jenny, one of his clients, standing at the opposite side of the pavement, staring at his bedroom window on many occasions. She would unexpectedly appear at Paul's local supermarket, pretending to be buying groceries and approaching him with a smile saying: 'I wasn't expecting to see you here'. On other occasions, Paul would come out of his local health centre after a morning's workout to be startled by a glimpse of Jenny's silhouette as she exited the centre.

Paul made many attempts to interpret the stalking, to explore the meaning for Jenny, to help her see the problem. But Jenny was adamant that it was pure coincidence and that his interpretations were a retaliation after she shared her sexual attraction towards him at the early phase of their work. Paul was becoming exasperated and angry, and had fantasies of ending the therapy to free himself of Jenny's intrusions. Supervision helped him vent his feelings but he felt stuck and immobilized by Jenny's resolve to continue stalking him. This example highlights the emotional impact on the therapist if he is the object of fascination, obsession and stalking.

Yours truly, a secret admirer

Storm, an attractive, articulate, female counselling psychologist, greets
Edward, her new male client in the reception area. As she introduces
herself, she notices how immaculately dressed Edward is with an air of
confidence that unnerved her. It's been 4 years since Storm qualified, and
for the first time, she feels a tremble, a kind of anxious anticipation and
begins to doubt whether she can handle a client like Edward. She greets
him in the reception area and asks him to follow her to the consulting
room. She walks in front and Edward follows in silence. As they enter
Storm's office, she points to the chair by the office window and asks him
to take a seat. Storm feels more alert and cautious than usual even though
she cannot make sense of it at this point. She gathers her thoughts and
asks him: 'What brings you here?' Edward gives Storm a penetrating look,
eyes her from head to toe and replies:

> The usual problem of finding attractive women with a certain look . . . slim,
> blond, intelligent and with large breasts irresistible . . . I have no problem
> conquering them . . . ha . . . ha . . . ha . . . . I shower them with gifts, com-
> pliments, tell them how beautiful they are, take them to expensive restau-
> rants, until they submit completely, almost become my slaves. Sexually, it
> can only happen in one position that I choose. If the woman tries to initiate
> or determine what the activity should be then I lose it . . . you know what
> I mean . . . my performance suffers.

He pauses, appears excited and continues, 'when I was reading therapist
profiles on the Internet and stumbled upon yours, I knew immediately
that you would be right for me . . . (pause)'. Storm responds by enquiring
what it is that in the client's mind 'made me right for you'. Edward replies,
'What you say in your profile, your experience, qualifications and the
location of your practice . . . it is perfect for me . . . (pause) you are too
attractive to be a therapist; don't get me wrong, I'm not complaining, just
curious, that's all'.
Storm feels trepidation, a mixture of anxiety, excitement and fear. In
the session that followed, Storm was conscious of her emotional response
to Edward's revelations and tried to contain how she felt and responded
by acknowledging his problem and then dealing with the practicalities of
therapy. This helped her regain her composure and be the therapist she
prided herself on being composed, contained, professional and attentive.
At the end of the session, Edward stood up, thanked Storm for listening
to him, remarking how he felt better already. Storm, on the other hand,

was aware of how exposed and objectified she felt, an experience tinged with anxiety. Her mind was bursting with thoughts for sometime after the session with Edward. She felt flattered but disgusted with herself for feeling this way. She promised herself to be extra careful with him, extra professional and ensure that she instituted firm boundaries. After all, she thought to herself, 'I'm not in the business of flattery, so I must be careful not to lose sight of Edward's seductive manoeuvres'.

Edward's charm never ceased to amaze his therapist. Sessions with him were characterized by incessant material about his conquests, his obsessions with women and his stubborn attempts to win over a Viennese medical doctor he had met during a travel to Canada a year earlier. He described her as 'a rare creature of grace, beauty and abundant intelligence' and spoke of the calls he made at any hour, the flowers and gifts he sent this woman, the trips to Vienna to meet her and his frustration that she was somewhat interested, but not quite. Storm kept copious notes of all the sessions with this client, and months passed when in one session Edward announced:

> I am afraid I couldn't help myself. I Googled you. He looked away and pressed a knuckle to his slightly open lips, and looked back at his therapist. I am sorry I did it. I held off for ages. But I couldn't resist, and I feel like I know too much about you now. I was drinking and the more G & T's I drank the more I thought I had to do it. I have been resisting doing it for months, but the information is there – and actually I knew I shouldn't have done it, but I guess at least I have told you. I feel like I know you so much better. I sort of feel I understand you better now. To trust you I need to know more about you.

Storm was reluctant to speak to her supervisor in detail about her own feelings towards her client and tried to process them on her own. It was troubling for her to deal with such intense feelings alone. Nevertheless, she feared that if she disclosed feeling seduced and gratified to her supervisor, she would be chastised.

When Storm began to receive bouquets of flowers and a new teddy bear each week sent to her office address, with little cards saying, 'from a secret admirer', her instinct told her that they were from Edward. One teddy bear called 'Cuddly' had a knife stuck to his chest; Storm found this disturbing. She felt that Cuddly was turning his rage against himself, now as the victim of unrequited love, with undertones of suicidal ideation. Storm interpreted this as a risk to violent acting out, including suicide. The harassing phone calls and inappropriately and sexually explicit text messages to her mobile also became regular. Although the number had been withheld, Storm had strong suspicions that these, too, were from Edward. She spoke to her supervisor immediately. This helped her to contain her feelings of being flattered and to focus on helping Edward understand and deal with his rage.

Feeling flattered

Another example that can be described as 'sexualisation of aggression' (Glasser, 1979) is that of Nico, an attractive and successful solicitor in his mid-30s. He sought therapy at the recommendation of an ex-girlfriend who found a therapist for him through a website search. Nico checked the therapist's profile on the website and mentioned during the assessment session that her photo had attracted him. She reminded him of his first girlfriend, he said, who had lost her virginity to him. Nico was an articulate, warm and compliant client.

Penelope, his half-Spanish therapist, was struck early on by how much Nico seemed to enjoy relating his sexual experiences to her, with particular emphasis on how the woman he was dating was bowled over by his sexual technique, giving her orgasms, the like of which she had never experienced nor would with any other man. She found herself in a double bind of both being 'taken in and not taken in' by Nico. Once, when she arrived directly from an appointment, he had seen her from the other end of the street outside the building where her practice was.

> I was at my café – the one across the road from you – just here – where by the way – they make an astonishingly good cappuccino – and there you were – at the end of the road. I could make you out from a distance as you have such a particular look to you. You have that Mediterranean sultry beauty. Just wonderful!

Penelope knew that Nico had lodged himself firmly in her mind, something she found disturbing, and wondered to what extent she was being drawn into a sadomasochistic relationship, which masked Nico's predicament. However, this did not lessen the difficulty she had in maintaining a distance from the client, who steadily attempted to undermine her by a relentless stream of seductive comments that she understood to be attacks on the therapy. Despite this, Penelope found herself succumbing to him in various ways. She started to feel very attractive in the sessions with him, beautiful at times, and her confidence as a woman was growing. Her sex life with her partner was enhanced and she was aware that she was becoming dependent on Nico's validation of her. It seemed to be the opium for an otherwise stressful professional phase she was going through.

Nico recounted how time after time with 'his women' he had ended the relationship when he fell in love with someone else, leaving the woman, in his words, 'broken' and 'on the floor'. Penelope took this as a warning, discussed her feelings with a colleague and managed to help Nico become aware of how his underlying aggression manifested in punishing women through means of sexual triumph over them. She then, in consultation with her supervisor, understood Nico's relational difficulties as making hate, not love, and that she had allowed herself to collude countertransferentially with Nico's seduction techniques. The joyful intensity with which his hatred surfaced was captured in his narrative of leaving women, *broken* and *on the floor*. Finally, Penelope felt that something in her previously 'love struck' affective composure had shifted, which allowed more neutral professional feelings to surface.

The previous examples are a testament to what Mullen et al. (2000) define as the intimacy type of stalker or obsessive relational intrusion stalker (Spitzberg & Cupach, 2003). The former state that any profession which 'comes into contact with the isolated and disordered and in whom sympathy and attention is easily reconstructed as romantic interest' (p. 48) could become a target. A study by Romans, Hayes, and White (1996) showed that a sizeable number of university counsellors had been stalked by a present or past client (5.6%). Hence, we must not underestimate the importance of knowing how to handle such situations.

Clients who fall into the category of the 'intimacy stalker' are convinced that they are sexually attracted to the therapist and feel justified in pursuing their romantic goal using inappropriate, hyperintimacy tactics. They feel justified that their actions are driven by pure desire for romantic love and, as such, are morally unquestionable. If delusional in some way, these clients will go as far as to harbour the belief that sexual desire is mutual, that the therapist is a fellow enthusiast in the attraction. Inexperienced therapists on the receiving end of client declarations of love, especially where this gratifies the therapist in some way, are more likely to blame themselves or feel guilty than experienced therapists who learned through experience to more easily recognize obsessive, stalking patterns. After the initial novelty of being seduced, charmed and validated by the client, a therapist may feel guilty, frightened, angry and shaken up. A study by Ladany et al. (1997) showed that therapists who experienced sexual desire or attraction towards a client felt distracted, guilty, embarrassed and afraid. Most therapists, as some studies suggest (Ladany et al., 1997; Rodolfa et al., 1994), do not talk to supervisors about sexual attraction out of fear of being judged. Avoidance in seeking guidance is potentially risky in that therapists, by relying solely on their own personal reflections, may miss out on learning to manage by obtaining the more objective view of a supervisor or colleague. However, dangers may lie here too.

Pseudo-love

If a client truly experiences sexual feelings, desire or romantic love for their therapist, they believe this to be true. It is their subjective reality, and as such, they genuinely feel it is their right to pursue happiness, albeit with a person who is not available or indeed interested. Stalkers with attachment difficulties resulting in loneliness and social isolation are prone to pseudo-love, as this kind of love resides in their mind, can be preserved as an ideal and ultimately protects the person from a disappointing reality. In the words of Pathe, Mullen, and Purcell (2001):

> All whose profession brings them into regular contact with people who are lonely or have a mental disorder are vulnerable to being stalked. Teachers, health care providers and lawyers appear to be at particular risk, attracting intimacy-seekers and socially incompetent, resentful and even predatory stalkers. Occasionally, the termination of a long-term therapeutic relationship can give rise to rejected stalking patterns (p. 399).

Pseudo-love is a distorted idea of how intimate, sexual relationships work; it can therefore be differentiated from mutual love where both parties share the same reality.

Internet stalking

A decade ago, the idea that a patient would be able to obtain factual, personal information about his/her therapist depended upon the therapist's own choice to disclose it. As far as the patient was concerned, he/she would rely solely on the little that was accessible to him/her; for example, the consulting room, the area where the therapist lived, the appearance of the therapist and the rest consisted of fantasy and imagination. The notion of an email address, mobile phone, telephone number or any kind of self-publicity or marketing was simply not present. In some theoretical modalities, factual information about the analyst where this might be available would not be disclosed due to the risk of destroying the emergence of transference, a pivotal aspect of psychoanalytic technique. Now, most therapists' profiles are available on the Internet. A distinguished psychoanalyst at a seminar held in London 5 years ago laughed at the suggestion of a trainee that by having an internet website, she might find patients. 'That would be very inappropriate, to disclose information about yourself', she told the trainee.

The reality is that most therapists, at least while setting up their practices, currently rely on Internet websites housing their profiles for referrals. For the most part, this has benefits. Patients are able to make more informed decisions in choosing a therapist. On a pragmatic level, information about therapists means that choice is afforded to prospective patients and therapists can widen their net to ensure that they can be more strategic as they develop their careers by growing their practices.

However, there is potential risk as we enter a more open and transparent age of psychotherapy, which is that for a group of patients prone to stalking, the Internet becomes an important vehicle accommodating voyeuristic or intrusive behaviours. There is little professional guidance for therapists on the consequences of their personal information being available through social networking sites such as Facebook or LinkedIn.

It seems that the development of social media is also encouraging therapists to search for information on their clients. A survey by DiLillo and Gale (2011) reported that 97.8% of student therapists (mostly in PsyD programmes) who participated reported searching for at least one client's information using search engines in the past year. The ethical implications are discussed in this survey, and a recommendation that promotes clear policies is made. Another recommendation is that supervisors and faculty should discuss the ethical implications of such practices with trainees.

Impact of stalking on victims

Stalking by casual acquaintances and friends, ex-intimates, strangers, work contacts and professional contacts will have an adverse impact on victims. Typical responses include fear, hypervigilance, distrust, loss of control, even post-traumatic stress disorder (Pathe et al., 2001). Discussions with colleagues in the psychology and psychotherapy field who, either during therapy treatment or once therapy ended, experienced prolonged intrusion such as repeated 'hang-up' phone calls in the early hours, surveillance, sexually explicit text messages and other stalking behaviours report experiencing fear and anxiety, coupled with helplessness, which impacts on their professional practice. One colleague mentioned feeling paranoid, a symptom that coincided with the break-up of her marriage. Individuals who are stalked may seek advice or counselling from health professionals or take out injunctions. Therapists, however, are trained to expect to be able to contain their feelings as well as those of their clients and continue to work with challenging client behaviours. This is a major dilemma for therapists, given that (as far as we know) there are no clear professional guidelines on how to handle being stalked by clients.

Clinical strategies

If therapists encounter stalking behaviours from clients, they could consider using some of the following clinical strategies:

- Think carefully of any personal information you place on Internet sites, as this will be exposed to potential clients, some of whom may use it to psychologically threaten or stalk you. Therapists who are in the public eye do not have control over personal information being available on the Internet. Some might consider having a different professional name, even though this may have other psychological implications, such as identity confusion.
- It is futile to suffer in silence if you're feeling anxious, afraid and stressed due to client harassment or intrusion. Speak to a colleague or supervisor first, explore and reflect on your feelings and agree on a clear strategy appropriate to the particular situation. This might involve terminating your work with a client or referring on to an appropriate service.
- Consider referring a client to a specialist clinic dealing with stalkers, especially when you feel that therapy interventions were ineffective in reforming stalking behaviours.
- If the talking cure has not managed to contain your client's endless intrusions into your personal life (as was the case with Roberto, the Italian psychologist in our example), it may be viable to report incidents to the police. Retain any evidence, such as text messages, mobile unsolicited calls, cards or letters. You may need to pass these on to the police.
- Therapists, after considerable psychological pressure from persistent stalking, could experience post-traumatic stress. Consult a therapist to help you work through stress that is likely to adversely impact on your personal and professional life.
- Feeling guilty and anxious that your supervisor will morally judge you if you feel attracted to a client will not help you work through these feelings. If you don't trust your supervisor, it may be time to find someone you can trust.

- It is important that trainings include modules on how to handle sexual attraction and its manifestation in stalking and encourage experiential work with role play. This can help empower the trainee and enable them to move beyond the taboo.

Conclusions

Although some psychotherapists interpret the question 'why can't we be lovers?' to mean 'why not', and a small minority become sexually involved with clients (to the client's as well as the therapist's detriment), the profession of psychotherapy makes it clear that sexual relationships between clients and therapists are prohibited. We have postulated that stalking is a relational and interactional problem and that health professionals are at risk of stalking behaviours due to the nature of the setting. A study by Abrams and Robinson (2011) found that of the 1,190 responding physicians, 14.9% reported having been stalked. Although both male and female patients were stalkers, their motives and stalking behaviours were dissimilar. They postulate that health professionals are at an increased risk of being stalked by patients who may have feelings of love, anger or resentment.

Therapists who become the object of sexual attraction by an intimacy stalker are often in a double bind. They may feel seduced and charmed by the stalker's unremitting sexual advances while at the same time they may become fearful, anxious and guilty. The chapter has not addressed issues of same gender and same sexuality dyads and types of stalking encountered in therapy. We highlighted through specific examples that hyperintimacy tactics adopted by intimacy stalking clients are not to be confused with authentic intimacy as postulated by Berry in Chapter 3, but are a result of pseudo-love. We hope that our discussion in this chapter will provide the impetus for further discourse on stalking within psychotherapy relationships to enlighten the field and to help develop an open dialogue around the handling of stalking clients.

References

Abrams, K. M., & Robinson, G. E. (2011). Stalking by patients: Doctors' experiences in a Canadian urban area. *Journal of Nervous and Mental Disease*, 199(10), 738–743.

Celenza, A. (2010). The guilty pleasure of erotic countertransference: Searching for radial true. *Studies in Gender and Sexuality*, *11*(4), 175–183.

De Botton, A. (2006). *On love*. Retrieved from http://www.goodreads.com/work/quotes/14280312-essays-in-love

DiLillo, D. K., & Gale, E. B., (2011). *To Google or not to Google: Graduate students' use of the Internet to access personal information about clients.* Faculty Publications, Department of Psychology. Paper 556. Retrieved from http://digitalcommons.unl.edu/psychfacpub/556

Giovazolias, T., & Davis, P. (2001). How common is sexual attraction towards clients? The experiences of sexual attraction of counselling psychologists toward their clients and its impact on the therapeutic process. *Counselling Psychology Quarterly*, *14*(4), 281–286.

Glasser, M. (1979). Some aspects of the role of aggression in the perversions. In I. Rosen (Ed.), *Sexual deviation*. Oxford: Oxford University Press.

Jeanrond, W. G. (2007). *Love enlightened – The promises and ambiguities of love.* pp. 253–281. Retrieved from http://www.cato-theo.net/Love-enlightened (viewed: 12/05/2013).

Ladany, N., O'Brien, K. M., Hill, C. E., Melincoff, D. S., Knox, S., & Petersen, D. A. (1997). Sexual attraction toward clients, use of supervision, and prior training: A qualitative study of predoctoral psychology interns. *Journal of Counseling Psychology*, *44*(4), 413–424.

Mann, D. (1994). The psychotherapist's erotic subjectivity. *British Journal of Psychotherapy*, *10*(3), 244–254.

Mann, D. (1999). Erotic narrative in psychoanalytic practice: An introduction. In D. Mann (Ed.), *Erotic transference and countertransference: Clinical practice in psychotherapy* (pp. 1–25). London: Routledge.

Mullen, P. E., Pathé, M., & Purcell, R. (2000). *Stalkers and their victims*. Cambridge, UK: Cambridge University Press.

Pathe, M., Mullen, P. E., & Purcell, R. (2001). The management of stalkers. *Advances in Psychiatric Treatment*, *7*, 335–342.

Pope, K. S., Keith-Spiegel, P., & Tabachnick, B. G. (1986). Sexual attraction to clients: The human therapist and the (sometimes) inhuman training system. *The American Psychologist*, *41*(2), 147–158.

Rodolfa, E., Hall, T., Holms, V., Davena, A., Komatz, D., Antunez, M., & Hall, A. (1994). The management of sexual feelings in therapy. *Professional Psychology, Research and Practice*, *25*(2), 168–172.

Romans, J., Hays, J., & White, T. (1996). Stalking and related behaviors experienced by counselling center staff members from current or former clients. *Professional Psychology: Research and Practice*, *27*, 595–599.

Spitzberg, B. H., & Cupach, W. R. (2003). What mad pursuit? Obsessive relational intrusion and stalking related phenomena. *Aggression and Violent Behavior*, *8*(4), 345–375.

Part II

Research-Informed Theoretical and Clinical Perspectives on Sexual Attraction in Therapy

11

Skilled Handling of Sexual Attraction in Therapy

A Grounded Theory of What Makes the Difference

Anthony Arcuri and Doris McIlwain

Only in the last 30 years do we see occasional research into psychotherapists' sexual attraction to clients. Prior to the mid-1980s, the literature contained brave admissions of sexual feelings towards clients, with conflicting explanations of their occurrence in terms of transference and countertransference[1] (e.g., Davis, 1978; Searles, 1959).

Then Pope, Keith-Spiegel, and Tabachnick (1986) published their landmark study exploring the prevalence of psychotherapists' sexual attraction to clients, psychotherapists' reactions to such experiences and how training programmes addressed the issue. Subsequently, primarily US-based studies enhanced understanding of the experience of attraction and the multiple influences on handling it in this sensitive context (e.g., Giovazolias & Davis, 2001; Ladany et al., 1997; Nickell, Hecker, Ray, & Bercik, 1995; Pope, Sonne, & Holroyd, 1993; Rodolfa et al., 1994).

Alongside was a reawakening of psychodynamic theorists and practitioners to analyzing sexual attraction to clients. We say 'reawakening' not only because of Searles's (1959) and Davis's (1978) earlier work but also recognizing Freud's papers on the issue in his writings on technique (Freud, 1912/2001, 1915/2001). Since the late 1980s, case studies of *erotic*

---

[1] Transference is where a therapy client's templates of loving established in past relationships emerge in the present in ways that script others into fulfilling the roles played by those in the past. Countertransference is where this occurs in the therapist.

Sexual Attraction in Therapy: Clinical Perspectives on Moving Beyond the Taboo – A Guide for Training and Practice, First Edition. Edited by Maria Luca.
© 2014 John Wiley & Sons, Ltd. Published 2014 by John Wiley & Sons, Ltd.

countertransference punctuated the psychodynamic literature (e.g., Davies, 1994; Field, 1989; Tansey, 1994).

Meetings held in the early 1990s on this topic by the American Psycho-analytic Association and the American Psychological Association marked 'the realization that the erotic nature of therapy cannot be foreclosed by silence' (Mann, 1999, p. 3). Yet literature relating to psychotherapists' sexual attraction to clients remains fragmented within and across theoretical and research paradigms. No cohesive, clear understanding of the process by which psychotherapists *handle* attraction exists. The profession needs such insight.

We offer here a theory – grounded in data – of how Sydney-based psychotherapists handled sexual attraction to clients in the mid-2000s. The theory necessarily takes a reflective stance on practitioners' phenomenological experience.

We explain our theory development, outline characteristics of psycho-therapists that leave them vulnerable to sexual attraction and influence their handling of it before discussing how psychotherapists appraise their sexual attraction and why. We explore how these processes inform psychotherapists' handling of sexual attraction, highlighting implications for practice, training and further research.

Arriving at Theory

Where an area lacks integrated theory, building a grounded theory offers a start. We interviewed 11 practising psychotherapists about hypothetical experiences of sexual attraction to clients (hypothetical to comply with our university's ethics committee). Many participants discussed their actual experiences of sexual attraction to clients.

From 35 respondents to an advertisement, we interviewed 11 partici-pants. The first we selected via purposive sampling (based on a judgement that he would provide a rich account). The remaining 10 were chosen using 'theoretical sampling' (given their potential to thicken and connect existing theoretical concepts) and included six males and five females, ranged in age from mid-20s to mid-60s (and in years practising from 1 to 40), and utilizing various theoretical orientations.

We adapted Strauss and Corbin's (1998) evolution of Glaser and Strauss's (1967) grounded theory to analyze the interviews. We coded for concepts and their evolving relationships until a theory was born. We kept in mind the influence of our own theoretical frameworks on the final model (see Arcuri & Mcilwain, 2010).

Our theory demonstrates that psychotherapists handle sexual attraction to clients via an iterative process, influenced by their unique characteristics (e.g., theoretical orientation, age). The process involves an appraisal of the sexual attraction and its manageability, shaped perhaps by whether it feels overwhelming, seems shared by the client or is driving pervasive fantasies. This appraisal informs the evaluation of options for handling it, which might include reflective coping options or interpersonal options such as referring the client on or taking the issue to supervision. Finally, after implementing these options, their consequences are evaluated. Please see Figure 11.1 for a diagrammatical representation of this theory and further for a detailed exploration of its components.

Vulnerability to Attraction? The Psychotherapist's Characteristics

Characteristics that influence the handling of sexual attraction include therapists' personal and professional identities (i.e., values, moral and ethical principles, boundaries, beliefs), which, in turn, are influenced by maturational characteristics, training history, theoretical orientation, relationship status and gender.

A poignant example of the influence of personal and professional identities was Corey's revelation that, because of his 'naturally looser boundaries around sex and monogamy' and his previously held belief that it is common for psychotherapists to have sex with their clients, he currently relies heavily on ethical guidelines for psychologists. Recently acquired professional beliefs about the best interests of clients powerfully shape his decision making regarding sexual attraction.

Rebecca experienced a different incongruity: her personal values are more stringent than the ethical guidelines regarding sexual contact with former clients. She believes that psychotherapists should not engage in sexual relationships with former clients under any circumstances, while her registration board's ethical guidelines suggest psychologists may in limited circumstances have sexual relationships with former clients at least 2 years following termination of psychotherapy.

The interview data sharpened the issue under investigation, from the start, distinguishing between the feeling of attraction and what is done in consequence of that feeling. Our participants expressed unanimously the belief that the initial experience of sexual attraction cannot be controlled and therefore is not unethical. However, ethicality became pertinent when assessing psychotherapists' intrapsychic and behavioural responses to their

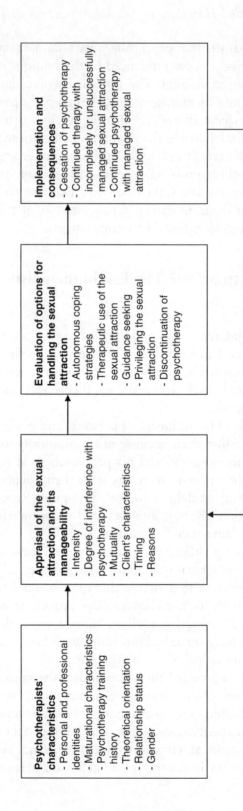

Figure 11.1. A grounded theory of psychotherapists' handling of sexual attraction to clients.

sexual attraction. These beliefs are consistent with those expressed by participants in previous research (e.g., Nickell et al., 1995; Pope, Tabachnick, & Keith-Spiegel, 1987) and by the few scholars who have explored this issue in the literature (Herring, 2001; Ladany et al., 1997; Pope et al., 1993).

Ethical guidelines should communicate that, while the experience of sexual attraction to clients is not unethical, it must be handled ethically, ensuring no sexual misconduct or hindering of psychotherapy. Handling the sexual attraction may also require consultation with senior colleagues and/or supervisors.

Participants expressed considerable personal guilt about experiences even of attraction, and this guilt may be a barrier to being quickly able to see that attraction is happening. While Rachel and Anita suggested that psychotherapists' sexual attraction to clients was ethical, they saw their own experiences of such attraction as 'wrong', invoking a cultural 'taboo'. So, psychotherapists' views about the ethicality of sexual attraction to clients *in general* may differ from their views of their own attraction in particular. The latter is consistent with the myth identified by Pope, Sonne, and Greene (2006, p. 28) that

> *Good* therapists (i.e., those who don't sexually exploit their patients) never have sexual feelings about their patients, don't become sexually aroused during therapy sessions, don't vicariously enjoy the (sometimes) guilty pleasures of their patients' sexual experiences, and don't have sexual fantasies or dreams about their patients.

Perhaps the intended message of scholars and educators that sexual attraction to clients is natural, common and even expectable has not penetrated deeply into the minds of psychotherapists. There is still considerable inner judgement.

Greater age and experience as a psychotherapist increase one's *felt* ability to handle sexual attraction to clients, perhaps due to learning gained from handling past attractions, and the development of more general knowledge, confidence, competence, professional boundaries and emotional awareness.

Psychotherapists' age was seen as important to some, where, for the men, increasing age was associated with decreasing 'libido' or 'sexual charge', making sexual attraction feel less difficult to manage. This finding concurs with previous research on sexuality and ageing (e.g., Morley, 2001; Segraves & Segraves, 1995). Participants' accounts of their changing libido or 'sexual drive' may reflect social discourse as well as biological behavioural determinants.

Women therapists noted challenges different from males'. Younger women, Bridget noted, frequently feel like 'everybody's property', which may interfere with their ability to confront sexual attraction to clients. She added that as women's 'confidence' increases with age, they become able to explore more freely their options for handling their sexual attraction. Gender differences are likely to go well beyond those revealed here. Sehl (1998) found that men were more likely than women to report frequent use of their sexual attraction for therapeutic ends.

Most participants reported no training in handling sexual attraction to clients, consistent with previous research (e.g., Blanchard & Lichtenberg, 1998; Paxton, Lovett, & Riggs, 2001; Pope et al., 1986; Sehl, 1998). This omission often leads psychotherapists to display erroneous beliefs about such attraction (Housman & Stake, 1999) and may unintentionally reinforce the view that it 'is abnormal, and is not to be acknowledged, let alone studied and discussed' (Pope, 2000, p. 608). In keeping with previous research, past education was often presented in the context of ethical decision making with a black-and-white focus proscribing sexual relationships with clients.

So, psychotherapists develop their beliefs based partly on their ethics training regarding the prohibition of sexual contact with clients. As Corey's case shows, this remains a crucially important area of education. It is not nuanced enough. Our participants voiced difficulty distinguishing taboos, feelings and ethics associated with sexual *contact* versus *attraction*. As Nickell et al. (1995, p. 325) suggest, 'Assessments of student and therapist beliefs about issues of sexual attraction to clients should be included as a component of training programmes and in supervision'.

Psychotherapists' theoretical orientations contribute to their conceptualizations of their sexual attraction to clients. Bridget's training in systems therapy, Edward's psychodynamic approach and Trevor's identification with Gestalt therapy allow them to understand some instances of sexual attraction as products of the therapeutic interaction and to use them therapeutically. This is in keeping with Gerber (1995, p. 118), who notes,

> Whether sexualized reactions are examined in psychotherapy depends to some extent on the therapist's perspective and training. For example, psychoanalysis has a potential built-in protective factor in that counter-transference reactions are a focus of the psychotherapy. In other forms of psychotherapy, however, interpretations of these reactions might be considered less important.

Indeed, other than with reference to psychodynamic concepts, our participants were unable to articulate how their favoured theoretical constructs conceptualize and suggest handling sexual attraction to clients. Similarly, the extant literature appears devoid of non-psychodynamic theoretical explanations of, or potential responses to, the phenomenon (Pope et al., 1986).

Some participants saw their relationship status as partly influencing their handling of sexual attraction to clients. Being in a committed romantic relationship might render such attraction less acceptable, while being single and/or sexually unfulfilled might create a stronger investment in the sexual attraction [which echoed Berry & Worthington's (2001) findings].

Appraisal of the Sexual Attraction and Its Manageability

Our participants handled sexual attraction to clients first by appraising its qualities, and consequently its manageability, to evaluate options for managing it, prior to implementation. Psychotherapists engage in appraisals of at least some of the following elements of their attraction: its intensity, degree of interference with psychotherapy, mutuality, timing, reasons for its emergence and client characteristics.

Markers of a minimally intense sexual attraction identified by our participants included admiration, curiosity, feelings of warmth and desire to engage in nonsexual touch. In contrast, a highly intense sexual attraction might entail sexual fantasy, preoccupation with the client, feelings of love, care and concern, and desire for a romantic and/or sexual relationship. In addition, highly intense experiences of sexual attraction were associated with experiences of anxiety, guilt, unsettlement and self-doubt.

Appraisals of intensity strongly influence therapists' choice of methods for handling it. Minimally intense sexual attractions might be handled using autonomous coping such as psychic management techniques alone, whereas highly intense sexual attractions might require more interpersonally oriented coping with one's supervisor or by discontinuing therapy.

Of major concern to practitioners is appraising how much sexual attraction interferes with psychotherapy, particularly regarding its intensity. At low levels, it might interfere minimally or might even be of therapeutic benefit (e.g., by enhancing therapeutic effort), while at high levels, it might interfere greatly (e.g., by impairing judgement, objectivity and the ability to implement specific therapeutic interventions).

Our participants appraised the mutuality of their sexual attraction by observing verbal and/or non-verbal signals from clients, and/or verbal confirmations of mutuality. Existing literature indicates that between 64% and 83% of psychotherapists report that at least one past instance of sexual attraction was mutual (Bernsen, Tabachnick, & Pope, 1994; Pope et al., 1986; Rodolfa et al., 1994).

The clients' attributes taken seriously in terms of attraction were their presenting problems (including history), emotional stability and age. Existing research suggests that particular care should be taken when psychotherapists experience sexual feelings towards sex offenders (Gerber, 1995), sexual abuse victims (including psychotherapist–client sexual abuse; Sonne & Pope, 1991) and older clients (Hillman & Stricker, 2001).

Discovering the meanings of the felt attraction and its relevance to therapy – that is, has it emanated primarily from the therapist, is it predominantly indicative of clients' issues, or has it emerged from key elements of the therapeutic relationship – shapes decisions about how to handle it. Some consider when it began during psychotherapy. For Edward, early occurrence suggests its development from 'his own issues', while later occurrence implicates the 'transference relationship'. Simon, who would likely discontinue therapy involving mutual attraction, would not terminate a therapy when this attraction emerged near the therapy's expected ending. Others consider where sexual thoughts occur, with some viewing the occurrence of such thoughts while not in the presence of clients as more likely due to their own characteristics.

Decisions regarding how to handle sexual attraction depend on the perceived manageability of the attraction, in turn influenced by the therapists' personal characteristics (e.g., self-efficacy, self-control), appraisals of their sexual attraction, and prior incomplete or unsuccessful attempts at managing it.

Most challenging and least manageable, according to most of our participants, are intense levels of sexual attraction (e.g., Rachel noted that she 'just couldn't work' if the attraction were strong) and mutual sexual attraction.

Some saw the presence of certain client characteristics (such as 'borderline features' or emotional instability) as making sexual attraction more difficult to manage, requiring particular objectivity and sensitivity. Some believed that they could manage their sexual attraction in most, if not all, circumstances.

Handling the Sexual Attraction: Evaluating Options

Participants indicated that they would next evaluate the ethicality and potential consequences of their options for handling their sexual attraction, including autonomous coping strategies, therapeutic use of the sexual attraction, guidance seeking, privileging the sexual attraction (i.e., express-ing it in a personally gratifying way, such as inviting sexual contact) and discontinuation of psychotherapy.

Psychotherapists are likely to attempt to manage their sexual attraction to clients using autonomous coping strategies (psychic and/or behav-ioural). Commonly favoured psychic management techniques included acknowledgement and awareness of the sexual attraction, as also reported in previous research (e.g., Giovazolias & Davis, 2001; Ladany et al., 1997) and recommended by scholars (e.g., Searles, 1959; Solomon, 1997).

Other techniques employed included self-analysis, 'self-talk', 'self-control'/'willpower', mindfulness and – particularly among beginning therapists – compartmentalizing, disregarding or shutting off the sexual attraction. Psychotherapists are likely to use psychic management tech-niques that are consistent with their theoretical orientations (e.g., psy-chodynamic therapists might employ self-analysis, whereas dialectical behavioural therapists might use mindfulness).

Psychotherapists differed markedly in their views about the conse-quences of disallowing sexual thoughts about clients. Some suggested that allowing such sexual thoughts could encourage inappropriate cognitions that lead to unethical behaviours, a line of reasoning first identified by Pope et al. (1993). Others conceptualized the forbidding of these sexual thoughts as psychic repression (removing them from awareness due to the pain of felt guilt), which could endanger themselves, psychotherapy and the clients (this was also the prevailing sentiment among scholars; e.g., Mann, 1994; Pope et al., 1993; Searles, 1959; Tansey, 1994).

Such a divergence in beliefs seemed to stem from identification with different theoretical orientations: those in favour of disallowing sexual thoughts were from cognitive-behavioural (or learning theory-based) backgrounds and those in favour of allowing these thoughts were from psychodynamic backgrounds. More research is needed given the diver-gence of beliefs on this thorny issue.

Behavioural management strategies – either used alone or supplemen-tary to psychic management techniques – include psychotherapists': attempting to behave as they would with other clients, steering the therapy away from content that might evoke sexual thoughts or feel-ings, and not scheduling these clients in the last appointment of the day to minimize the likelihood of the relationship continuing after-hours. Moving the direction of therapy away from certain issues seems a problematic choice in that therapy is diverging to manage therapist issues rather than being focused on client issues, but it may be a useful short-term solution.

Therapeutic Use of the Sexual Attraction

When psychotherapists appraise their sexual attraction as relevant to psychotherapy, they may attempt to use it to enhance understanding of therapeutic issues and/or as points of discussion with these clients.

Our participants suggested they might reflect on their attraction's meanings regarding the client's needs and ways of relating to people, and use it to guide treatment and elucidate areas of therapeutic focus (as also recommended by several theorists; e.g., Gabbard, 1994; Pope et al., 1993; Rosiello, 2003).

Whether to discuss one's sexual attraction with clients is a hotly debated issue in the literature, which produced mixed opinions among our sample. Consistent with most participants in past research (e.g., Gibson & Pope, 1993; Pope et al., 1987), our therapists who viewed their sexual attraction as never relevant to psychotherapy saw self-disclosing sexual attraction as always unethical and potentially harmful to the client, the therapeutic relationship and their professional reputations. A number of scholars have argued that psychotherapists should never share or explore openly their sexual attraction with clients (Gabbard, 1994; Gorkin, 1985; Kernberg, 1994).

So, it is of interest that some participants in our research saw disclosure as unethical and risky *only when* (1) the client is emotionally unstable or not mature enough to engage in sexual relationships generally; (2) the sexual attraction emerges primarily from the psychotherapist's characteristics and not from those of the client; or (3) the psychotherapist discusses the sexual attraction in a direct – or 'raw' – manner. These views echo those expressed by only a minority of participants in past research (e.g., Gibson & Pope, 1993; Goodyear & Shumate, 1996; Harris, 2001).

Nonetheless, Dalenberg (2000) discovered via her survey of former clients whose psychotherapists had self-disclosed sexual attraction to them that clients are most likely to benefit from such self-disclosures when their psychotherapists make clear statements of boundaries and acknowledge the normalcy of the human sexual response in intimate settings, and when the clients understand why the topic is being discussed (i.e., in response to their, rather than the psychotherapists', needs).

How directly therapists discuss their sexual attraction with clients is a consideration that has attracted debate among theorists and one that arose for several of our participants. Jørstad (2002) argues that direct disclosures of sexual attraction to clients can sometimes be beneficial to these clients, whereas Bridges (1998) and Fisher (2004) argue that such disclosures are unethical and risk harm to these clients, the therapeutic process, the psychotherapists' careers and the mental health profession.

In our study, Trevor indicated that, after careful consideration, he might directly discuss his sexual attraction with a client for the client's benefit. Anita suggested that direct disclosure of sexual attraction to clients would be unethical but that indirect disclosure with reference to 'approved language', such as transference and countertransference, would be appropriate. Similarly, Edward suggested that he might discuss sexual attraction with clients in a non-sexualized way in terms of intimacy and closeness within the therapeutic relationship.

These approaches are consistent with Fisher's (2004, p. 117) acknowledgement of 'a therapeutic middle ground', in which explicit disclosures of sexual feelings are avoided in favour of indirect disclosures, such as acknowledgements of caring and warmth within the therapeutic relationship. Nonetheless, Trevor and Anita thought that supervision should be sought before psychotherapists discuss their sexual attraction with clients, a stance strongly supported by Fisher (2004) and Pope et al. (1993).

None of our participants had ever received guidance or training regarding the therapeutic use of sexual attraction to clients, even though some indicated that they would implement, or have implemented, such an intervention. However, participants trained in theoretical orientations that construct the therapy relationship as a therapeutic tool (such as psychodynamic orientations) were much more likely to view their sexual attractions as therapeutically useful than were those trained in other theoretical orientations.

Guidance Seeking

Our participants saw seeking guidance regarding 'difficult-to-manage' sexual attractions as ethically sound practice, while the literature recommends seeking guidance, preferably from supervisors or senior colleagues, notwithstanding the perceived difficulty level of the sexual attraction (e.g., Gabbard, 1994; Nickell et al., 1995; Pope et al., 1993).

While psychotherapists believe guidance should be sought, the reality is that there are barriers to doing so. Our participants' feared negative consequences included embarrassment or awkwardness, being judged negatively (e.g., as unprofessional or weak), receiving inadequate guidance and being reported for unethical practice to a professional registration body.

Psychotherapists-in-training face unique barriers, identified by our participants as underdeveloped 'professional self-esteem', which can enhance concerns about competence and others' perceptions, and fear of being deemed unfit by supervisors to graduate from one's training programme or to gain registration with a professional body.

Highly experienced psychotherapists may also face particular barriers. Among our participants, Martin reported that seeking guidance from peers (a common mode of supervision for senior practitioners) would be extremely challenging, given that he would be concerned about maintaining his reputation for remaining in control during psychotherapy. These barriers are consistent with and supplement previous research (e.g., Ladany et al., 1997; Noonan & Lane, 2001; Rodolfa et al., 1994).

Barriers to seeking guidance are diminished when psychotherapists have access to sources of guidance perceived as trustworthy, open-minded and able to provide adequate assistance regarding coping strategies, behaving ethically, using sexual attraction therapeutically and/or discontinuing psychotherapy (in keeping with previous research; e.g., Rodolfa et al., 1994; Shepard, 2000). Where guidance is lacking or requires supplementation, a small number of our participants indicated that they would confide in non-psychotherapist, understanding friends (who can provide emotional support).

We found that psychotherapists employ autonomous coping strategies for manageable attractions but are more likely to seek guidance for difficult-to-manage attractions (e.g., highly intense and interfering with psychotherapy). Manageability may be an unidentified contributing factor in previous research, suggesting that slightly more than half of psychotherapists are likely to seek guidance when sexually attracted to clients (Giovazolias & Davis, 2001; Pope et al., 1986).

Our participants and those from prior research (Housman & Stake, 1999; Paxton et al., 2001) have found that seeking professional guidance can enhance understanding of the meanings of the sexual attraction and can lead to positive therapeutic outcomes.

Privileging the Sexual Attraction: Seeking Personal Rather Than Therapeutic Benefit

Part of handling sexual attraction to clients may involve privileging (or giving expression to) the sexual attraction for personal rather than therapeutic benefit. We acknowledge that some psychotherapists might privilege the sexual attraction for personal benefit under the guise of therapeutic benefit (Pope et al., 1993). It is in such situations that interpersonal coping methods are most relevant so that the person experiencing the attraction can have access to intersubjective resources as a 'reality check' to their appraisals and their means of addressing attraction issues.

We suggest that consciously privileging sexual attraction to clients is less likely when therapists see such privileging as unethical and potentially detrimental to themselves, psychotherapy and/or the clients. For our participants, privileging sexual attraction while in the presence of clients (excluding sexual contact, which will be discussed separately) include sexually suggestive language (verbal or body language); special treatment of clients, including extended or unnecessary 'therapeutic' contact; manipulating clients to meet their needs (e.g., to be liked or seen as attractive); and socializing with clients. Anita disclosed that she was more accommodative of a client to whom she was attracted and took greater care of her physical appearance in his presence. These findings are consistent with, and supplement, previous research (e.g., Pope et al., 1987).

A few discussed privileging sexual attraction while away from the client. Corey and Trevor expressed concerns that engaging in vivid sexual fantasizing about clients could alter their perceptions of these clients and thus change therapeutic relationships in negative ways. However, some suggested that they permit themselves to 'indulge' in sexual fantasizing about clients at what they deem non-harmful and manageable levels. Corey revealed that he discussed his sexual attraction to a client with another person for the purpose of 'getting off on' it (which he thought was unethical).

Engaging in behaviours that appear to privilege therapists' sexual attraction to clients may be expected, given that their needs to express their attraction are not often met in more appropriate domains, such as supervision. Consistent with previous research, we suggest that psychotherapists might benefit from gaining reflective distance on their experiences. Supervisors and senior colleagues should encourage psychotherapists to reflect on their fantasies and behaviours.

Finally, our participants declared unanimously that engaging in sexual relationships with clients is unethical and likely to result in multiple negative consequences for themselves (such as de-registration with professional bodies and social embarrassment), the therapeutic relationships (e.g., abuse of the power differential) and the clients (such as psychological damage and exploitation of trust and vulnerability), as past research would concur (e.g., Pope & Vetter, 1992; Wincze, Richards, Parsons, & Bailey, 1996). Correspondingly, none of our participants indicated that they have engaged or would engage in such behaviour. Nonetheless, past research demonstrates that a small percentage of psychotherapists have done so (e.g., Celenza, 2005; Viztum & Chen, 1993).

Discontinuation of Psychotherapy

Decisions regarding continuance of psychotherapy where therapists are sexually attracted to clients are influenced primarily by their perception of the attraction's manageability and secondarily by their assessments of the consequences and ethicality of continuing psychotherapy.

A number of therapists viewed continuing psychotherapy in the presence of unmanageable sexual attraction as unethical; rather they would discontinue psychotherapy provided they had access to adequate referral networks (highlighting the importance of the availability of such networks). Among these participants, highly intense, greatly interfering and/ or mutually experienced sexual attractions were seen as potentially too difficult to manage.

Simon suggested that he would consider the client's presenting problems in deciding on whether to continue therapy (e.g., he would be more likely to discontinue psychotherapy when the client's issues were sex related). Trevor suggested that he would decide whether to continue therapy in consultation with his peer supervision group (a highly recommended course of action), whereas Erin and Simon suggested that they would make such decisions in consultation with their clients (which, as indicated previously, should be implemented with caution and careful deliberation).

Where discontinuing therapy was seen as necessary, participants deliberated about whether to provide their clients with the genuine reasons for doing so. Opinions were mixed. Several indicated that offering real reasons would be unethical and/or likely to result in negative consequences (such as exacerbating mutual attraction or the client's distress, or appearing 'creepy'). Others were unsure, and some would seek guidance. Simon thought it would be unethical to mislead clients and would provide the genuine reasons for ending therapy.

Implementation and Consequences

In deciding what to do, psychotherapists appraise their sexual attraction in terms of its manageability and consider their options accordingly. The decision-making process can be cyclical: decisions are reached, rescinded and renegotiated before being implemented. Some actions may be implemented after varying degrees of deliberation, while others may be implemented immediately, possibly without conscious consideration.

For example, a psychotherapist might discuss tentatively her sexual attraction with her client after several discussions with her supervisor (a process similar to that described by Trevor), whereas another psychotherapist might begin flirting with his client as soon as he experiences sexual attraction (a process described as unethical by several participants).

Consequences of implementing options included cessation of psychotherapy, continued psychotherapy with incompletely or unsuccessfully managed sexual attraction (found to be prominent in Luca and Boyden's study in Chapter 13), or continued psychotherapy with managed sexual attraction. Where the sexual attraction is incompletely or unsuccessfully managed and therapy continues, the context of the attraction (e.g., its intensity) and the psychotherapists' perceptions of its manageability may change, which, in turn, informs further attempts at handling it, thus indicating the process's cyclical nature.

Several participants suggested the handling process cycled through autonomous coping strategies, which, if not completely successful, were followed by guidance seeking and ultimately by the discontinuation of psychotherapy. Not all psychotherapists in all cases cycle through different approaches in this way or at all. Psychotherapists might find relief in knowing that handling sexual attraction to clients need not occur as a one-off event but can unfold as a process over time, involving both individual efforts and those supported by supervisors and/or senior colleagues.

Finally, we found that psychotherapists can, in some cases, manage their sexual attraction to clients effectively and continue psychotherapy, sometimes with therapeutic benefit. This finding may provide hope to psychotherapists who may be uncertain about the possibility of managing sexual attraction to clients effectively.

This chapter has outlined a number of domains requiring further research to explore the spectrum of complexities that arise in handling sexual attraction, such as the efficacy of attempts to ignore or avoid acknowledging its existence, ways of separating the ethicality of 'attraction' from behaviours that may arise from that attraction, and whether and in what circumstances disclosure of attraction may be a coping option and when it may be destructive to the therapeutic process. However, in short, we feel that the practitioners we spoke to have shared experiences that are likely to resonate with clinicians. We feel that our model reveals attributes that may render a practitioner more (or less) vulnerable to unbidden attraction. We hope that it opens up the discussion in ways that intersect with existing research literature, and promotes consideration of training and support options for practitioners.

Clinical Strategies to Manage Sexual Attraction

- The experience of sexual attraction to clients is not unethical. We encourage therapists to reflect on whether they hold a double standard where they view other therapists' attraction as ethical but their own as unacceptable. Ethical considerations become pertinent only in the *handling* of the sexual attraction to ensure it does not hinder the process of psychotherapy or indeed lead to sexual misconduct.
- If psychotherapists reflect on their values, principles, boundaries and beliefs, and canvas the full range of elements of their sexual attraction, they could enable a richer and more honest exploration and perhaps revision their approaches to handling their sexual attraction.
- We encourage psychotherapists to seek the guidance of senior colleagues and supervisors to assist in this reflective process and to develop appropriate courses of action.
- Sexual attraction can be used therapeutically by reflecting on its meanings in terms of the client's needs and ways of relating to people, and as a guide for treatment planning and the elucidation of areas of therapeutic focus.
- When considering whether to self-disclose sexual attraction to a client, psychotherapists are encouraged to seek the guidance of a supervisor or a senior colleague, particularly to help clarify the purpose, and the potential risks and benefits, of such a disclosure.
- Seeking professional guidance can also help psychotherapists reflect on their fantasies and behaviours relating to clients to whom they are sexually attracted in order to understand the degree to which they are privileging their sexual attraction, even if they believe they are not doing so.
- If a sexual attraction is deemed unmanageable, one might discontinue therapy and refer the client to another therapist. Again, we advise seeking professional guidance in this instance, including about how to explain it to the client.
- The handling of sexual attraction to clients need not occur as a one-off event but can unfold as a process over time, involving both individual efforts and those supported by supervisors and/or senior colleagues.

Optimal Supervision and Training Conditions

- Educators and supervisors should broach the topic of sexual attraction to clients with their trainees in an accepting and open manner, and model appropriately 'boundaried' behaviours and high levels of personal reflection and insight.
- Sources of guidance need to be perceived as trustworthy, open-minded, unlikely to criticize or punish, and competent to provide adequate assistance in sexual attraction issues.
- Scholars of different theoretical backgrounds need to articulate their respective theoretical positions regarding the experience and handling of sexual attraction to clients, as they do in this book (including how it might or might not be used therapeutically, and when and how to discontinue therapy). Psychotherapy training programmes should include such theory in their curricula.
- Training in sexual attraction issues should be delivered outside the context of ethics classes, in discussion-based rather than didactic formats, where sexual attraction can be distinguished from sexual misconduct, and complex cases illustrating nuanced issues can be explored with reference to the role of the therapeutic relationship.

References

Arcuri, A., & Mcilwain, D. (2010). Psychotherapists' handling of sexual attraction to clients: A grounded theory. In L. Richards (Ed.), *Handling qualitative data: A practical guide*. London: Sage Publications. Retrieved from companion website http://www.uk.sagepub.com/richards/homeP2.htm

Bernsen, A., Tabachnick, B. G., & Pope, K. S. (1994). National survey of social workers' sexual attraction to their clients: Results, implications, and comparison to psychologists. *Ethics & Behavior, 4,* 369–388.

Berry, J. T., & Worthington, E. L., Jr. (2001). A general model of coping with sexual attraction in professional relationships: A study of psychologists, ministers, and managers. *Marriage & Family: A Christian Journal, 4,* 285–308.

Blanchard, C. A., & Lichtenberg, J. W. (1998). Counseling psychologists' training to deal with their sexual feelings in therapy. *The Counseling Psychologist, 26,* 624–639.

Bridges, N. A. (1998). Teaching psychiatric trainees to respond to sexual and loving feelings: The supervisory challenge. *The Journal of Psychotherapy Practice and Research, 7,* 217–226.

Celenza, A. (2005). Sexual boundary violations: How do they happen? *Directions in Psychiatry, 25,* 141–149.

Dalenberg, C. J. (2000). *Countertransference and the treatment of trauma.* Washington, DC: American Psychological Association.

Davies, J. M. (1994). Love in the afternoon: A relational reconsideration of desire and dread in the countertransference. *Psychoanalytic Dialogues, 4,* 153–170.

Davis, H. (1978). The use of countertransference feelings in resolving resistance. *Psychoanalytic Review, 65,* 557–568.

Field, N. (1989). Listening with the body: An exploration in the countertransference. *British Journal of Psychotherapy, 5,* 512–522.

Fisher, C. D. (2004). Ethical issues in therapy: Therapist self-disclosure of sexual feelings. *Ethics & Behavior, 14,* 105–121.

Freud, S. (1912/2001). The dynamics of transference. In J. Strachey (Ed.), *The standard edition of the complete psychological works of Sigmund Freud, volume XII (1911–1913): The case of Schreber, papers on technique and other works.* London: Vintage.

Freud, S. (1915/2001). Observations on transference-love (Further recommendations on the technique of psycho-analysis III). In J. Strachey (Ed.), *The standard edition of the complete psychological works of Sigmund Freud, volume XII (1911–1913): The case of Schreber, papers on technique and other works.* London: Vintage.

Gabbard, G. O. (1994). Sexual excitement and countertransference love in the analyst. *Journal of the American Psychoanalytic Association, 42,* 1083–1106.

Gerber, P. N. (1995). Commentary on counter-transference in working with sex offenders: The issue of sexual attraction. *Journal of Child Sexual Abuse, 4*(1), 117–120.

Gibson, W. T., & Pope, K. S. (1993). The ethics of counseling: A national survey of certified counselors. *Journal of Counseling and Development, 71,* 330–336.

Giovazolias, T., & Davis, P. (2001). How common is sexual attraction towards clients? The experiences of sexual attraction of counselling psychologists toward their clients and its impact on the therapeutic process. *Counselling Psychology Quarterly, 14,* 281–286.

Glaser, B. G., & Strauss, A. L. (1967). *The discovery of grounded theory: Strategies for qualitative research.* Chicago, IL: Aldine Publishing Company.

Goodyear, R. K., & Shumate, J. L. (1996). Perceived effects of therapist self-disclosure of attraction to clients. *Professional Psychology, Research and Practice, 27,* 613–616.

Gorkin, M. (1985). Varieties of sexualized countertransference. *Psychoanalytic Review, 72,* 421–440.

Harris, S. M. (2001). Teaching family therapists about sexual attraction in therapy. *Journal of Marital & Family Therapy, 27,* 123–128.

Herring, B. (2001). Ethical guidelines in the treatment of compulsive sexual behavior. *Sexual Addiction & Compulsivity, 8*, 13–22.

Hillman, J., & Stricker, G. (2001). The management of sexualized transference and countertransference with older adult patients: Implications for practice. *Professional Psychology, Research and Practice, 32*, 272–277.

Housman, L. M., & Stake, J. E. (1999). The current state of sexual ethics training in clinical psychology: Issues of quantity, quality, and effectiveness. *Professional Psychology, Research and Practice, 30*, 302–311.

Jørstad, J. (2002). Erotic countertransference: Hazards, challenges and therapeutic potentials. *Scandinavian Psychoanalytic Review, 25*, 117–134.

Kernberg, O. F. (1994). Love in the analytic setting. *Journal of the American Psychoanalytic Association, 42*, 1137–1157.

Ladany, N., O'Brien, K. M., Hill, C. E., Melincoff, D. S., Knox, S., & Petersen, D. A. (1997). Sexual attraction toward clients, use of supervision, and prior training: A qualitative study of predoctoral psychology interns. *Journal of Counseling Psychology, 44*, 413–424.

Mann, D. (1994). The psychotherapist's erotic subjectivity. *British Journal of Psychotherapy, 1*, 244–254.

Mann, D. (1999). Erotic narrative in psychoanalytic practice: An introduction. In D. Mann (Ed.), *Erotic transference and countertransference: Clinical practice in psychotherapy*. London: Routledge.

Morley, J. E. (2001). Androgens and aging. *Maturitas, 38*, 61–73.

Nickell, N. J., Hecker, L. L., Ray, R. E., & Bercik, J. (1995). Marriage and family therapists' sexual attraction to clients: An exploratory study. *American Journal of Family Therapy, 23*, 315–327.

Noonan, H., & Lane, R. C. (2001). The erotic transference: The adult male patient and the female therapist. *Journal of Psychotherapy in Independent Practice, 2*, 37–56.

Paxton, C., Lovett, J., & Riggs, M. L. (2001). The nature of professional training and perceptions of adequacy in dealing with sexual feelings in psychotherapy: Experiences of clinical faculty. *Ethics & Behavior, 11*, 175–189.

Pope, K. S. (2000). Therapists' sexual feelings and behaviors: Research, trends, and quandaries. In L. T. Szuchman & F. Muscarella (Eds.), *Psychological perspectives on human sexuality*. New York: John Wiley & Sons.

Pope, K. S., & Vetter, V. A. (1992). Ethical dilemmas encountered by members of the American Psychological Association: A national survey. *The American Psychologist, 47*, 397–411.

Pope, K. S., Keith-Spiegel, P., & Tabachnick, B. G. (1986). Sexual attraction to clients: The human therapist and the (sometimes) inhuman training system. *The American Psychologist, 41*, 147–158.

Pope, K. S., Sonne, J. L., & Greene, B. (2006). *What therapists don't talk about and why: Understanding taboos that hurt us and our clients*. Washington, DC: American Psychological Association.

Pope, K. S., Sonne, J. L., & Holroyd, J. (1993). *Sexual feelings in psychotherapy: Explorations for therapists and therapists-in-training.* Washington, DC: American Psychological Association.

Pope, K. S., Tabachnick, B. G., & Keith-Spiegel, P. (1987). Ethics of practice: The beliefs and behaviors of psychologists as therapists. *The American Psychologist, 42,* 993–1006.

Rodolfa, E., Hall, T., Holms, V., Davena, A., Komatz, D., Antunez, M., & Hall, A. (1994). The management of sexual feelings in therapy. *Professional Psychology, Research and Practice, 25,* 168–172.

Rosiello, F. (2003). On lust and loathing: Erotic transference/countertransference between a female analyst and female patients. In J. Drescher, A. D'Ercole, & E. Schoenberg (Eds.), *Psychotherapy with gay men and lesbians: Contemporary dynamic approaches.* Binghamton, NY: The Harrington Park Press/The Haworth Press.

Searles, H. (1959). Oedipal love in the countertransference. *International Journal of Psycho-Analysis, 40,* 180–190.

Segraves, R. T., & Segraves, K. B. (1995). Human sexuality and aging. *Journal of Sex Education and Therapy, 21,* 88–102.

Sehl, M. R. (1998). Erotic countertransference and clinical social work practice: A national survey of psychotherapists' sexual feelings, attitudes, and responses. *Journal of Analytic Social Work, 5,* 39–55.

Shepard, J. K. (2000). Female trainees' experience of having sexual feelings toward a male patient while being supervised by a male supervisor. *Dissertation Abstracts International: Section B: The Sciences & Engineering, 61,* 2782.

Solomon, M. F. (1997). On love and lust in the countertransference. *The Journal of the American Academy of Psychoanalysis and Dynamic Psychiatry, 25,* 71–90.

Sonne, J. L., & Pope, K. S. (1991). Treating victims of therapist-patient sexual involvement. *Psychotherapy: Theory, Research, Practice, Training, 28,* 174–187.

Strauss, A., & Corbin, J. (1998). *Basics of qualitative research: Techniques and procedures for developing grounded theory.* Thousand Oaks, CA: Sage Publications.

Tansey, M. J. (1994). Sexual attraction and phobic dread in the countertransference. *Psychoanalytic Dialogues, 4,* 139–152.

Viztum, E., & Chen, E. (1993). Patient-therapist sexual contacts. *Sihot/Dialogue: Israel Journal of Psychotherapy, 7,* 85–92.

Wincze, J. P., Richards, J., Parsons, J. P., & Bailey, S. (1996). A comparative survey of therapist sexual misconduct between an American state and an Australian state. *Professional Psychology, Research and Practice, 27,* 289–294.

12

The Self-Preservation Society

A Discourse Analysis of Male Heterosexual Therapists and Discourses of Sexual Attraction

John Penny and Malcolm Cross

The Context

Therapists, clients and sex: an ongoing 'problem'

Sexual attraction, and in particular acting out of sexual desires in the context of psychotherapy, continues to be a problem within the domain of psychotherapy. In the following chapter, we seek to briefly set out the history and background of this phenomenon and illustrate using the contemporary discourse of a number of practising male therapists that the risks remain. In 1973, Kardener, Fuller, and Mensh surveyed physicians' and psychiatrists' experiences of erotic and non-erotic contact with patients. They found that 5% had had sex with patients. In 1979, Pope, Levenson, and Schover found 7% of psychologists conducting psychotherapy had had sexual contact with clients. Seven years later, Pope, Keith-Speigel, and Tabachnick (1986) conducted a similar survey and found that 95% of male psychotherapists questioned had been sexually attracted to clients. Further, 9.4% of those men had acted out those feelings. Eight years later, Rodolfa et al. (1994) reported an 88% attraction rate. Again, 4% of therapists questioned had acted out. Seto (1995) reported that complaints against psychologists in North America were on the rise, and in 2005, a third of a century after the Kardener et al. study (1973), Ladany et al. (1997) were still reporting some 5% of therapists admitting to sexual misconduct with patients.

Sexual Attraction in Therapy: Clinical Perspectives on Moving Beyond the Taboo – A Guide for Training and Practice, First Edition. Edited by Maria Luca.
© 2014 John Wiley & Sons, Ltd. Published 2014 by John Wiley & Sons, Ltd.

But the problem of how to manage sexual attraction in psychotherapy goes right back to its origins. Breuer and Freud grappled with the implications of the obsession and infatuation of the former with Anna O (Breuer & Freud, 1895/1974). From that earliest moment, sexual attraction between analysands and analysts, labelled in the psychodynamic school as erotic transference and countertransference, was regarded as dangerous and problematic, a view crystallized by Freud (1915) in 'Observations on Transference Love', written in response to the increasingly widespread problem of therapists having sex with patients, a phenomenon that was arguably turning psychoanalysis into a laughing stock (Gay, 1995). Glen O. Gabbard, a formidable voice against sexual enactment in psychotherapy, relates the inappropriate sexual behaviour of such luminaries as Carl Jung, Otto Rank, Karen Horney and Frieda Fromm-Reichmann (Gabbard, 1994).

It seems that, despite paper after paper ringing alarm bells about sexual misconduct, almost nothing has changed. Acting out of sexual attraction seems to be still affecting between 1% and 5% of therapists, and inadequacies in training and supervision continue to be blamed (Halter, Brown, & Stone, 2007). Ladany et al. (1997), in reviewing literature on sexual attraction and acting out, note 'the consistency of findings across these studies is impressive' (p. 413).

We would argue that down the years, a number of discourses have been applied to the problem, all of which share the property of helping therapists minimize personal responsibility for inappropriate actions.

A failure of training

A prominent discourse calls for increased education and training; for instance, Edelwich and Brodsky (1982) and Pope et al. (1986) were critical of the lack of training and guidance on the management of sexual attraction. Rodolfa et al. (1994) (who provided a comprehensive review of such papers to that date) surveyed to see what had changed in training but found that almost nothing had. Five years later, Hamilton and Sprull (1999) were similarly critical of training. They suggested that systemic and pedagogic elements of training, notably the shift to briefer models, had reduced the concern over transference and countertransference. Training was not, they suggested, dealing adequately with the management of sexual attraction (although the moratorium on enactment was loud and clear) and supervision was found to be reluctant to deal honestly with trainees' feelings. These criticisms are raised again and again down the years (Bartell & Rubin, 1990; Gilbert, 1987; McCarthy & Holliday, 2004; Noel, 2008; Wester & Vogel, 2002).

The client causes the problem

Freud started the ball rolling with discourse that attributed the problem of sexual enactment in therapeutic dyads to the female client. In Freud's 'Observations on Transference Love' (1915), he recognizes that the phenomenon will 'occur without fail' (p. 383). However, the attraction, he points out, is not about the analyst and therefore is not something he should take pride in: the attraction belongs to the analytic situation, not to 'the charms of his own person'. The analyst must be 'proof against every temptation' (Freud, 1915, p. 383), resisting the discomfort of not playing the traditional male role when a woman expresses her love as Sabbadini demonstrates in Chapter 9.

It's not a problem after all . . .

As recently as 2001, Giovazolias and Davis found that more than half of the counselling psychologists who reported being sexually attracted to clients felt it had been beneficial to the therapy, but the team acknowledge that these respondents do have a vested interest in putting a positive spin on this. Only 6.3% of counselling psychologists reporting attraction felt it had a negative impact on therapy. Seven years earlier, only 43% of participants in the Rodolfa et al. study (1994) of US counselling psychologists reported sexual attraction as having a negative impact on therapy.

In fact, acting out may be a good thing

Down the years, attempts have been made to suggest that acting on sexual attraction may be a good thing. Sandor Ferenczi kissed his patients (Masson, 1988); heavyweight therapist William Reich made a case for sexual enactment as a therapeutic tool (Reich, 1968); and Glen Gabbard (1996) relates the sad tale of the fall from grace of an eminent psychiatrist who magically believed that sexual intercourse with him would prove salvific and so cure his patient.

A profile of the typical offender

Halter et al. (2007) summarize literature looking at factors associated with sexual misconduct by therapists. Wary of overvaluing 'predictive' profiling, they nonetheless draw out some broad conclusions. Offenders tend to be older males; victims tend to be female. Sexual misconduct is associated with the therapist having a history of being sexually abused. He may have suffered from insecure attachments, or lack current emotionally intimate relationships outside his job. And here, we would suggest, are some important clues as to why the institution of psychotherapy has been unable to put its house in order: perhaps this is not a professional problem but one associated with gender. Perhaps the problem lies in masculinity?

Masculinity

Masculinity is a menu of discourses that change from situation to situation. The menu offers hegemonic definitions, the prevailing ideal of a given institution that changes over time. Connell (1995) defines hegemonic masculinity as 'the configuration of gender practice which embodies the currently accepted answer to the problem of the legitimacy of patriarchy, which guarantees the dominant position of men and the subordinate position of women' (p. 77).

When worlds collide

Being constantly and unendingly produced through discourse, gender has no existential coherence. Identities are not settled and unitary, but rather, they shift constantly in talk, drawing upon cultural resources to make and remake identity in changing and fluid contexts. As they grow and develop, boys learn, and are taught, about their world and appropriate ways to be in that world. Levant (2001) describes how boys are taught, by reinforcement of approved behaviours and punishment of deviation, the culturally approved standards of masculinity. These standards come together in what Pollack and Levant (1998, p. 21) call a 'code of masculinity', which is defined to a large degree diametrically to feminine characteristics.

In developing their version of masculinity, men must make choices. Some choices men make may be automatic; others require active resolution of dilemmas, such as reconciling individual views and values about masculinity with the variations of masculinity prevalent in the immediate social and cultural context (Wetherell & Maybin, 1996). One key dilemma that men must solve, we would suggest, is conflict between masculinity and the demands of other social and cultural institutions in which they are situated, because, of course, masculinity is interwoven with other institutions that exert influence on its construction.

How to avoid falling to pieces

The psychoanalytic paradigm and ideas of the discursive construction of gender and sexuality share the idea of the subjective experience of a cohesive sense of self, struggling to maintain cohesion in the face of fragmentation. Both paradigms see the individual as a multivariously situated series of identities that are sourced from the world outside the body. In the discursive tradition, there are multiplicities of discourses that swirl in the cultural space, spoken by the individual who positions him or herself in relation to these discourses. The trick is to maintain the illusion of cohesion. Henriques, Hollway, Urwin, Venn, and Walkerdine (1984) suggest that key questions have to be asked in relation to the fragmented self: how are the fragments held together and how is subjective experience of continuity to be explained? Butler (1999) suggests that the production of gender lies in cultural codes circulating through language and that the performance of gender, by using these outer-world codes, gives the illusion of a cohesive self on the inside.

However, working as a therapist can present challenges to masculinity and with challenge comes the potential for fragmentation. Wester and Lyubelsky (2005) point out that men are expected to be warm and caring in the family (and of course, professional when working as therapists), a role that may have been internalized as feminine. O'Neil, Helms, Gable, David, and Wrightsman (1986, p. 335) named this switch between one role and another as 'male gender role conflict'. Similarly, Adler (1927/1992) wrote of the 'masculine protest', the anxiety felt by men when they perceive themselves to be in a feminized position of weakness. Gough (2004) argues for a psychoanalytic understanding of masculinity, suggesting that such a reading can identify masculine anxieties and defences around the potential surfacing of feminine desires such as seeking (or perhaps giving) comfort. One defensive strategy he identifies is the reframing of powerful women (seen as such from disempowered masculine positions) as figures of ridicule. Similarly, Benwell (2003) suggests that dichotomous gender categories may be less about preserving patriarchy and more about constructing certainty and security.

Myriad discourses comprise the sense of self and we should be mindful of their existence in the background as we concentrate on the foreground discourses associated with masculinity and psychotherapy. Both these institutions are central to the constructions of identity that the research participants have in their professional context. When they work in harmony, or when opposing institutions are allied in different settings and at different times, the sense of self is secure: the problem comes when we have to be different people *at the same time*. Building on Davies and Harré's (1990) insight that to experience contradictory positions challenges the sense of self as continuous and unitary, we would go further and suggest that the sense of threat is correlated to the centrality of the institutions to one's sense of self, and that gender identity and professional identity are core identity markers for men.

Methodology

Eight male therapists who responded to a call for participants were interviewed online via email exchanges or synchronous 'chatting' in a secure chat room. Data were analyzed using a fusion of Foucauldian and critical discourse analyses. Foucauldian discourse analysis seeks to address issues of power and examines how the speaker (or writer) is positioned by discourse and how discourse reproduces power relations. Fusion of the ideas of Foucault with critical discourse analysis allowed focus on both the immediate conversational features and the wider dominant discourses underpinning meaning (see, e.g., Burman & Parker, 1993; Fairclough, 1992; Parker, 1992).

As analysis revealed discourses, each was named and the cultural and historical contexts in which they emerged were considered. It became possible to see how discourses could annex other discourses that enjoy power, to explore who might benefit from the discourse and to consider who might be disadvantaged by it.

Our arguments proceed on the basis that conscious experiencing of a simultaneous clash of identities brings a conflict in moral codes and expected behaviours. This clash of identities, we would suggest, stimulates moral anxiety predicated on the fear that masculine impulses could override professional codes, and that such a clash evokes particular anxiety when contemporary hegemonic constructs of masculinity – that permit sexual attraction, and potentially enactment thereof – clash contemporaneously with professional standards of restraint. It is our contention that the discourses spoken by participants in relation to sexual attraction are deployed to restore congruence between identities, and to minimize the sense of the self as fragmenting.

Interlude

Although you will only get the vaguest sense of the therapists who agreed to take part in this work from the extracts that we have space to offer, you should be assured that every single participant was seeking to make sense of experiences of sexual attraction that had, to a greater or lesser degree, caused them professional disquiet. They were, as men, striving to make sense of what had occurred: they were not seeking to be manipulative or to minimize the intensity of their experience. These are sincere men.

As to the reading we have made of their contributions, you may feel we have been somewhat harsh, even that we have exploited their honesty. We would make two observations. Firstly, discourses derived from the institution of psychotherapy had not provided these men with the explanations they sought. We would suggest that their honesty is exploited by our colluding with the notion that this institution can indeed provide such explanations. Secondly, it is important to hold onto the idea that it is the discourses that speak the man, and not vice versa. Participants speak of their experiences of sexual attraction using the discourses available to them. We would suggest that our duty of care is to highlight these discourses so these men can become empowered as to their effect. Our reading is therefore offered as an invitation to resist.

We believe that these men were bold in coming forward to talk about a contentious and almost taboo subject. We have therefore made great efforts to defend their anonymity. We provide only the most basic information about each participant, and any detail that might reveal, or even hint at, their identity has been changed. Extracts presented for your consideration are typical of discourses that occur over multiple contributions.

How Therapists Manage Sexual Attraction: Using Discourses of Masculinity

The discourse of physical attraction: rabbits in the headlights

When the participants first meet their clients, the attraction that occurs is apparently immediate, physical, places the male therapist in a passive position and is experienced as residing in the client. The therapists are like rabbits caught in the headlights of a car: passive, powerless to act, unable to look away.

> I remember being struck quite forcibly . . . by how attractive she was.

> She had a full figure, but it was also trim. She wore a business suit, with a skirt rather than trousers. She had dark blonde hair and very penetrating blue eyes . . . she certainly embodied an archetypal sexy woman – the saucy secretary type. (Freddie, 36, white British, heterosexual integrative counsellor)

Freddie's picture is of a curvaceous blonde, but not one in tune with contemporary tastes, who is fat. She is attractive in a way that is firmly in tune with hegemonic masculinity. Freddie's description of Lelia's physique almost compels agreement that she is attractive to warrant one's own sense of masculinity. Indeed, 'she was a very sexy lady' (not 'I thought she was'). It is not that he *found* her to be attractive; she *is*, as a pre-existing state. So attractive is she that the effect, like the rabbit facing the oncoming car, is constructed as physically assaulting. Discourse used to describe sexual attraction often borrows from discourse of rape. Were Freddie's words taken literally, he is describing an attack. Elsewhere in his discourses, he uses, in the context of Lelia's attraction, such words and phrases as 'intrude', 'intrusive', 'captivated', 'hooked in'. The imagery is explicitly used in Dominic's account: he feels cast as the rapist and later, when his client gains agency, feels raped. The descriptors Freddie uses certainly place the attraction wholly within Lelia. She wears a business suit that emphasizes her power, but with a skirt rather than trousers, implying perhaps that she chooses to emphasize how attractive she is, thus shifting more responsibility for the attraction onto her. The imagery is from the world of Benny Hill and the *Nuts* photo-spread. 'Saucy secretary' changes Lelia's status from the professional businesswoman implied when describing her clothes. The image suggests not only attractiveness, but the implied construction that she would be 'game' too: the saucy secretary is not a prudish image. Arthur treads a similar path:

> a professional woman (PhD education, high status job) sat on the chair, one leg on the arm of the chair, twiddling her long blonde hair and being 'very girlie'. (Arthur, 43, white British, heterosexual cognitive behavioural therapist)

The reference to a 'professional woman' may be read, not as contextualized by the bracketed phrase but by 'very girlie'. The latter phrase evokes the idea of the girlie magazine, particularly when connected to the pose this client is given. The profession evoked now is that most ancient profession (Kipling, 1888/1983), prostitution. Like Freddie, Roger can be read as a heterosexual man who knows what sort of woman is attractive:

> Generally I'm attracted to tall, long haired, beautiful women with slim figures and largish breasts. Strange huh? (Roger, 50, white British, heterosexual integrative psychotherapist)

These descriptions also offer a hegemonic view and one that, by the use of the word 'generally', fits many women and not just Lana. Roger implies

the attraction he feels is quite normal and uses an ironically worded rhe-
torical question as a call to agree. By stressing her physical attraction as
so hegemonic, he places himself squarely as a typical man. The appeal of
long hair, slim figures and 'largish' breasts is not explained. These features
come preloaded as attractive: it is inherent in the construct. By referring
to such preloaded features, he can create pressure to agree that she is
attractive. Neither man describes features like knees or ears that might
not be seen as such shorthand attributes of attraction. Nor is enough
detail given for us to refute her attractiveness. Like Freddie, Roger constructs the attraction as pre-existing, something that is brought into the
room by Lana, a position reinforced by her sharing her sexual attraction
towards him before he says what it is about her that is attractive. She is
thus also the agent of the attraction process: she starts it; he is the recipient of it.

The importance of the physical in attraction is seen in Simon's change
of attitude to his unnamed client:

> Initially there were no attraction issues, the client was down, dowdy, and
> presenting as totally non sexual to me. (Simon, 59, heterosexual integrative
> counsellor; ethnicity not shared)

> Part of this process was being able to talk about 'sex' and 'sexuality' in the
> counselling room. This talk, and faced with a client who now dressed and
> appeared smart and attractive and who openly wished to have a sexual
> experience with me, had the effect of sexually arousing me. (Simon)

Notice that the sexually explicit talk alone is not enough: her physical
appearance has to change too for her to become 'sexually arousing', and
it is she who *makes* the changes and he who *experiences* the effects of
those changes: again, the client is the agent of the attraction; and again,
the man is the passive recipient of it. Indeed, she has even usurped the
traditional male role of managing relationship development. Contrarily,
Tony apparently concedes he has a role in constructing the attraction:

> She took care over her appearance, she wore some make up, her physical
> appearance and her almost flirty manner I found attractive. (Tony, 45, white
> British, heterosexual psychodynamic counsellor)

Although acknowledging that he *found* these things attractive (not 'they
were'), the ordering of the sentence may give a clue as to where he feels
most of the responsibility lies. His part in the attraction comes last, not

first. The features are established, *flirtatiously* presented (an active position for the client, implying perhaps the motive of encouraging Tony to find her attractive), and then he reacts to them.

An apparently negative case is found in the narrative given by Arthur, who also seems not to react to the attraction:

> She wasn't immediately 'stunning' or excessively pretty. She was smart and although clearly in her forties had weathered well so to speak. (Arthur)

Again, the qualities and quantities of attraction belong to the client: the positioning is very different if the description begins with 'I did not experience her as . . .' rather than 'She wasn't'. What, however, Arthur *has* done is to engage with the same process as the other therapists; he has just arrived elsewhere. His narrative makes an assessment of Valerie's attractiveness based on hegemonic norms, firstly as a 'stunner' (a shorthand hegemonic term for an attractive and sexually available woman), then as an innocent, childlike 'pretty' figure and finally as an older, attractive woman. The second sentence can be read as stating the hegemonic 'truth' of attraction as age related, a position that Arthur may be uncomfortable with: the last three words acknowledge this as a borrowed phrase rather than his own.

So, physical attractiveness is something the clients seem to bring with them. The features described are preloaded with attraction; institutional masculinity rather than individual men reacts to these women. If things stay as they are, these men are expected by hegemonic masculine norms to take back agency and engage with this attraction. The obvious way to do this would be to engage directly with the attraction, especially where the client is mutually attracted, and to act on it. However, in the world both inside and outside psychotherapy, this can be frowned upon, especially if the therapist is in a relationship that is framed as monogamous. Further, psychotherapy forbids the enactment that masculinity expects. A conflict between selves could develop: fragmentation could occur. This attraction needs reframing, and quickly.

It's natural to be sexually attracted to a client: discourses of embodiment

> *We are sexual beings and this is part of how we relate to others, in my view.*
> *(Charlie, 51 white British, heterosexual gestalt counsellor)*

This fundamental position underlies the narratives and may therefore be regarded as a position close to the dominant discourses of the institutions of masculinity and psychotherapy. Charlie frames sexual attraction in a construct of men (and possibly, by implication, women; it depends who 'we' are) as sexual beings. Using discourses of embodiment and organic inevitability, he minimizes the possibility of another position. This rather bold statement ends with a rider that allows masculinity wriggle room should it be needed: there might be other points of view and perhaps, by implication, he could be persuaded to them. Tony also seeks to normalize the attraction he feels as an inevitable embodied reaction to an attractive woman:

> I am thinking about my own libido and how to be at ease with that part of myself both personally and professionally. So the attraction was part of that process. (Tony)

Tony shows how the attraction is used as part of his thinking about managing embodied sexual arousal. He draws a distinction between two institutions, one of which seems to be psychotherapy ('professionally'). The other is likely to be masculinity because of the sexual element ('libido'). With a meta-discourse of attraction being inevitable and part of the embodied male experience as a given, he implies an ongoing struggle to match the demands of the two institutions.

All in the mind: fantasizing about the client and imagining sexual enactment

> *I did have some sexual fantasies and I'm sure these affected my sex life but as far as I am aware not notably. I did not feel that the situation affected my personal relationship as I have a good, rich relationship and a satisfying sex life. (Charlie)*

This extract illustrates very clearly the interweaving of discourses to position sexual attraction. A number of positions seem to be taken in rapid succession here. Firstly, Charlie owns his sexual fantasies, confirming his status (and typicality) as a heterosexual male who knows how to react to an attractive female. He notes that these fantasies become transferred into his personal relationship, in which we can read through discourse of *counterbalance*, discussed further. Then, the first position is retracted and a new one is constructed in which he has a rich relationship with satisfying sex, hence lessening the impact his client is having. This position suits psychotherapy more comfortably than the first. If the client was having a sexual impact, then Charlie could be read as straying towards the unprofessional end of the professional hierarchy. In the second position, sexual fantasy is largely contained within appropriate boundaries and the relationship outside is warranted as successful (which raises his status as a successful man). Finally, he returns to the first position and reconstructs it using the discourse *retrospection of doom* (also described further), implying that different personal circumstances could have created more difficulty. This third position evokes a traditional message: behind every successful man is a woman. It seems that for Charlie to be successful with sexually attractive clients, a counterbalance of sexual outlet is needed and his partner provides that.

Part of the unease about sexual fantasies may be that they turn *rabbits* from a discourse in which the man is passive into one where he is agent. This could draw him rather too close to acting on the attraction, something psychotherapy will not tolerate. It is not likely that other institutions will react well either, not least monogamy. Indeed, even masculinity may not like the lack of control over emotion that acting out would represent because of damage potentially done to other practitioners: you don't let your mates down.

Hegemonic masculinity expects that if women activate sexual arousal, men should act on it. This is the classic lad-mag scenario of uncomplicated sex (Penny, 2007). Fortunately, two discourses can be, and are, accessed by our participants to both prevent acting out becoming an issue, supporting monogamy as a reason not to act, and avoid the inflicting of damage on constructs of masculinity. Echoing one of the defences deployed by the ego to manage internal conflict in the psychodynamic paradigm, therapists can 'displace' sexual attraction elsewhere.

Counterbalance: the displacement of sexual enactment

The 'elsewhere' is onto wives and partners. It is almost as if these wives/partners are required by the construction of their gender role in these narratives to take some responsibility for the management of this sexual tension. There is an underlying discourse that implies that, if femininity caused this masculine reaction (the assumption that underlies the discourse *rabbits*), femininity should be responsible for its management.

Bill's narrative makes the link between wives and clients and between *all in the mind* and *counterbalance*:

> The erotic transference occurred briefly after perhaps two of the sessions
> . . . when first answering your questions noted that the source of this was
> an image of a photograph of my wife when young. (Bill, 69, white British,
> heterosexual integrative counsellor)

'The' (not 'my') erotic transference occurs (apparently independently; no agency is present) and is retrospectively connected to his wife. Thus, his wife becomes embroiled in the attraction. It might be *Maggie* sat in the session, but it is his *wife* who is the past object being reflected in this client. With this identification in mind, we are told:

> The fantasy would have been (briefly) about having sex with her. There was arousal that I was aware of during one session and briefly afterwards. (Bill)

Bill's words suggest a defensive discourse to manage anxiety and feelings of guilt/shame about transgressing boundaries. It is as if the fantasy would seem less unprofessional if it is really about his wife rather than the client. Bill's words frame these events as a small aberration, a moment of reverie in which the resemblance to his wife dominates the space. The fantasy and arousal are diminished by the repeated use of 'briefly'. However, unease oozes from this extract, indicating perhaps some conflict between masculine and professional roles. Bill does not own the fantasy and the arousal: they are independent objects positioned away from him. Without the context, the second sentence could be about the client's reaction to *him*.

Perhaps Bill's unease is because the sexual attraction has continued to be positioned in the client and he is experiencing the arousal directly about her, and in the sessions, regardless of whether she is a transferential object or not.

> Thankfully, I am in a committed relationship which is fulfilling so I think that also helped firm the boundary. I wonder how it would have felt if I'd been out of relationship for a while. Probably more distracting. (Arthur)

Like Charlie, Arthur draws on the *retrospection of doom* ('Thankfully' and the second sentence) to show how dangerous this all could have been without his committed relationship, although his professionalism remains intact: there would have merely been more distraction. This relationship shores up his ability to resist. Dominic also counterbalances the attraction for a client by sex with his wife, making the connection explicit:

> I feel that through the most challenging periods I noticed a need to make love with my wife on the night before I saw Hazel and that if suppressed sexual tension was picked up in the room I probably tried to 'cleanse' this feeling in reaffirming my sexual bound with my wife through sex as well. (Dominic, 41, white British, heterosexual psychodynamic counsellor)

Dominic and Arthur show how sexual displacement can be explained as therapeutically valid, a necessary element in managing the attraction. The position taken shows them to be sexually virile, aware of their clients as sexually attractive, and alluring enough in themselves to attract wives and partners. Masculinity is happy, especially because the sex described is so focused on male needs. The displacement of sexual tension is positioned as therapeutically advantageous to the client, which satisfies psychotherapy that the practitioner is a safe pair of hands. Any argument that the wife/partner is being objectified as a source of sexual release is weakened by the implicit discourse that femininity caused this problem, and femininity should help solve it (the discourse of *rabbits*). That sex is happening somewhere else helps the male not to have sex with the client, as masculinity will acknowledge monogamous resisting of temptation. However, resisting sexually available females when no alternative is on offer is subject to challenge as a low-status masculine position and potentially places pressure on men to act.

The *Retrospection of Doom*

In managing sexual attraction to clients, *the retrospection of doom* can shore up *counterbalance*. There is a deal here: masculinity will agree with psychotherapy that therapists need not have sex with their clients if *counterbalance* is legitimized. However, no such agreement stands without this position being available. *Retrospection of doom* is used to make veiled threats to psychotherapy as to what *could* happen if 'legitimate' embodied masculine needs are not met. This device has been accessed by Dominic and Arthur (as discussed earlier) and by Simon:

> I am now 50+, have no sexual hang-ups, and no unmet needs in that area.
> If I was in my prime and handling such a delicate and explosive relationship
> I would not like to say what would have happened. (Simon)

The *doom* scenario supports discourse that pervades the structure of psychotherapy warranting age and experience. A younger and more inexperienced man, by implication, would have such sexual hang-ups and would therefore be unable to handle this therapy. Simon may be past his prime, but this is a position that brings advantages. While still sexually active, and so still exhibiting high-status masculinity, Simon can also use his age to raise his professional status: older therapists are a safer pair of hands. More subtly, Roger cautions:

I had to pay closer attention to my process to not let those feelings interfere in the therapy by blinding me to what she needed to achieve in therapy. (Roger)

Roger uses *doom* to show that he is working harder than usual (but not at the limits of tolerance ['closer']; that position might undermine his expertise) to ensure that the therapy stays on course, demonstrated by his opening oblique reference to internal supervision. But reading between the lines, a veiled warning can be seen that warns of embodied affect overriding coming professional identity.

Contraindicators

The client may also be legitimately resisted as a sexual object if the man can find some good reason, based on a perceived flaw in the female object, not to act: Arthur, for example, initially thinks his attractive female client is lesbian. Bill notes contraindicators very early on:

Curiously there were aspects of her presentation which I did not permit to get in the way. She was a smoker and this odour permeated her presence at times; her pallor was pale and unhealthy.

This extract blends *contraindicators* (the second sentence) with unconscious processes (especially 'Curiously' in the first sentence) to create a position in which Maggie only appears attractive in the therapeutic relationship, seen through the lens of transference. When later he does not act out, the groundwork is already laid that, actually, she is not attractive at all, so any potential conflict with masculinity's agenda is avoided. Having established that Lana was physically attractive but not emotionally so, Roger adds:

She was clearly willing but being married to a depressive, I didn't want another one in my life. The sad loneliness would have most probably turned into neurotic clinging. She dropped clear hints that she wanted to fuck me if I was willing. I made it clear that I was not.

Roger's narrative makes it clear that his decision is not about his virility, masculinity or confidence to seduce her. She is 'clearly willing': he need only say the word. The decision to turn her down is made in his own self-interest, and a clear act of agency and congruent with constructs of heterosexual hegemonic masculinity that portray sex as uncomplicated and focused on male needs. Roger is considering Lana as a woman rather than a client and therefore masculinity has had the final say on not acting out, rather than psychotherapy.

Freddie offers perhaps the most candid contraindicator of them all:

> The client showed no indication that she was attracted to me. Indeed as I wrote before, she seemed to be warning me off. Had she been open to the idea however, or showed any indication that what I felt was mutual, then things might have been more challenging. Had I been single, I guess seduction could have been a distinct possibility. She was that hot!

Freddie's narrative vacillates whether the attraction is or is not mutual. In contrast with Roger, Freddie is in a low-status position where he seems to be unattractive to 'the client'. There is no danger of acting out because she is not interested. However, Freddie's masculinity is rescued by deploying *doom* and *counterbalance* in the penultimate sentence. He may not be having sex with *the client*, but that he is having sex elsewhere is implied. Further, the client is given very high status indeed as an attractive woman, which positions her rejection of Freddie as more reasonable and places him in a position where other men might be inclined to empathize rather than judge.

Concluding Thoughts

Previous literature on sexual attraction in the therapeutic dyad has emphasized discourses from psychotherapy: transference, training, supervision, the prizing of intimacy in the dyad. Our analysis has shown that discourses of masculinity also play an important, perhaps crucial, role in the management of sexual attraction between male heterosexual therapists and their clients.

By deploying the discourses we have described, supported by devices such as fantasies and contraindicators, therapists can respond to sexual feelings in ways that are congruent to dominant constructs of heterosexual masculinity, protecting the patriarchal dividend, without any inappropriate acting out being required. Psychotherapy can approve of this outcome and is gently encouraged to support this management process by reminders through *doom* of what might happen were the process to be challenged. The client may be safe(r) from acting out by the therapist, but she continues to be sexually and physically attractive.

Because sexual attraction and sex roles can be constructed as inevitable, the discourse of *rabbits* can position physical attraction in the female client. By positioning sexual attraction as pre-existing, the woman (and womankind) becomes responsible for it. Gabbard, an influential voice on the subject of inappropriate enactment of sexual attraction, articulates the standard response to attraction in unequivocal terms: 'We . . . can never blame the patient for the analyst's transgressions. The patient has no professional code of conduct and is entitled to test the limits of the analytic setting' (Gabbard, 2006, p. 199). However, Gabbard's underlying assumption is still that the attraction is situated in the client. The positioning of responsibility on clients is widespread in psychotherapy: Schaverien (1997) notes that female analysands in the early days of psychoanalysis were seen as 'needy and seductive' (p. 5). McCartney (1966), cited by Masson (1988), describes the behaviour of female patients who *require* him to act out their sexual transference. This discourse perpetuates the position that the client is the cause of the response the therapist feels. Psychotherapy accepts the *feelings* as legitimate; only the *enactment* of them is not permitted. There is potential conflict with masculine discourses that describe sexual arousal as a naturalistic embodied experience. Responsibility for this conflict can then be placed in the female client. Thus, men who enact sexual attraction inappropriately may be able to retain a masculine position of strength and resistance, of going down fighting against unassailable odds.

Ongoing experiencing of sexual attraction, despite a moratorium on enactment, meets masculine needs. Responding to sexual attraction addresses gender role conflict (O'Neil et al., 1986) and the masculine protest (Adler, 1927/1992). Fragmentation is averted and conflict avoided.

Psychodynamic therapists understand anxiety as a communication that repressed material is rising into conscious awareness and appreciate that if one can bear this anxiety and pay attention to the rising material, then the anxiety can be relieved by engagement with the de-repressed material. This requires the rejection of defensive anxiety-reducing strategies. The place where institutional discourses interact is in individuals, who are inevitably going to experience times when conflicting discourses are incongruent in their attitudes, values and expected behaviours. By paying attention to this conflict, signalled by moral and neurotic anxiety, the individual has the opportunity to recognize the fragmentary nature of the self and perhaps exercise some agency to engage with this. Attention could become focused on the discourse that constructs identity, not on the individual identity that is the result of it.

We refrain from ending this chapter with clinical strategies in the belief that any such strategies direct attention away from engagement with, and possibly challenge to, institutional discourse and back to imagined deficit in the individual.

The title of this chapter was taken from the film *The Italian Job* (1969), directed by Peter Collinson, a film that famously ends with an unresolved cliffhanger as a coach hangs precariously over a huge drop, balanced by stolen gold at one end and the thieves who stole it at the other. By not providing an ending, Collinson has encouraged over 40 years of debate. Inspired by Collinson, and similarly refraining from offering solutions, we hope that others will be inspired to examine wider socio-cultural influences on the practice of psychotherapy by men and that individual therapists will be able to recognize anxiety as a signal to explore personal experience and, in particular, sexual attraction of discourse more deeply.

References

Adler, A. (1927/1992). *Understanding human nature*. C. Brett (trans.). Oxford: Oneworld.

Bartell, P., & Rubin, L. (1990). Dangerous liaisons: Sexual intimacies in supervision. *Professional Psychology, Research and Practice*, 21(6), 442–450.

Benwell, B. (2003). Masculinity and men's lifestyle magazines. In B. Benwell (Ed.), *Masculinity and men's lifestyle magazines*. Oxford: Blackwell Publishing.

Breuer, J., & Freud, S. (1895/1974). *Studies on hysteria* (The Penguin Freud Library, Vol. 3). Harmondsworth: Penguin.

Burman, E., & Parker, I. (1993). *Discourse analytic research: Repertoires and readings of texts*. London: Routledge.

Butler, J. (1999). *Gender trouble: Feminism and the subversion of identity* (2nd ed.). London: Routledge.

Collinson, P. (1969). *The Italian job*. London: Oakhurst Productions/Paramount British Pictures.

Connell, R. (1995). *Masculinities*. Cambridge, UK: Polity Press.

Davies, B., & Harré, R. (1990). Positioning: The discursive production of selves. *Journal for the Theory of Social Behaviour*, 20(1), 43–65.

Edelwich, J., & Brodsky, A. (1982). *Sexual dilemmas for the helping professional*. New York: Brunner/Mazel.

Fairclough, N. (1992). *Discourse and social change*. Cambridge, UK: Polity Press.

Freud, S. (1915). Observations on transference love. In P. Gay (Ed.), *The Freud reader*. London: Vintage.

Gabbard, G. (1994). Psychotherapists who transgress sexual boundaries with patients. *Bulletin of the Menninger Clinic, 58*(1), 124–135.

Gabbard, G. (1996). *Love and hate in the analytic setting.* Northvale, NJ: Jason Aronson.

Gabbard, G. (2006). Miscarriages of psychoanalytic treatment with suicidal patients. In A. Cooper (Ed.), *Contemporary psychoanalysis in America.* Arlington, VA: American Psychiatric Publishing.

Gay, P. (1995). *The Freud reader.* London: Vintage.

Gilbert, L. (1987). Female and male emotional dependency and its implications for the therapist-client relationship. *Professional Psychology, Research and Practice, 18*(6), 555–561.

Giovazolias, T., & Davis, P. (2001). How common is sexual attraction towards clients? The experiences of sexual attraction in counselling psychologists towards their clients and its impact on the therapeutic process. *Counselling Psychology Quarterly, 14*(4), 281–286.

Gough, B. (2004). Psychoanalysis as a resource for understanding emotional ruptures in the text: The case of defensive masculinities. *British Journal of Social Psychology, 43*(2), 245–267.

Halter, M., Brown, H., & Stone, J. (2007). Sexual boundary violations by health professionals – An overview of the published empirical literature. *Council for Healthcare Regulatory Excellence.*

Hamilton, J., & Sprull, J. (1999). Identifying and reducing risk factors related to trainee-client sexual misconduct. *Professional Psychology, Research and Practice, 30*(3), 318–327.

Henriques, J., Hollway, W., Urwin, C., Venn, C., & Walkerdine, V. (1984). *Changing the subject: Psychology, social regulation and subjectivity.* London: Routledge.

Kardener, S., Fuller, M., & Mensh, I. (1973). A survey of physicians' attitudes and practices regarding erotic and non-erotic contact with patients. *American Journal of Psychiatry, 130*(10), 1077–1081.

Kipling, R. (1888/1983). *Soldiers three.* Harmondsworth: Penguin.

Ladany, N., O'Brien, K., Hill, C., Melincoff, D., Knox, S., & Petersen, D. (1997). Sexual attraction toward clients, use of supervision, and prior training: A qualitative study of predoctoral psychology interns. *Journal of Counseling Psychology, 44*(4), 413–424.

Levant, R. (2001). The crisis of boyhood. In G. Brooks & G. Good (Eds.), *The new handbook of psychotherapy and counselling with men: A comprehensive guide to settings, problems and treatment approaches* (Vol. 1). San Francisco, CA: Jossey-Bass.

McCarthy, J., & Holliday, E. (2004). The counselling and help-seeking of males: A diversity perspective. *Journal of Counselling and Development, 82*(1), 25–30.

McCartney, J. (1966). Overt transference. *Journal of Sex Research, 2*(3), 227–237.

Masson, J. (1988). *Against therapy*. London: Fontana.

Noel, M. (2008). Sexual misconduct by psychologists: Who reports it? *Dissertation Abstracts International: Section B: The Sciences and Engineering*, 68(10-B), 6975.

O'Neil, J., Helms, B., Gable, R., David, L., & Wrightsman, L. (1986). Gender Role Conflict Scale: College men's fear of femininity. *Sex Roles*, 14(5/6), 335–350.

Parker, I. (1992). *Discourse dynamics*. London: Routledge.

Penny, J. (2007). Making multiple masculinities in men's magazines: Constructions and portrayals of 21st century man and attendant implications for counselling psychology. *Counselling Psychology Review*, 22(2), 5–13.

Pollack, W., & Levant, R. (Eds.) (1998). *New psychotherapy for men*. New York: Wiley.

Pope, K., Keith-Speigel, P., & Tabachnick, B. (1986). Sexual attraction to clients: The human therapist and the (sometimes) inhuman training system. *American Psychologist*, 41(2), 147–158.

Pope, K., Levenson, H., & Schover, L. (1979). Sexual intimacy in psychology training: Results and implications of a national survey. *American Psychologist*, 34(8), 682–689.

Reich, W. (1968). *The function of the orgasm: Sex-economic problems of biological energy*. London: Panther.

Rodolfa, E., Hall, T., Holms, V., Davena, A., Komatz, D., Antunez, M., & Hall, A. (1994). The management of sexual feelings in therapy. *Professional Psychology, Research and Practice*, 25(2), 168–172.

Schaverien, J. (1997). Men who leave too soon: Reflections on the erotic transference and countertransference. *British Journal of Psychotherapy*, 14(1), 3–16.

Seto, M. (1995). Sex with therapy clients: Its prevalence, potential consequences, and implications for psychology training. *Canadian Psychology*, 36(1), 70–86.

Wester, S., & Lyubelsky, J. (2005). Supporting the thin blue line: Gender-sensitive therapy with male police officers. *Professional Psychology, Research and Practice*, 36(1), 51–58.

Wester, S., & Vogel, D. (2002). Working with the masculine mystique: Male gender role conflict, counselling self-efficacy, and the training of male psychologists. *Professional Psychology, Research and Practice*, 33(4), 370–376.

Wetherell, M., & Maybin, J. (1996). The distributed self: A social constructionist perspective. In R. Stevens (Ed.), *Understanding the self*. London: Sage.

13

An Elephant in the Room

*A Grounded Theory of Experienced
Psychotherapists' Reactions and
Attitudes to Sexual Attraction*

Maria Luca and Mark Boyden

Our idea for this chapter had been percolating for some time, mostly due to our own personal experiences of encountering client sexual attraction in our work. Sexual attraction, and in particular the reactions of experienced therapists to client sexual attraction towards them, is still a reasonably under-researched topic and one demanding attention. Evidence from discussions with colleagues suggests that sexual attraction in the therapy relationship is an elephant in the room. It is certainly a subject that induces fear, guilt and shame in therapists, resulting in avoiding exploring the phenomenon as the Markovic study in Chapter 15 also showed. As a result, the purposive (Covington, 2000), meaningful aspects of this therapy experience may remain elusive and the therapy itself incomplete.

The recent film *A Dangerous Method* (Cronenberg, 2011) reminds us of the risks therapists face in responding to the erotically charged therapy by becoming sexually involved with patients to the detriment of the therapeutic relationship. Central to a successful psychoanalytic treatment is the notion that if patients experience romantic feelings or 'fall in love' with their analysts, then the 'Oedipal transference' could be resolved, and patients, through the technique of optimal frustration stemming from unrequited love, would be helped to relinquish certain hopes for instinctual gratification (Davies, 2003).

As the centrality of sexual attraction has gained momentum in the literature, (Borys & Pope, 1989; Gabbard, 1994, 1995; Ladany et al., 1997;

Sexual Attraction in Therapy: Clinical Perspectives on Moving Beyond the Taboo – A Guide for Training and Practice, First Edition. Edited by Maria Luca.
© 2014 John Wiley & Sons, Ltd. Published 2014 by John Wiley & Sons, Ltd.

Pope, Keith-Spiegel, & Tabachnick, 1986; Rodolfa et al., 1994), the significance of the therapist's power and authority is reported to lend a certain sexual appeal. The personality and attributes, gender and sexual orientation of the therapist as contributing factors to sexual attraction developing in the dyad are also being continuously scrutinized (Lester, 1985; Schaverien, 1997). In recent years, some studies such as Ladany et al.'s (1997) document the troubling feelings of fear and guilt, reported by therapists, when they experience sexual desire towards a client. However, as Bonasia (2001) postulates, 'while it may be deemed perfectly normal for an analyst to have erotic feelings towards patients of either sex, psychopathology is . . . involved only if he acts out' (p. 249). While it is well documented in the literature that some therapists become sexually involved with their clients with the occasional involvement resulting in marriage, it seems that sexual involvement between therapists and their clients is declining (Borys & Pope, 1989).

In this chapter, we will illustrate, using a grounded theory method, how experienced psychotherapists of different theoretical modalities react and make sense of client sexual attraction towards them. As members of the therapy profession, psychotherapists, counsellors and psychologists seem to lack the confidence to engage in sexual attraction in ways that facilitate client process. As psychotherapists, we witness the most intimate dramas unfold in the security of the therapy relationship. We are infected and affected by our clients' worlds with negative and positive feelings stirred up in us, transporting us to the highs and lows of existence. If love, eros, romantic and sexual desires are characterized by a quality of reciprocity, or at least hope for reciprocity, then the question for the profession is how do we react/respond to our clients' sexual desires and to what extent can our reactions/responses be deemed therapeutic? We will present the results of a study that examined therapists' lived experiences of sexual attraction towards them.

Methodology

Two psychotherapists were recruited through selective sampling (due to their long experience of practice and supervising) for the pilot studies and to help develop sensitizing concepts. An additional 10 psychotherapists recruited through a snowball method signed a consent form to participate in the study. They had an average of 14.6 years' post-qualification experience ranging between 8 and 27 years. All were white, four were heterosexual men and one was gay, and five were heterosexual women. Two were humanistic, three integrative, one cognitive analytic/integrative, two psychoanalytic, one interpersonal/relational and one a transactional analyst. Nine were accredited psychotherapists with the United Kingdom Council for Psychotherapy (UKCP) and one with the British Psychoanalytic Council (BCP). Two held PhDs and two were in the process of completing. The inclusion criteria consisted of (1) being a psychotherapist with more than 5 years' post-qualification experience and (2) having experience of client sexual attraction in clinical practice. Ethical approval was granted from a university ethics committee and pseudonyms are used to refer to participants.

Data were analyzed using a constructivist grounded theory, along the lines of our epistemological position that recognizes the researcher's subjectivity and agency in the construction of the story presented in this chapter. Charmaz (2000) captures the constructivist researcher as 'the researcher composes the story; it does not simply unfold before the eyes of an objective viewer' (p. 522). Researcher observations prior to collection of data (what Blumer, 1969 has termed 'sensitizing concepts') were taken into consideration and scrutinized during the data analysis. Therefore, knowledge and readings acquired prior to conducting this research could not be postponed as Glaser and Strauss (1967) advocated. Embracing researcher and participant subjectivity, exercising human agency (Patton, 2002), as well as believing that these enrich and provide a meaningful and embodied understanding of human phenomena informed this study.

Our analysis of the data was influenced by the constructivist/ interpretivist paradigm advocating that 'human science involves understanding as interpretation' (Rennie, 1988, p. 134). This modern constructivist grounded theory actively repositions 'the researcher as the author of a reconstruction of experience and meaning' (Mills, Bonner, & Francis, 2006, p. 2). It is associated with 'a way of understanding that views people as existing within multiple horizons of meaning, as striving to make sense of their experience, as constituted by their cultural and historical context, as engaged in dialogue' (McLeod, 2001, p. 28) and as unique. In line with this principle, we employed Rennie's (2000) 'double hermeneutic' to deal with issues of agency such as the way a researcher chooses to represent, disclose and interpret participant experience. The double hermeneutic advocates that 'the participants are trying to make sense of their world; the researcher is trying to make sense of the participants trying to make sense of their world' (Smith & Osborn, 2003, in Nuttall, 2006, p. 434). Hence, 'the analysis of the data involved a "circling of consciousness" using immersion in the data, engagement, constant abstraction and reflexivity' (Luca, 2009, p. 200). These principles enhanced theoretical sensitivity, 'a multidimensional concept that includes the researchers' level of insight into the research area, how attuned they are to the nuances and complexity of the participant's words and actions, their ability to reconstruct meaning from the data generated with the participant' (Mills et al. (2006, p. 4). These were the main repository of ideas through which potential categories were identified until the conceptual frame had been built. We began developing sensitizing concepts (through open coding) from the initial generation of data from two interviews with experienced psychotherapists. This process is described as theoretical sampling (Charmaz, 1990) and helps researchers decide what data to collect next to help confirm or refute initial categories that emerge. Sensitizing concepts are synonymous with developing hypotheses grounded in the data, not from the researchers' own preconceived ideas about phenomena. Theoretical sampling indicated that experienced psychotherapists felt guilty, frightened and careful in working with sexual attraction. Paradoxically, the same therapists regarded sexual desire as it develops in therapy to have therapeutic potential. We felt that by interviewing more experienced psychotherapists of different theoretical modalities, we would maximize the views, similarities and differences between this group of practitioners. When interviews were completed and analyzed using open coding, we were able to develop and link concepts into conceptual groups (axial coding). Our theoretical framework developed through identifying the core categories (selective coding) that best captured the meaning of conceptual groups. A re-examination of data showed that there were no new conceptual perspectives in the data, a point of data saturation where the analysis was concluded.

To ensure trustworthiness of the research findings and data analysis, we adopted Elliott, Fischer, and Rennie's (1999) standards of good practice. These include 'trustworthiness of observations' found in researcher transparency and reflexivity and 'trustworthiness of researcher' (McLeod, 1995) where researchers create a secure base and participants perceive them as trustworthy. This was achieved through researcher involvement in the interviews and a dialogical approach to interviewing. Researcher transparency is a principle connected with researcher agency and subjectivity being made available to the reader through relevant disclosure. Reflexivity refers to both researcher 'ownership of perspective' (Elliott et al., 1999) and to 'self-awareness and agency within that awareness' (Rennie, 2004). Figure 13.1 shows the theoretical framework that developed, which will be discussed in the findings.

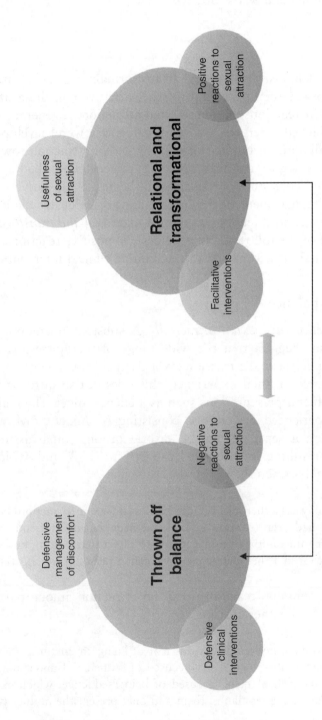

Figure 13.1. A grounded theory of experienced therapists' reactions and handling of sexual attraction.

Findings

The findings demonstrate that far from normalizing sexual attraction, experienced psychotherapists tend to react negatively in these situations, moralizing their reactions to client sexual attraction. A general picture of feeling destabilized emerged. Two core categories were developed from the analysis alluding to implicit or explicit sexual attraction towards the therapist: one category captures a lived experience described as *thrown off balance* and consisting of various sub-themes: (1) negative reactions, (2) defensive management of discomfort and (3) defensive clinical interventions. The second category was named *relational and transformational* and consisted of the following sub-themes: (1) positive reactions, (2) usefulness of sexual attraction and (3) facilitative clinical interventions.

Thrown off balance

Negative reactions to sexual attraction   A substantial amount of data from this study suggest that the wide range of therapists' reactions to implicit or explicit sexual attraction towards them from clients has thrown them off balance. In their experience, this does not seem to be the case with other difficult presentations such as a client's anger. The majority of therapists experienced discomfort, consisting of anxiety, awkwardness, confusion, fear, a sense of danger, disorientation, embarrassment and vulnerability resulting in a reduced capacity to think and avoidance in handling sexual attraction.

> In my early days as a therapist I didn't address it [sexual attraction] because I couldn't. I had been overpowered. I remember that it disoriented me. It left me feeling uncomfortable, and it was so direct that I didn't know how to respond to it in a therapeutic context or in a personal context (Hugh)

Fear was a common reaction to sexual attraction among participants in our study. As one therapist put it:

> At the forefront of my mind was this fear of being an unethical therapist, and – Oh my God! – what if I'm accused of seducing? I understand that women are terrified of being accused of being seductive, which explains why they placate the woman in them and only present the mother (Gail).

What also became clear was that some therapists' fear was captured in describing sexual attraction as 'too dangerous' as a therapist put it:

You are aware of a felt sense but it's too hot to handle, it's too dangerous, so you sort of park it and take a step back and say: "Okay, it's too hot to handle at the moment but I recognise you are there. I see you are important. I will come back to you after the session is over, but you are going to have to just stay there for a moment" (Kane)

Several therapists felt guilty if they believed that they might have unwittingly encouraged the client's desire, leading them to feel confused and guarded. Kane gave a very honest example, highlighting how his confusion over sexual matters in everyday life found its way into his therapy room:

As an adolescent I had terrible problems with it because [with] women dressed attractively, your instinct is to look and look and look, but the actual social propriety is that you mustn't look at all and you must pretend you are not being interested.

He went on to describe it as a double bind (Bateson, 1972) that, given the intimacy of the therapy situation, emerges naturally only to clash with the counterintuitive and decidedly asymmetrical constraints of the therapeutic relationship.

A number of participants handled the attraction by deflecting or ignoring its presence, stating that in such situations, they would not want to work with a client:

It would make me feel uncomfortable and unsafe, and I think I probably wouldn't want to continue working with them, to be honest with you. So maybe I have somehow prevented it from happening. I would see [sexual attraction] as interfering with the work rather than enhancing it . . . I have unconsciously tried to avoid it and tried not to let it come into the work (Caley)

Kyle also voiced his fears that the clients 'could see you as seductive. . . . It could be too much for them'. Another therapist, Pam, stated that 'I used to feel frightened and revolted and I managed them by going to see [my supervisor]. I managed them at the time just by acknowledging them; it was all I could do'. Hugh referred to training supervision, in which 'there was a time when it was scary for me to admit it, you mightn't be understood by your peers or by a tutor, you might be labelled'. He added that "talking about it, discovering that it was a common event, that it was human' came as a relief". Caley's description captures therapists' negative reaction to sexual attraction: 'I wouldn't want it in the room unless it erupted into the room'. The word eruption illustrates that it is only through force that sexual attraction could enter Caley's consulting room.

Defensive management of discomfort   One of the most universal responses among the therapists was that of fear: not just fear of behaving in an unethical way but of having the power to hurt the client experiencing unrequited sexual feelings for the therapist. In Omar's words, 'I don't think I really had the nerve to challenge him with what was going on'. Peter felt that 'one has to be able to hold the context and hold the intensity of the bubble. If you burst the bubble too early, you can shame the patient . . . but if you damage the context in the moment you have big problems, so the question is: how do you hold these two factors?' Pam would use a breathing technique to manage her discomfort: 'I would just sort of breathe through it'. This might be taken to indicate that the effect the phenomenon had on Pam may have been quite intense.

The data suggest that some therapists have formed the impression that sexual attraction must be handled 'differently' from other aspects of the therapeutic relationship in some often non-definable way. This might take the form of feeling they must inform the client that they did not share the sexual attraction or 'go professional', as Peter put it. This also seemed to result for some in espousing the notion that the best course of action is to ignore what seemed to be happening, based on the belief that saying anything at all would be harmful to the client: 'Unless it becomes an obstacle in the therapy – unless it becomes a resistance – if it's part of the flow, I don't see there is any particular point in naming it or doing anything with it actually' (Kane). Peter puts it as 'I think that I consciously forgot it (sexual attraction) so that I just had to deal with the other presenting issues'.

Defensive clinical interventions   It became evident from the data that by tightening up therapeutic boundaries, by becoming more formal and less relational with the client, the danger of sexual attraction becoming overwhelming could be contained:

> My demeanour would change. . . . . I would be much more authoritative. . . . I would become very firm, if I noticed a client displaying sexual attraction. Inexperience or fear . . . being out of your depth, can cause you to use the wrong interventions or have inappropriate understanding of your client, and they will sense that. (Gail)

Sanitizing sexual attraction was also a way of avoiding acknowledgement of it. This is captured in Caley's words: 'I always imagine that my clients look on me as a maternal figure rather than a sexual being . . . [or] like a goddess maybe. . . . idealization, yes'. Speaking of a specific client, Caley added the following:

> Whether it was something that he felt and suppressed or wasn't spoken about, or whether it came out in the form of idealisation. Because I know that I was very idealised in his mind. I think when you idealise somebody it can kind of take . . . It doesn't take the attraction away but it kind of makes it impossible to express it. . . . Some could be – what do you call it? – idealisation anything where there is an increased level of a sense of affection, maybe, that could have a blurred boundary to it.

Becoming firm with a client and keeping rigid boundaries can also tie in with another response elicited by the research findings. Therapists commented on 'bracketing' their own thoughts and responses: 'It's a kind of relaxation and disengagement. . . . This [SA] is not therapeutic for the person so I am not going to engage with this so I somehow manage to disengage myself. I do it physically. . . . It's a kind of relaxation' (Kane).

Relational and transformational

Positive reactions to sexual attraction Although virtually all therapists experienced some level of discomfort, a minority of them found the fact that a client was sexually attracted to them to be a narcissistically validating experience. Therapists described a boost of confidence as well as feelings of affirmation, arousal, excitement, enjoyment, flattery and power. In some cases, this positive experience was associated with shame in what was seen by them as a pathological narcissistic need to be validated by a client in this way. Their reaction to this kind of validation was therefore paradoxical and is associated with the therapeutic ethos that as therapists, if seduced or flattered, we should not act upon our own needs for validation and focus on a professional handling of client erotic desires.

Gail mentioned a number of positives – in addition to anxieties – about working with sexual attraction. She described a 'kind of arousal' emerging from a heightened sense of working relationally, which she understood to be a therapeutic response to a client's seductiveness and an opportunity to be seized to help the client understand their emotional situation. According to Gail, this arousal could cause a heightened level of stimulation in the therapeutic interaction, which could be an ally to the therapeutic alliance. At the same time, she described what she thought was the need for a skilled approach that only comes from experience:

> It is important that the therapist does not become caught up and seduced by the sense of personal gratification and validation; the intimacy of therapy lends itself to clients developing what they perceive to be sexual attraction towards the therapist. We need to recognise it as such, contain our feelings so that we don't become sexually involved with clients.

Omar, also referring to therapist validation, stated:

> Narcissistic gratification that as a therapist, you feel whenever . . . someone else feels attraction towards you, but you have to . . . put that in the context of where it is taking place, and be both mature enough to understand what it means and disciplined enough not to act upon it.

What is captured in the above-mentioned therapists' descriptions is a kind of tension between the idea that sexual attraction can deepen the work, but at the same time, as therapists, we should not act upon our own needs to be validated or gratified.

Sue also highlighted, from an analytic standpoint, that working openly with client sexual attraction could bring a dimension of humour into the therapy, even though her remark could also be seen as a defensive reaction:

> The idea of having erotic dreams about me so intrigued him that every time he had one he brought it into therapy and we used it as material. He was quite astounded . . . but we both thought it was rather funny actually.

Usefulness of sexual attraction   Some therapists' descriptions of how they managed sexual attraction in their work illustrate that despite their discomfort, they found it useful. They made use of their discomfort by becoming more interested in reading, talking to supervisors and generally enhancing their knowledge of sexual attraction. The example from Pam shows her positive attitude to sexual attraction: 'it's that slightly kind of rabbit in the headlights moment, but safely done it's incredibly useful'. Sue, in a rather ironic tone, stipulates what she perceives to be a common occurrence in older male therapists but includes a positive connotation to it:

You get an awful lot of older male therapists, particularly attractive or not particularly attractive, attracted to the rather young, pretty female clients. What a "surprise"! What a surprise as they (also) would be attracted to them in real life; it's what they do with the feelings of attraction [as professionals in the consulting room] that's enormously important and if handled carefully it can benefit clients.

As well as arousal, other positive aspects of working with the client's sexual attraction in the room, as Gail saw it, were 'vitality' and the sense of 'feeling more alive'. 'It makes you feel connected', she added. It also brought about personal and professional growth in the therapists. Not only Gail but also Peter, Omar and Kyle all began to delve into more literature about working with sexual attraction, gaining not only practical knowledge sitting in the consulting room with a client but also multi-perspective theoretical knowledge as well. Hugh commented that 'Theory is used to inform the intuitive feelings now'. Kane felt more able to discuss sexual attraction with colleagues and felt he gained some confidence. These therapists also said they regarded what they learned both theoretically and practically as a catalyst for growth and development. It is worth noting here that all these therapists except Kane incorporated a large proportion of psychoanalytic theory in their way of working.

Facilitative clinical interventions   Despite their immediate discomfort to sexual attraction, some therapists stated how they managed to become motivated and learned to handle it. They reported using some clinical interventions they had found facilitative, such as *responding with non-shaming delicacy, normalizing sexual attraction, discussing sexual attraction safely, collaborating openly with the client, understanding and working openly with sexual attraction.*

Peter aptly put it: 'everything can be talked about but with a non-shaming delicacy and "going professional" doesn't do that. I think if you talk about it earlier on its kind of there and it's just ordinary'. This very delicate approach seems geared towards both keeping the therapeutic alliance intact and making it clear that the therapist is both hearing and understanding the client, meaning that the client experiences less discomfort in addressing what is still seen as 'a hot potato' in Kyle's description. Hugh favoured delicacy in approaching sexual attraction, rather than the previously discussed flexing of the frame: 'Putting a boundary in kindly, was important; specifically because I did it kindly; I didn't reject, I didn't scare, I didn't prohibit and I made what he knew to be the case explicit, so hopefully I also did it safely'. Hugh also discussed the idea of asking the client to explore the notion of 'What do you need from me, or what do you need from yourself, to be able to make that a positive experience for you?' As Gail stresses:

> We have created such a taboo of the sexual aspect of being human; and it is a normal experience that can be transformational for the client; if we don't fear it and normalise it instead it can potentially help the client.

Kane refers to a paradox, with underlying anxiety, in working with sexual attraction: 'I would suggest that's a good thing to be open, but of course it opens the door to Pandora's Box in some ways'.

Some therapists spoke about how they learned from experience to use more facilitative clinical interventions than when they were relatively inexperienced: 'I made mistakes that I've learned from. . . . I would have done it differently if it were now. Understanding it more and acknowledging it in an open, but sensitive manner' (Gail). Hugh also speaks of being more open with sexual attraction now than in his past experience: 'I would bring it into the arena now . . . I am now quite comfortable about the fact of sexual attraction in the room'. As Omar described:

> They have to tell you . . . things that might be embarrassing or difficult . . . and [if] you then ignore them or you don't respond to them by trying to understand them, . . . then I think you are letting them down.

The theoretical framework that we developed has led to the emergence of some clinical strategies in handling sexual attraction.

Clinical Strategies in Handling Sexual Attraction

- If a client is sexually attracted to you and you feel the timing is right to open this up and explore, do so with a sensitive, non-shaming attitude to prevent client defensiveness. The risk of clients becoming defensive decreases if an alliance has developed.
- Be mindful of the language you use in bringing client sexual feelings to the fore, as this will impact on whether the client enters into dialogue or closes up altogether. If this is the first time you broach the subject, it is more effective if you offer your understanding tentatively, as food for thought rather than 'this is how it is'. Tentative interventions invite clients into collaboration with the potential of deepening the work.

- In reflecting about a client's sexual desire and the feelings it evoked in you, consider how your interventions and behaviour are in the best interests of your client or to gratify your own needs. If the latter, discuss with a supervisor, colleague or a therapist.
- Managing client sexual attraction by tightening the frame through becoming more authoritative, firm, intellectualizing or disengaging may communicate fear and avoidance to clients, than willingness to treat all client material seriously. If afraid or uncomfortable, try to understand and situate your fears. This will help you manage your feelings better so they do not get in the way of professionally handling sexual attraction.
- If you feel immobilized or detect a reduced capacity to think, talk to a supervisor or colleague. An impasse can be defused once acknowledged to open the way to creative, effective therapeutic dialogue.
- Clients' therapy will only go so far as the therapist is able to travel. Examine your attitudes to client sexual attraction as these will impact on the level of depth you are psychologically prepared to delve into. A closed, judgemental or rejecting attitude may not be in the best interests of your client. Sexual attraction is part of the human condition and will inevitably find its way into the consulting room. Normalize it if you detect it in a client. It has the potential for transformational work.
- At times, it is appropriate to note sexual attraction, but not discuss with the client, if judged to be detrimental. Appropriate timing of openly working with sexual attraction is also important and can only be judged by the therapist.

Concluding Thoughts

This study demonstrates the paradoxical feelings and challenges, including moralizing, discomfort, embarrassment, confusion and vulnerabilities, that working with sexual attraction poses for therapists. Sometimes the thorny issue of sexual desire in therapy hastily brings therapy to an end, as one participant disclosed. The therapists in our study were *thrown off balance* when they encountered sexual attraction in their work. Some viewed the experience as a dangerous enemy threatening their equilibrium, while others felt it as an ally, with transformational qualities that could deepen the work. Being on the receiving end of client sexual attraction led some therapists to a reduced capacity to think, therefore becoming less able to facilitate a client's process. Some, especially the humanistic participants, managed their discomfort by denying the existence of client erotic desires, or worse, ending the work with a client due to fear of acting out inappropriately. Therefore, being thrown off balance led participants to a more defensive management of their discomfort such as becoming more authoritative, firm, intellectualizing, disengaging and sanitizing their responses and focusing instead on other issues, away from the sexual attraction. Therapists' reactions in this study resonate with Freud's (1910) idea that therapists must 'develop the thick skin we need' (Bonasia, 2001, p. 250) to control our amorous affective responses to client erotic desires. However, as Bonasia (2001) maintains, 'instances of sexual acting out are also a consequence-the most conspicuous, but certainly not the only one-of the silence that has fallen upon sexuality and the sexual counter-transference' (p. 251).

Participants thought back to the past and how, when relatively inexperienced, they were more avoidant, embarrassed and anxious, resulting in feeling immobilized and unable to do any work around sexual attraction once it manifested in therapy. This suggests that the more experienced they are, the less likely therapists will avoid handling sexual attraction. In a paradoxical fashion, some therapists made use of their negative reactions to sexual attraction by becoming motivated to learn how to handle it. Some sought the advice of supervisors, while others took it to their personal therapy, as the feelings were too intense to handle in supervision alone. Not all participant experiences were negative. Some mentioned the potential usefulness, vitality and transformational quality that sexual attraction can bring to therapy if utilized appropriately for the client's benefit. The positive reactions from some participants included the feeling of arousal and vitality that sexual attraction from clients induces, while stressing the importance of being mindful and not falling into the trap of narcissistic gratification. A number of participants rose above their fear and anxiety and used facilitative interventions to handle sexual attraction. These included responding sensitively and in a non-shaming delicacy, normalizing sexual attraction, working openly with sexual attraction in a safe way, collaborating with clients and showing understanding, rather than fear when on the receiving end of client erotic desire.

In conclusion, therapists in this study who tolerated the intensity and openly worked with sexual attraction reported that it led to greater understanding and integration. In contrast, those who found the experience intolerable reported a loss in their capacity to think, at times resulting in premature termination. Ethics and professionalism were the driving forces in participants' reactions and handling of sexual attraction, a finding consistent with previous studies (Ladany et al., 1997; Pope, Sonne, &

Holroyd, 1993). By not attending to what might be implicit or explicit sexual desire, we ultimately deny clients the opportunity to explore their emotional needs as they present themselves through sexual attraction. Therapists recognize increasingly that love, eroticism, romantic and sexual desires are central to the therapy process but often go unrecognized or neglected by therapists who feel inept or fearful in giving them the centrality they deserve. It is therefore fundamental that training programmes include modules on handling sexual attraction in therapy, as Harris and Timm in Chapter 8 recommend.

References

Bateson, G. (1972). *Steps to an ecology of mind: Collected essays in anthropology, psychiatry, evolution, and epistemology. Part III: Form and pathology in relationship*. University of Chicago Press, 1999, originally published. San Francisco, CA: Chandler Publishing.

Blumer, H. (1969). *Symbolic interactionism*. Englewood Cliffs, NJ: Prentice Hall.

Bonasia, E. (2001). The countertransference: Erotic, erotised and perverse. *International Journal of Psycho-Analysis, 82*(2), 249–262.

Borys, D., & Pope, K. (1989). Dual relationships between therapist and client: A national study of psychologists, psychiatrists, and social workers. *Professional Psychology, Research and Practice, 20*(5), 283–293.

Charmaz, K. (1990). 'Discovering' chronic illness: Using grounded theory. *Social Science and Medicine, 30*(11), 1161–1172.

Charmaz, K. (2000). Grounded theory: Objectivist and constructivist methods. In N. Denzin & Y. Lincoln (Eds.), *Handbook of qualitative research* (2nd ed., pp. 509–535). Thousand Oaks, CA: Sage.

Covington, C. (2000). Opening the mind to reality. *Journal of Analytical Psychology, 45*(1), 21–37.

Cronenberg, D. (2011). *A dangerous method*. Film. Retrieved from http://www.imdb.com/title/tt1571222/

Davies, J. M. (2003). Falling in love with love: Oedipal and post-Oedipal manifestations of idealization, mourning and erotic masochism. *Psychoanalytic Dialogues, 13*(1), 1–27.

Elliott, R., Fischer, C. T., & Rennie, D. L. (1999). Evolving guidelines for publication of qualitative research studies in psychology and related fields. *British Journal of Clinical Psychology, 38*(3), 215–229.

Freud, S. (1910). *The future prospects of psychoanalytic theory*. London: Hogarth Press.

Gabbard, G. O. (1994). Sexual excitement and countertransference love in the analyst. *Journal of the American Psychoanalytic Association, 42*(4), 1083–1106.

Gabbard, G. O. (1995). The early history of boundary violations in psychoanalysis. *Journal of the American Psychoanalytic Association, 43*(4), 1115–1136.

Glaser, B., & Strauss, A. (1967). *The discovery of grounded theory*. London: Weidenfeld and Nicolson.

Ladany, N., Melincoff, D. C., O'Brient, K. M., Hill, C. E., Knox, S., & Petersen, D. A. (1997). Sexual attraction toward clients, use of supervision, and prior training: A qualitative study of predoctoral psychology interns. *Journal of Counseling Psychology, 44*(4), 413–424.

Lester, E. (1985). The female analyst and the erotized transference. *International Journal of Psycho-Analysis, 66*, 283–293.

Luca, M. (2009). A therapist's portrait of a clinical encounter with a somatizer. In L. Finlay & K. Evans (Eds.), *Relational centred research for psychotherapists: Exploring meanings and experience*. London: Blackwells.

McLeod, J. (1995). *Doing counselling research*. London: Sage.

McLeod, J. (2001). *Qualitative research in counselling and psychotherapy* (reprinted, 2006). London: Sage.

Mills, J., Bonner, A., & Francis, K. (2006). Adopting a constructivist approach to grounded theory: Implications for research design. *International Journal of Nursing Practice, 12*(8), 8–13.

Nuttall, J. (2006). Researching psychotherapy integration: A heuristic approach. *Counselling Psychology Quarterly, 19*(4), 1–16.

Patton, M. Q. (2002). *Qualitative research and evaluation methods* (3rd ed.). Thousand Oaks, CA: Sage.

Pope, K. S., Keith-Spiegel, P., & Tabachnick, B. G. (1986). Sexual attraction to clients: The human therapist and the (sometimes) inhuman training system. *American Psychologist, 41*(2), 147–158.

Pope, K. S., Sonne, J., & Holroyd, J. (1993). *Sexual feelings in psychotherapy: Explorations for therapists and therapists-in-training*. Washington, DC: American Psychological Association.

Rennie, D. L. (1988). Grounded theory: A promising approach to conceptualization in psychology? *Canadian Psychology, 29*(2), 139–150.

Rennie, D. L. (2000). Grounded theory methodology as methodical hermeneutics – Reconciling realism and relativism. *Theory and Psychology, 10*(4), 481–502.

Rennie, D. L. (2004). Reflexivity and person-centered counseling. *Journal of Humanistic Psychology, 44*(2), 182–203.

Rodolfa, E., Hall, X., Holms, V., Davena, A., Komatz, D., Antunez, M., & Hall, A. (1994). The management of sexual feelings in therapy. *Professional Psychology, Research and Practice, 25*(2), 168–172.

Schaverien, J. (1997). Men who leave too soon: Reflections on the erotic transference and countertransference. *British Journal of Psychotherapy, 14*(1), 3–16.

Smith, J. A., & Osborn, M. (2003). Interpretative phenomenological analysis. In J. A. Smith (Ed.), *Qualitative psychology: a practical guide to research methods* (pp. 51–80). London: Sage.

14

Therapists' Disclosures of Their Sexual Feelings to Their Clients

The Importance of Honesty – An Interpretative Phenomenological Approach

Anna Marshall and Martin Milton

This book is testament to the fact that sexual feelings in therapy warrant our attention – both as therapists and also as researchers. The literature shows that therapists' sexual attraction towards their clients is a common occurrence in that most therapists feel sexually attracted to a client at some point in their professional lives (Gabbard, 1994, 1995; Pope et al., 1986). These sexual feelings could be described as a mixture of 'real' and transferential feelings between client and therapist (Gelso & Carter, 1985). Regardless of the origins, it is at the therapist's discretion whether or not their sexual feelings are disclosed to the client.

The British Psychological Society's (BPS) *Ethical Principles for Psychologists and Code of Conduct* (2009) highlights that psychologists should refrain from engaging in a sexual relationship with clients. It does not, however, include any guidelines on *disclosing* sexual feelings to the client. Its guidance is that psychologists should 'restrict the scope of disclosure to that which is consistent with professional purposes' (p. 11). The word 'restrict' gives therapists the responsibility to decide what they feel is appropriate to disclose. It is the therapists' responsibility to ensure that their actions are always undertaken in an ethical manner.

In light of this, this chapter reports on a study that explores sexual attraction and self-disclosure. To do this, the chapter will look at

Sexual Attraction in Therapy: Clinical Perspectives on Moving Beyond the Taboo – A Guide for Training and Practice, First Edition. Edited by Maria Luca.
© 2014 John Wiley & Sons, Ltd. Published 2014 by John Wiley & Sons, Ltd.

definitions and then explore relevant literature. The chapter will then present the findings of the study.

Sexual Feelings

It will always be a challenge to define sexual feelings as they vary from person to person. However, for the purpose of this chapter, we will define sexual feelings as a subjective desire to be sexually intimate with another. It has been noted that 84% of therapists develop sexual feelings towards a client in practice (Pope et al., 1986; Rodolfa et al., 1994). This is different from sexual 'involvement' of course. The rate of sexual involvement between therapist and client appears to be in decline (Borys & Pope, 1989). It is clear that there is a substantial difference between *having* sexual feelings and *acting on* them. However, the two have not always been understood as separate and thus has resulted in therapists feeling guilt, fear and embarrassment around acknowledging these feelings (Ladany et al., 1997).

Historically, when sexual feelings between therapist and client have been written about, they were almost exclusively conceived of as transference or countertransference. Freud (1915, 1963) explained that a therapist's erotic feelings towards a client were a reaction to the client's transference, a phenomenon associated with the therapy. The therapist's feelings were a direct response to the client's and not their own individual feelings. Freud acknowledged that 'transference love' occurs frequently and advised that it should be repressed and not acted out as it could potentially destroy therapy and damage the relationship (Freud & Jung, 1974). Many psychoanalysts have attempted to adhere to Freud's teachings. However, important as this is, strict guidelines potentially lead the therapist to feel guilty and ill-equipped to appropriately manage the transference feelings.

Mental health professionals have adopted a variety of ways to manage sexual feelings. Some discuss feelings in supervision or therapy, while others manage their feelings by disclosing them to their clients (Pope et al., 1987; Stake & Oliver, 1991). When adopting this second strategy, two crucial steps have been suggested to help. The first is to 'normalize' sexual feelings, that is, to help therapists become aware that these feelings will occur in their professional lives at some point. The second strategy is to separate out our conceptualizations of sexual feelings and sexual involvement, suggesting that the profession approach these two states differently from one another (Bridges, 1998; Gorton, Samuel, & Zebrowski, 1996; Hamilton & Spruill, 1999).

Self-Disclosure

There is a long-standing debate whether self-disclosure (of anything, not just sexual feelings) of the therapist is beneficial to the therapeutic process (see Spinelli, 1995). In the last 30 years, there has been a shift from the intrapsychic approach to the interpersonal (Stolorow et al., 1987), which does of course require practitioners to consider when, why and how to self-disclose. One of the key principles of counselling psychology, object relations theory, existential psychotherapy and client-centred therapy is to focus on how the therapist is in relation with the client (Duffy, 1990). Like others, Horvath and Bedi (2002) found the therapeutic relationship plays a significant role in achieving positive outcomes for therapy. Thus, more therapists are considering and using self-disclosure as a tool to relate in therapy. Jourard (1971) described self-disclosure as permitting the true self to be known to others – and this includes an understanding that what we experience and what may be disclosed are influenced and affected by the person we are in relationship with. By expressing ourselves to others, we draw a more intimate relationship with them. However, it could be argued that therapists' self-disclosures would disrupt the therapeutic process and bring intrusion of reality at the expense of the personal and psychological material. Another concern is that the motivations behind the therapists' disclosures are often unclear and therefore they have a potential to confuse the needs of the client with therapist's needs (Hanly, 1998). In cases where there has been sexual misconduct, self-disclosure is seen as the first step towards crossing the boundary of sexual involvement (Gutheil & Gabbard, 1993, 1998; Simon, 1995; Somer & Saadon, 1999). As noted previously, self-disclosure of sexual feelings does not indicate that there will be sexual involvement between therapist and client; the majority of self-disclosure cases are thought not to have led to transgressions (Gabbard, 2001; Simon, 2001).

While we can acknowledge these different perspectives, it is clear that self-disclosure is practised among therapists; however, it seems that few therapists disclose their sexual feelings (Fisher, 2004). Davies (1994) discussed a case study where she disclosed her sexual feelings to a male client in order to help the client see how he could be sexually desired and reduce his revulsion around sexual feelings. The client's initial reaction was one of horror. However, Davies eventually saw her self-disclosure as a success. She reported that the client was able to experience eroticism in a new arena where his feelings were acknowledged and accepted and were separate from his own feelings of revulsion. Slavin et al. (1998) discussed another case where a therapist developed sexual feelings towards his client who was abused as a child. The client began to sense his feelings and responded negatively by refusing to talk with him. He eventually disclosed his feelings to her, which validated the patient's perception of his sexual feelings. The disclosure facilitated a discussion around the client's fear of sensing sexual feelings but simultaneously feeling unable to talk about them, which echoed the previous abusive relationship. The honesty in the therapeutic relationship led to therapeutic benefits.

Gabbard (1994, 1996) suggests that many therapists get stuck in the predicament between silently managing their sexual feelings and self-disclosing their feelings to the client. Fitzpatrick (1999) highlighted that there is often a middle ground when managing sexual feelings. She worked with a client who had low self-esteem and he began to question in sessions whether she had sexual feelings for him. Fitzpatrick was aware that silence could reinforce his self-hate; equally, she recognized that disclosure could confuse or gratify him and disrupt therapy. She decided to comment on their rapport and explained that she had 'loving feelings' towards him. She concluded that a choice of words can enable a practitioner to be 'explicit without causing confusion over boundaries' (p. 123). However, it is difficult to know where the middle ground lies and it comes down to the therapist's own understanding of 'middle ground'. Pope et al. (1993) highlighted the importance of a therapist having a therapeutic rationale when considering disclosing such feelings to the client (see also Spinelli, 1995).

At this point, the chapter will look at our research study, which asked the question, how do therapists self-disclose their sexual feelings to their clients?

The Study

This study aimed to explore (1) how therapists understand their sexual feelings for a client and (2) how they decide to disclose their sexual feelings to the client. We used interpretative phenomenological analysis (IPA) for several reasons. The study is phenomenologically oriented and IPA is a method that tends to lead to findings of the kind that practitioners find useful. IPA explores how one experiences an aspect of the world and makes sense of that world (Smith, Flowers, & Larkin, 2009). IPA is an integrative approach – while prioritizing participants' responses, the researcher also adopts an interpretative role (Smith et al., 2009). Ethical approval was granted by the Faculty of Arts and Human Sciences at the University of Surrey. The inclusion criteria required therapists to have disclosed their sexual feelings to a client but not acted on their feelings during the therapy.

The four research participants were all therapists with a formally recognized accreditation or were eligible for accreditation by the United Kingdom Council for Psychotherapy (UKCP), the BPS and the United Kingdom Association of Humanistic Psychology Practitioners, (UKAHPP). Two were male and two female, aged between 30 and 50 years old. All participants had at least 3 years of post-qualification clinical experience.

Semi-structured interviews were used in this research and to allow participants the freedom to express themselves. The schedule was developed to cover three broad areas: (1) the development of sexual feelings towards the client, (2) the process in which therapists made the decision to disclose their sexual feelings and how the feelings were presented and (3) exploring the impact the disclosure had on the therapeutic process and relationship.

The semantic content and language was explored in each transcript, and keywords or phrases were used to encapsulate the essence of the data and these were transformed into themes. This was repeated for each transcript and resulted in master themes.

The recommendations of various authors (Smith, 2004; Smith, Jarman, & Osborn, 1999; Yardley, 2000) are followed to establish credibility. The reader should note that all identifying information has been removed to ensure confidentiality. Pseudonyms have been used for the participants.

Findings

The interviews identified several themes around the therapists' disclosures of their sexual feelings, and this chapter focuses on one prominent theme: *honesty in the therapeutic relationship*. This master theme has been broken down into several sub-themes and the relationship between them and is presented in a diagram (see Figure 14.1).

Honesty in the therapeutic relationship is the overarching theme in the data. As Julia exclaimed:

> A moment where you are completely honest with each other; I felt like it was a bit of a relief, it felt like it was really, like a genuine moment.

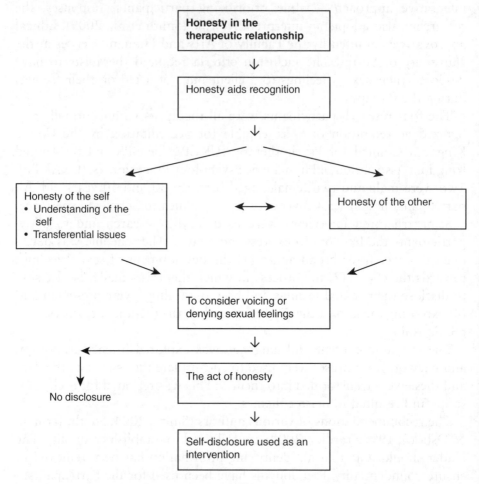

Figure 14.1. The therapists' process of self-disclosing their feelings.

This overarching theme 'contains' various sub-themes, including *honesty aids recognition, honesty with the self, honesty with the other, consider voicing or denying sexual feelings* and *the act of honesty*.

Honesty aids recognition

This sub-theme highlights how the participants felt that honesty around themselves, clients and therapeutic relationships led them to recognize their sexual feelings. Once the feelings were recognized, there was a need to explore them. Mark described his attempts to unpick his sexual feelings when a client had a resemblance to a former partner. He said, 'This is not the person I had a relationship with 15 years ago, it's a different person. You always have to acknowledge that'.

So Mark acknowledged his sexual feelings in relation to his client and separated them from his past relationship.

Honesty with the self

This theme addresses the participants' awareness of their feelings and their exploration as to why these feelings occurred. Sarah gives an example of this. She remembers her thoughts during a session:

> I was aware that I was attracted to him, [. . .], I wasn't sure if it was coming from him or not, [. . .] but it might be just coming from me. Because I thought oh this is just my stuff. You know if I met him in a social situation I would be attracted to him.

Sarah demonstrates that confusion can occur when exploring where the sexual feelings originate from. If the feelings are from the therapist, they take on a different meaning than erotic countertransferential feelings. One's own feelings inform the therapist about themselves, whereas the transferential feelings are informative about the client's process. In this extract, Sarah attempts to explain why she had these sexual feelings:

> At the time I wasn't in a relationship, I was lonely and when I do erotic transference workshops that I teach, what I write is that if the client is attracted to you "what's that about?" But if you are attracted to the client, all the things you need to look at, are: are you lacking something in your life, because if it is, you have to go and deal with it.

Sarah suggested it is useful to consider the reason for sexual feelings occurring in a therapeutic relationship. She felt her sexual feelings were related to a sense of personal loneliness, suggesting sexual feelings can occur when there is something 'lacking' in a person's life. She stated 'you have to go and deal with it' indicating that a therapist's feelings is something the therapist needs to deal with and that having sexual feelings in the therapeutic relationship is problematic.

Henry was curious about the intensity of his sexual feelings for his client, making him question whether he was having a midlife crisis. He said, 'So feeling this deeply about a client in this sexually charged way is new for me [. . .] Am I having a midlife crisis?'

Reflection can lead to a consideration of negative, worrying possibilities, but this is not all. Julia also considered that the sexual feelings were due to her vulnerability and highlighted that the client's vulnerability 'touched' something in her. Julia's use of words, such as 'touch', also demonstrated the intimacy in the relationship. She said:

> It was probably his vulnerability that touched something in me and perhaps I got in touch with my own vulnerability and perhaps that's what he was triggering in me.

Julia felt that the client 'was triggering' her vulnerability, suggesting that her sexual feelings developed from the relationship with her client, not solely from her personal issues.

A consequence of the therapists' being *honest with the self* is that it is felt to lead to a deeper understanding of the countertransferential element of the feelings. Mark and Henry explored the countertransferential aspect of the therapeutic relationship to understand their feelings in greater depth: Henry said:

> The counter-transference of my own narcissistic wound where my mother is beautiful and she was a cold fish and I feel rejected [. . .] and they are both around the thirty mark which is how old my mum was when she had me.

Mark similarly felt that his feelings towards a client were related to a past romantic relationship. 'So these qualities reminded me of [. . .] my past girlfriend [. . .] this definitely initiated positive transference in terms of how I saw the client'.

In summary, the therapists were aware of their sexual feelings and felt it important to explore whether these feelings were transferential or feelings originating in their personal histories. The participants who 'owned' their sexual feelings felt there was a reason for their feelings and that they were due to something lacking in their lives.

Honesty with the other

As well as these therapists' explorations of their own sexual feelings, they formulated and explored the client's presentation in an attempt to understand the feelings. Therapists' reflections of their work with clients help in understanding their own sexual feelings:

I [. . .] felt the client was quite scared, I don't want to use the word fragile, I'm not sure if it is the right word, I know what an enormous effort it was for him to allow himself to become attached to someone. (Julia)

Julia understood that it was 'an enormous effort' for the client to form a relationship. Thus, part of her attraction was that she felt privileged that the client had chosen her to 'attach' himself to. She said, 'On my part it made me feel a bit special because you know, I felt quite privileged. It brought out some feelings in myself as well as towards him'.

Mark understood his client to be misunderstood. He said:

The impression I got [. . .] was that she was feeling quite lonely, she was feeling quite angry, a low motivation, didn't care about anything. Didn't have many friends in her life. Didn't feel understood.

Thus, Mark's sexual feelings could also have derived from a need to be the one to understand the client.

When trying to understand the client's possible influence on these feelings, Sarah discussed how clients with a history of sexual abuse tend to push boundaries within the therapeutic relationship, which can lead to sexual feelings developing in the relationship:

[. . .] I've noticed [. . .] that it is quite often in the room and [. . .] it's like in that sort of compulsion to repeat. [. . .] it comes up on you, if I flirt with you, are you going to act on that and I think it is part of the therapy, its therapeutic.

Sarah is invoking the idea that when one has sexual feelings for a client it is possible that the client is 'acting out' his or her issues with the therapist. This also warrants consideration.

The theme *honesty aids recognition* has highlighted how therapists' honest reflection can lead to a recognition and understanding of *both* therapists' and clients' feelings.

As seen in Figure 14.1, once therapists are open to themselves about the presence of sexual feelings and consider what meaning they might have, the next theme is relevant. This was termed 'consider voicing or denying sexual feelings'. This theme addresses how therapists think about sexual feelings and self-disclosure. Some therapists discussed how they made their decision to disclose their feelings. While the option of not speaking about them was possible, therapists felt obligated to be, as they saw it, honest and genuine with their clients, that the idea of *not* being honest could damage the therapeutic relationship. Julia states:

> One human being who asked another human being, can you like me after everything after all the personal things I have told you [. . .] I couldn't in good conscience say no.

There are a few ideas to note in this extract. Firstly, Julia felt obliged to express her feelings; she had to be honest. To deny her feelings would feel like a rejection. Secondly, Julia views the interaction as 'one human being who asked another human being'. The labels of 'therapist' and 'client' are not significant, creating a more intimate interaction. Similarly as follows, Sarah indicates that she is almost obliged to disclose her feelings as she acknowledges that she is a very special person in (the patient's) life:

> I am a very special person in her life and I'm not going to deny that. I'm not going to deny her that.

The consequences (such as the possible breakdown of the therapeutic relationship or the rejection of the patient) of *not* being honest appear to be key in deciding to disclose sexual feelings to clients. When deciding whether to self-disclose or not, the therapists felt an obligation to the client or themselves to be honest and that to deny feelings could risk, or be, an act of rejection. Therefore, it was important not to deny their feelings.

The act of honesty

As shown in Figure 14.1, this theme is how the movement is made from the decision-making process to an act of self-disclosure. Julia felt a sense of relief:

> you have to contain the clients thoughts, feelings and wishes as well as your own in therapy and [to] have a moment where you are completely honest with each other; I felt like it was a bit of a relief, it felt like it was really, like a genuine moment.

Julia illustrates the struggle inherent in therapists containing feelings and the difficulty in deciding the appropriateness of self-disclosure. Julia found the process difficult and experienced the self-disclosure as positive ('genuine'). Sarah said, 'My take is to be honest and then to work with, [. . .] I'll see on their faces their reaction'.

Sarah found she could work through the client's response; thus, it felt safe to disclose. Thus, the act of being honest was a relief and was understood to be the most appropriate decision. The desire for the act of honesty is an initial stage in the process of disclosing and the therapist can take the opportunity to explore the impact of the self-disclosure with the client.

Self-disclosure of sexual feelings is experienced as a process extending beyond the verbal – and this leads to the final sub-theme, *self-disclosure as an intervention*. Participants speculated as to how their self-disclosure impacted on the client, the relationship and the process of therapy. Mark viewed his self-disclosure positively. He said, 'It had a positive impact not only for this session but generally for the working alliance as well'. Mark stated that he 'would do it for any other client', illustrating that it is not something exclusive to this client. He viewed self-disclosure as a therapeutic 'tool'. Julia felt that the disclosure could be healing to the client: 'He felt he could actually be liked and be loved if he showed people who he truly was'.

Sarah used her self-disclosure and relationship as an intervention 'to show him you can have an attraction [but] you don't have to act on it, if it's not appropriate. He told me that it was really, really significant the work he had done with me'. Sarah adds that the therapist should only use self-disclosures to help the client:

> You have to keep in mind the ethical implications of it [. . .], you knew that these feelings could only be used in the benefits of the therapy [. . .] and I have to use it in a way that would help my work.

This theme can only be speculative, of course, as the therapists are reporting their clients' experience. But it is clear that therapists feel that their self-disclosure played a significant part in the therapeutic process.

Discussion

These findings highlight two important aspects. Firstly, sexual feelings in the therapeutic relationship are complex, with varied meanings for the therapist, client and the relationship. Secondly, self-disclosure of sexual feelings is a relational act.

These findings illustrate the fact that these feelings – and what to 'do' with them – can be confusing as they pertain to the meaning they have, that is, whether the sexual feelings are related to the individual therapist, whether they are transferential or a mixture of both.

The feelings that were considered transferential appeared to feel more manageable as the formulation can assist therapists in understanding why these feelings occurred and what they mean, as if therapists can detach themselves from the feelings. This process can demystify and reduce the romance of the sexual feelings. In this transferential dimension, the therapist's interventions and responses are less controlled and this could be when the therapist feels encouraged to self-disclose his or her feelings.

It is, of course, difficult to separate 'transferential' feelings from one's own feelings, as feelings are unique to the individual and it is possible for feelings to be understood as both at the same time. Bergmann (1987) stated, 'I have found that the transferential love is a very early and dependent form of love, such love is not unknown in real life but they are ill suited to the slings and arrows of everyday experiences. Transference love can be the beginning of a capacity to love but by itself it is not life equivalent' (p. 225). Mann (1997) believed there is little difference between authentic and transference love. He viewed them as both genuine and real feelings that can occur both in the therapeutic setting and in other settings.

Our study suggests that the sexual feelings that are thought to 'belong' to the therapist might be more confusing and potentially problematic. Rodolfa et al.'s (1994) survey found that over half of the participants reported that authentic sexual feelings made them feel anxious and guilty. Adrian (1996) also found that these sexual feelings could be so intense that they leave the therapist feeling anxious and uncomfortable as if the feelings were unethical. It could be that when therapists experience their sexual feelings to be 'authentic' or 'individual', they have a sense of vulnerability and exposure in the therapeutic relationship. Therapists were more inclined to explore the meaning of feelings as a way to manage their anxiety or guilt.

From the participant's perspective, the experience of self-disclosure was viewed positively, reinforcing findings in existing literature. Asheri (2004) highlighted the importance of the therapist's exploration of the client's sexuality and erotic desires and that shying away from their own feelings can encourage the client to withdraw. She believed that being able to show your humanity by being honest in the therapeutic context is part of the most intimate process between client and therapist. This is supported in these findings. Similarly, Giovazolias and Davis (2001) found that the therapists who chose to disclose their feelings found their attraction to benefit the therapy compared with the therapists who did not disclose (disclosure is discouraged by Harris and Timm in Chapter 8).

A criticism, which could be applied to these research studies, ours included, is that they only explored the therapist's perspective of the experience of self-disclosure. Clients might have experienced therapist disclosure of sexual feelings differently. Therapists could potentially hold a biased opinion, as they were accountable for the disclosure. While, the therapists felt that they self-disclosed for the benefit of the client and not for their own needs or desires, it is clear that we do not know whether this captured the experience of clients or not. They understood their self-disclosure as a benefit for the client, but it was based on their own understanding, feelings and assumptions of the client and the relationship. One therapist described their self-disclosure of sexual feelings as a 'relief' which could be construed as a benefit for the therapist more so than the client. Many authors have argued that self-disclosure should not burden the client or put the client in the position where they feel they need to care for the therapist (Fisher, 2004; Pope et al., 1987). Gabbard (1994) highlighted that, even if the self-disclosure was ethically bound, there is still no way for therapists to know if their message was received in the way it had been intended to be received. This highlights the fact that the clients' experience of receiving therapist self-disclosure warrants research and reflection.

Strategies to Manage Sexual Feelings

Martin et al. (2010) developed a framework with certain components that they felt were fundamental to managing the therapist's sexual feelings towards the client. It involved five steps, which are detailed as follows:

- The therapist identifies his or her sexual feelings, which can be accompanied by secondary emotion such as anxiety, guilt and shame.
- The therapist understands that it is an emotion that is important to explore and he/she is motivated to explore and reflect on the feeling.
- The therapist reflects on his or her own processes and how he/she has become 'involved' with this feeling, reflecting on his/her current and past experiences and his/her own 'vulnerabilities'. In addition exploring the personal and professional implications of his/her feelings.
- Then moving to focus on the client, the therapist builds a formulation using his/her sexual feelings to inform the client's formulation. To seek further support from clinical supervision.

- Finally, using new understanding of the relationship with the client for therapeutic benefit and awareness of therapist sexual feelings as a therapeutic intervention whether it is 'explicit or not'.

Conclusion

The general consensus of all health professionals is not to act on any sexual feelings as it can cause immense harm to the client. However, there appears to be little consensus on how to *manage* such sexual feelings. This is an issue as sexual feelings are common and there are currently no guidelines around managing sexual feelings and how the therapist should understand such feelings. However, as Pope et al. (2006) noted, it may not be possible to have guidelines around a topic that is so specific to the individuals involved. As Asheri (2004) stated, feelings are not a linear process and there needs to be a fluidity and flexibility in this arena. Fear and embarrassment needs to be taken out of the therapist's sexual feelings so that calm reflection can lead to ethical therapeutic practice. A small-scale qualitative study like ours cannot hope to answer the question of 'is honesty the best policy' with any finality. But it does contribute to the important ever-continuing debate around whether or not to disclose feelings, as does the very existence of this book. We hope that readers will find a way to be open to their feelings – sexual or of any kind – and reflect on them thoughtfully and openly so that risk is minimized. Where self-disclosure of a therapist's sexual feelings is chosen, it can be construed as a way of being genuine, ethical and authentic with the client's best interest at heart. However, therapists would be encouraged to critically think about the possibility that every good therapist's intention does not necessarily produce a positive outcome.

References

Adrian, C. (1996). Therapist sexual feelings in hypnotherapy: Managing therapeutic boundaries in hypnotic work. *International Journal of Clinical and Experimental Hypnosis*, 44(1), 20–32.
Asheri, S. (2004). *Erotic desire in the therapy room, dare we embody it? Can we afford to?* Paper presented at the United Kingdom Council of Psychotherapy. Retrieved from http://www.yobeely.f2s.com/articles/eroticdesire.html
Bergmann, M. (1987). *The story of one man's quest to know what love is*. New York: Columbia University Press.

Borys, D., & Pope, K. (1989). Dual relationships between therapist and client: A national study of psychologists, psychiatrists, and social workers. *Professional Psychology, Research and Practice, 20*(5), 283–293.

Bridges, N. A. (1998). Teaching psychiatric trainees to respond to sexual and loving feelings. *Journal of Psychotherapy Practice and Research, 7*(3), 217–226.

British Psychological Society (2009). *Code of conduct 2006.* Retrieved from http://www.bps.org.uk/system/files/documents/code_of_ethics_and_conduct.pdf/

Davies, J. M. (1994). Love in the afternoon: A relational reconsideration of desire and dread in the counter-transference. *Psychoanalytic Dialogues, 4,* 153–170.

Duffy, M. (1990). Counseling psychology USA: Patterns of continuity and change. *Counselling Psychology Review, 5*(2), 8–12.

Fisher, D. (2004). Ethical issues in therapy: Therapist self-disclosure of sexual feelings. *Ethics and Behavior, 14*(2), 105–121.

Fitzpatrick, K. (1999). Terms of endearment in clinical analysis. *Psychoanalytic Quarterly, 68,* 119–125.

Freud, S. (1915). Instincts and their vicissitudes. In S. Freud (Ed.), *The standard edition of the complete psychological works of Sigmund Freud, volume XIV. On the history of the psychoanalytic movement, papers on metapsychology and other works* (pp. 109–140). London: Hogarth Press.

Freud, S. (1963). Further recommendations in the technique of psychoanalysis: Observations on transference-love. In P. Rieff (Ed.), *Freud: Therapy and technique* (pp. 167–180). New York: Collier Books.

Freud, S., & Jung, C. G. (1974). The Freud-Jung letters: The correspondence between Sigmund Freud and Carl Gustav Jung. In W. McGuire (Ed.), *The Freud-Jung letters: The correspondence between Sigmund Freud and Carl Gustav Jung* (pp. 17–581). London: Hogarth Press.

Gabbard, G. O. (1994). Sexual excitement and counter transference love in the analyst. *Journal of the American Psychoanalytic Association, 42,* 1083–1106.

Gabbard, G. O. (1995). The early history of boundary violations in psychoanalysis. *Journal of the American Psychoanalytic Association, 43,* 1115–1136.

Gabbard, G. O. (1996). The analyst's contribution to the erotic transference. *Contemporary Psychoanalysis, 32*(2), 249–273.

Gabbard, G. O. (2001). Commentary: Boundaries, culture, and psychotherapy. *The Journal of the American Academy of Psychiatry and the Law, 29*(3), 284–286.

Gelso, C., & Carter, J. (1985). The relationship in counseling and psychotherapy: Components, consequences, and theoretical antecedents. *The Counseling Psychologist, 13*(2), 155–243.

Giovazolias, T., & Davis, P. (2001). How common is sexual attraction towards clients? The experiences of sexual attraction of counseling psychologists toward their clients and its impact on the therapeutic process. *Counselling Psychology Quarterly, 14*(4), 281–286.

Gorton, G. E., Samuel, S. E., & Zebrowski, S. M. (1996). A pilot course for residents on sexual feelings and boundary maintenance in treatment. *Academic Psychiatry, 20,* 43–55.

Gutheil, T. G., & Gabbard, G. O. (1993). The concept of boundaries in clinical practice: Theoretical and risk-management dimensions. *American Journal of Psychiatry, 150,* 188–196.

Gutheil, T. G., & Gabbard, G. O. (1998). Misuses and misunderstandings of boundary theory in clinical and regulatory settings. *American Journal of Psychiatry, 155*(3), 409–414.

Hamilton, J. C., & Spruill, J. (1999). Identifying and reducing risk factors related to trainee-client sexual misconduct. *Professional Psychology, Research and Practice, 30*(3), 318–327.

Hanly, C. (1998). Reflections on the analyst's self-disclosure. *Psychoanalytic Inquiry, 18*(4), 550–565.

Horvath, A. O., & Bedi, R. P. (2002). The alliance. In J. C. Norcross (Ed.), *Psychotherapy relationships that work: Therapists contributions and responsiveness to patients* (pp. 37–71). New York: Oxford University Press.

Jourard, S. (1971). *The transparent self* (rev. ed.). New York: Van Nostrand.

Ladany, N., O'Brien, K. M., Hill, C. E., Melincoff, D. S., Knox, S., & Petersen, D. A., et al. (1997). Sexual attraction toward clients, use of supervision, and prior training: A qualitative study of predoctoral psychology interns. *Journal of Counseling Psychology, 44,* 413–424. doi: 10.1037/0022-0167.44.4.413

Mann, D. (1997). *Psychotherapy, an erotic relationship: Transference and countertranference passions.* New York: Routledge.

Martin, C., Godfrey, M., Meekums, B., Madill, A., et al. (2010). Staying on the straight and narrow. *Therapy Today, 21*(5), 11–14.

Pope, K., Sonne, J., Greene, B., et al. (2006). *What therapists don't talk about and why: Understanding taboos that hurt us and our clients.* Washington, DC: American Psychological Association.

Pope, K. S., Keith-Spiegel, P., Tabachnick, B., et al. (1986). Sexual attraction to clients: The human therapist and the (sometimes) inhuman training system. *American Psychologist, 41,* 147–158.

Pope, K. S., Sonne, J. L., Holroyd, J., et al. (1993). *Sexual feelings in psychotherapy.* Washington, DC: American Psychological Association.

Pope, K. S., Tabachnick, B. G., Spiegel, P. K., et al. (1987). Ethics of practice: The beliefs and behaviours of psychologists and therapists. *American Psychologist, 42,* 993–1006.

Rodolfa, E., Hall, X., Holms, V., Davena, A., Komatz, D., Antunez, M., Hall, A., et al. (1994). The management of sexual feelings in therapy. *Professional Psychology, Research and Practice, 25,* 168–172.

Simon, R. I. (1995). The natural history of therapist self-disclosure: Identification and prevention. *Psychiatric Annals, 25,* 90–94.

Simon, R. I. (2001). Commentary: Treatment boundaries, flexible guidelines, not rigid standards. *The Journal of the American Academy of Psychiatry and the Law*, 29(3), 287–289.

Slavin, J. H., Rahmani, M., Pollock, L., et al. (1998). Reality and danger in psychoanalytic treatment. *Psychoanalytic Quarterly*, 67(2), 191–217.

Smith, J. A. (2004). Reflecting on the development of interpretative phenomenological analysis and its contribution to qualitative research in psychology. *Qualitative Research in Psychology*, 1(1), 30–54.

Smith, J. A., Flowers, P., & Larkin, M. (2009). *Interpretative phenomenological analysis: Theory method and research*. London: Sage.

Smith, J. A., Jarman, M., & Osborn, M. (1999). Doing interpretative phenomenological analysis. In M. Murrey & K. Chamberlain (Eds.), *Qualitative health psychology* (pp. 218–241). London: Sage Publications.

Somer, E., & Saadon, M. (1999). Therapist-client sex: Clients' retrospective reports. *Professional Psychology, Research and Practice*, 30(5), 504–509.

Spinelli, E. (1995). On disclosure. *Journal of the Society for Existential Analysis*, 6(1), 2–19.

Stake, J. E., & Oliver, J. (1991). Sexual contact and touching between therapist and client: A survey of psychologists' attitudes and behavior. *Professional Psychology, Research and Practice*, 22, 297–307.

Stolorow, R. D., Brandchaft, B., Atwood, G. E., et al. (1987). *Psychoanalytic treatment: An intersubjective approach*. Hillsdale, NJ: Analytic Press.

Yardley, L. (2000). Dilemmas in qualitative health research. *Psychology and Health*, 15, 215–228.

15

Systemic Family Therapists' Narratives on Sexual Attraction in Their Clinical Practice

A Narrative Analysis

Desa Markovic

Introduction

Literature within systemic family and marital therapy on sexual attraction in therapy is limited. Two studies from the 1990s make a mention of the subject of sexual attraction in marital and family therapy (Brock & Coufal, 1994; Nickell, Hecker, Ray, & Bercik, 1995). Harris (2001) discusses teaching family and marital therapists about sexual attraction in therapy, stating that this is an under-researched area and that little has been written about it. A long-standing absence of systematic research on the topic and the importance of addressing it in supervision and training have been acknowledged to an extent (Farris, 2002). However, there still exists a gap in literature, research and clinical practice, and reference to these issues in the training of systemic therapists is minimal.

The aim of this chapter is to discuss the findings of a research study on systemic family therapists' accounts of instances of sexual attraction in their practice and the meaning they ascribe to these instances as well as the course of action they decided to take. In addition, my hope was to open up discussion on this taboo subject in therapy and to generate ideas and suggestions for improving practice. Clinical strategies are proposed based on the key findings of the research analysis.

Sexual Attraction in Therapy: Clinical Perspectives on Moving Beyond the Taboo – A Guide for Training and Practice, First Edition. Edited by Maria Luca.
© 2014 John Wiley & Sons, Ltd. Published 2014 by John Wiley & Sons, Ltd.

Research Method

I interviewed 14 participants recruited through networking within the community of professionally registered systemic family and couple psychotherapists in the United Kingdom. Post-qualifying experience ranged from 5 to 30 years. Many have been supervising and teaching for a number of years. All but one completed training in the United Kingdom. This was a diverse group originating from five continents with a mixture of gender, ethnicity and sexual orientation, with an age range of 40–65. Ethical permission was obtained to use excerpts from research interviews under pseudonyms for publication.

I applied narrative analysis as an appropriate method for eliciting rich narratives and detailed accounts of therapists' thoughts, dilemmas and feelings. Working with narrative material requires dialogic listening (Bakhtin, 1981) to three voices: the voice of the participant narrator, the theoretical framework, and a reflexive monitoring of reading and interpretation. Hypotheses were generated while reading and analyzing the narratives, enriching an 'ever growing circle of understanding' (Lieblich, Tuval-Mashiach, & Zilber, 1998). Interviews evolved in a conversational manner, coherent with the open and flexible nature of narrative analysis, aiming to generate reflection and to facilitate the telling of lived experiences as well as of constructed meanings through imagining hypothetical scenarios. In the final shaping of the results, equal attention was paid to the unique, idiosyncratic meanings and to the shared patterns and commonalities of the themes. Results are a set of storied meanings representing a variety of constructions situated in professional, social, cultural, familial and institutional discourses.

Discursive Themes: A Spectrum

This section summarizes the outcome of narrative analysis relating to the discursive themes that transpired from the accounts. The themes reflect a diverse range of ideas, practices, meanings and emotions rather than generalizations.

A variety of narratives emerged on a 'spectrum of attraction' as one participant phrased it, about the instances of sexual attraction in therapists' clinical practice. Within this spectrum, a range from complete absence of such instances to stories and experiences of strong attraction were described. This reflected both the diversity of systemic practice and consistency, in that examples of attraction were presented as exceptional rather than a regular situation. Discursive themes are summarized as follows.

Sexual Attraction Does Not Occur in Systemic Therapy

Many therapists were certain that sexual attraction never occurred in their clinical sessions. A range of explanations was given for this, such as age difference between therapists and clients; for example, a middle-aged male therapist said, 'Given my age and that most of my clients are children it's not unusual there is no sexual attraction. I think I'm attractive to clients in other ways' (Brian).

Furthermore, typical systemic working contexts such as child and adolescent family services were constructed as not allowing for sexual feelings to occur: 'The family service context with the child in focus may filter out certain clients who might be more flirtatious' (Vera). Often groups of colleagues are observing sessions, thus 'witnessing the relationship' (Olga). In addition, sessions are frequently video recorded which 'may make both parties feel contained by that' (Mia). A strong narrative emerged that 'individual work lends itself more to moments of intimacy than group work' (Tom). Some therapists constructed their position within the family context as 'feeling parental' rather than sexually attracted. Therapists in private practice also confirmed the importance of the environment and stressed that 'private milieu can help such feelings develop' (Robert). Adam stated, 'Something about working from home allows for such expression and fantasy. There is no receptionist, no formality, it's very personal'. Some concerns were expressed that within the current economic pressures in the British National Health Service (NHS) context, conversations on the intricacies of the therapeutic relationship are getting lost: 'and while it is so important to have that reflective space, it is considered as a luxury rather than necessity' (Dina).

A pattern of narratives suggested that a relatively rare and irregular occurrence of such a phenomenon directly relates to the nature of the systemic approach. Fascinating stories of comparisons and contrasts between systemic and psychodynamic approaches all pointed in the same direction in that these occurrences would be typical for psychodynamic ways of working as opposed to systemic practice. Olga, who works both psychoanalytically and systemically in different settings, commented, 'In my individual psychodynamic work I can think of many examples but in my systemic work I can't think of any'. Striking hypotheses developed about how therapists' positioning in the therapeutic relationship determines sexual attraction. Tim's comment, 'Perhaps I haven't been on a lookout for it', alongside Emma's, 'Perhaps because I haven't encouraged that talk very much', suggested that therapists' chosen focus shapes or even creates occurrence of this phenomenon. Petra's narrative further developed such thoughts in a compelling reflection on her past psychoanalysis:

> I was around 20 and I felt attracted to my therapist and talked about it to her; I didn't want a relationship with her but I thought I had to disclose this because this is what therapy was about so I was talking about her place in my life, dreams and fantasies I had about her and she would interpret. Now I think the style of therapy brought that forth. As I shifted in my theoretical orientation I found that people didn't have that level of interest in me. I realised transference was a theory and a social construct that brought something forth.

Emma expressed that systemic therapy is about 'real lives and real sexual communication', whereas when working within a psychoanalytic framework, it is 'about dreams, distant memories, and unconscious material which encourages building on fantasy'. Another angle to this hypothesis was that perhaps systemic therapists being transparent about themselves and demystifying their 'persona' makes them become 'less of an intriguing mystery figure inviting fantasy and desire' (Mia).

Within the context of contemplating the impact of the therapist's position on the occurrence of this phenomenon, another perspective was offered: that a systemic 'lack of vocabulary' for these situations relates to the focus on the world of a client where therapists are not a central figure.

A wider context's impact on limiting conversations about sexual attraction was considered and a narrative transpired about the suppressive nature of family and cultural upbringing, which constrains talking about sexual issues openly:

> In my family there was no permission to talk about sex and I didn't develop a grammar for it; the educational influence and then therapy training didn't help. I've been raised by a general culture of cover-up (Adam)

Robert hypothesized that the professional practice framework describing sexual relationships with clients as unethical closes down conversations about it: 'To discuss sexual attraction would be tantamount to unethical behaviour, almost regarded in itself as unethical as to do the deed'. He went on to speak of how legal and ethical contexts constrained therapists' language:

> The effect that the area of sexual abuse has on people is interesting; for example would you describe a young person as beautiful, attractive, funny . . . or are there other ways to describe them that you would resort to . . .?

Trust and safety in supervision were regarded as major factors in conversations about sexual attraction. Some therapists did not feel supported enough in a supervision context to discuss sensitive subjects such as sex. Brian, a systemic supervisor, felt 'interrogated' in group supervision:

> When I said I had felt "attracted" to a client, it was immediately understood as sexual. A supervisee became visibly tense and started interrogating me, almost as if I had been unethical. I said to her, your whole posture and tone of voice changed, and you didn't even ask what kind of attraction I was talking about . . .

Opposing narratives developed in relation to how sex as a topic influences sexual feelings. Therapists who reported an absence of discussions on the topic of sex in their sessions believed that talking about sex is more likely to evoke sexual feelings: 'If you enter into the field of sexual intimacy, passion, attraction and so on, you start to perceive the person as a sexual being and as a partner' (Dina). This was a hypothetical construction, contrasted to the lived experience of others who reflected that talking about sex in therapy desexualizes it: 'Talking about sex from a professional position in a boundaried and sometimes technical way takes out the mystique and the sexy elements' (Robert).

Attraction in Therapy Is Not Sexual and Forms Part of Therapy

Therapists seemed to find it relatively easy to recall experiences of attraction but queried its sexual nature. They questioned the definition of sexual attraction and how it differs from other forms of attraction. For example, Dan recounted:

> There were a number of instances when female clients have said to me: "You are easy to talk to"; or "You understand me"; these indicate some attraction but is it sexual . . .?

Many emphasized the difference between noticing and feeling attraction. Some clients' stories about unusual sexual practices and fantasies were so intriguing that it raised a question of another distinction, being sexually attracted by the clients' stories or the clients themselves.

Therapists' questioning of the meaning of sexual attraction drew attention to the complexity and the multifaceted characteristics of both sexual attraction and the interpersonal quality of the therapeutic relationship. Many therapists spoke of feeling attracted to clients in a variety of non-sexual ways. Expressions involved *admiration, mind attractiveness* and being *in tune with a client*, the latter described in the following story:

> I was seeing this family from Iraq, they came to the second session all dressed in black and they hardly talked, they were just crying and crying, they all were so . . . distressed. Finally the father managed to say their whole family was killed in a bombing. And I just cried with them, I couldn't even say anything. I didn't think they would come back. I was surprised when they did. We talked about how that session had been experienced and they said they felt secure and contained; it gave them lot of hope that I could feel their pain. (Philip)

Some therapists indicated an overlap between sexual feelings and feelings of closeness and intimacy, stating the difficulty of separating them out. Sonia hypothesized on clients' experiences in general: 'I imagine clients often have such feelings, a sense of gratitude or gentleness towards therapists'. A narrative that warm personal feelings equal good therapeutic experience was developed: 'If it was a positive relationship and if there were elements of flirting I wouldn't associate it with a sexualised context' (Tim). 'Therapy generates certain unique intimacy' (Olga). 'Therapy is a kind of special closeness' (Adam).

Internal Management of Sexual Attraction Is Sometimes the Best Option

The idea of handling issues of sexual attraction by internal processing was also expressed by a number of therapists. Some would choose to *minimize* or *pretend it's not happening*, advocating that addressing sexual attraction directly would potentially create more problems than it would resolve. The choice of such responses depended on therapists' perception of clients' benefit, but sometimes related to the therapist's doubt as to the best course of action. Therapists' uncertainty came across in some accounts where they admitted their 'puzzlement' and 'feeling uncomfortable' such as 'fear of exposure', being 'muddled and getting into a tangle', 'getting it wrong' and fearing being 'accused by clients', or 'the possibility of being misunderstood by clients, colleagues, professional bodies . . .'. There was a powerful narrative of a lack of guidance within systemic training and supervision as to the ways of effectively handling instances of sexual attraction, however rare they may be. Mia, who trained oversees, felt well equipped as the training was more focused on practical aspects of therapy. Her narrative emphasized that 'too much theory can get in the way of being proactive', while Dina was critical of the 'limited usefulness of the systemic approach', stating that 'there is no steady theory you can rely on or draw on when it comes to phenomena like this'.

A theme emerged that managing sexual attraction internally avoids exacerbation of the issue. Dan recalled talking with a client about her sexual attraction to him, which became 'an obsessive and overwhelming story in her life and took a while to resolve'. As a result, he subsequently became purposefully 'guarded' and 'cautious'. Vera proposed 'not making too much of every little comment a therapist can hear', illustrating this with an example where she decided to treat her male client's end of session comment 'Have a good Valentine's Day' as a remark reflecting a social custom to which she responded accordingly.

A general theme stressed the importance of responding sensitively to clients' vulnerability. Reflections such as 'therapists should just leave it' are related to previous instances where 'it didn't go well to pick up on'. Mia attempted to address a client's seductive and playful ways of relating to her: 'I tried to be gently reflexive but she heard it as an accusation, as something she shouldn't do'.

Sexual Attraction Can Positively Contribute to Therapy

A therapeutically resourceful way of using attraction as a tool towards therapeutic change was illustrated by the following story:

> About a year into therapy my client openly admitted she had sexual feelings towards me. I thought it was more than sex; it was love in a way. Working with this therapeutically over time became an important part of her recovery (Robert).

Some narratives embraced both the importance of being explicit about the boundaries in the 'domain of production' and exploring issues of attraction therapeutically within the 'domain of explanation' (Maturana, 1985). Tom gave an illustration of this 'both/and', a systemically crucial principle, by example of a long-term client who expressed her sexual desire towards him:

> I gave her a very strong message about professional boundaries and I believe that has enabled the relationship to continue. We talked about her feelings for me in many sessions and through these conversations she resolved them and was able to move on in her life and relationships.

Tim recalled a client who increased his awareness of his sexuality through therapeutic conversations:

> He came to one session revealing: "I realise I feel attracted to men . . . Conversations we were having helped me realise that." He didn't say he was attracted to me but he did say I was a great influence.

Vera gave an example of a woman flirting with her in couple therapy, which she decided to address explicitly, using systemic active exploratory curiosity. This led to more specific conversations regarding the client's feelings of being sexually ignored by her husband, which helped him explore his own inhibitions. This opened up the couple's 'frozen' sexual communication and over time led to enhanced mutual understanding of their sexual needs.

Gender narratives are sometimes used to encourage clients' reflexivity: 'When I talk with clients about their sexual relationships, I ask how it is to talk about it with me as a woman' (Olga).

A therapist reflecting on her position as supervisor stated:

> I often ask my students how they think clients might perceive them, as a mother, sister, teacher, or a potential partner . . . and how this might influence therapy (Dina)

Sexual Attraction in Therapy Is an Indication of a Problem

There was a pattern of problematizing sexual attraction in therapy. Meanings such as clients 'crossing the boundaries' or 'not respecting therapeutic contract', or therapists 'sending the wrong signals' or 'being inadequately provocative' related to sexual attraction in therapy as improper. A hypothesis was offered that sexual attraction 'is a distraction technique, as a means of clients avoiding important subjects' (Sonia). Another narrative linked personality disorder clients getting sadistic pleasure from putting the therapist in a difficult position: 'they have a sense of your vulnerability . . . they like to tantalize you' (Vera). This suggests that some therapists' understanding of the type of sexual attraction is linked to their psychological formulation of the client's problem.

Certain lived experiences of clients' attraction to therapists were described as 'tricky' and 'uncomfortable'. One therapist felt 'manipulated by the client'. Others described examples of clients' inappropriate sexual attraction resulting in a premature end of therapy. Some clients' relentless pursuing behaviour triggered therapists' enforcement of boundaries, and in one situation, an external consultant was called in for support. A therapist phrased her particular experience as 'stalking' given its intensity and level of intrusion, a subject discussed by Luca and Soskice in Chapter 10. She depicted being 'powerless, angry, and annoyed' by persistent messages from her ex-client. Another described 'getting stressed and confused between being playful and professional' with a client she 'liked very much' whose attitude to her was 'very seductive, using humour a lot', 'not sexual but somewhere on the edge' (Mia).

Stories of therapists' sexual attraction to clients were thoughtfully shared. Therapists resorted to self-supervision and consultations with supervisors, colleagues and teams to make sense of their feelings and consider the best way forward. A therapist reflected on her self-supervision following feelings of sexual attraction to a client:

> I started to notice my questioning was becoming intrusive, not reflective, asking questions out of perverse sexualised, selfish curiosity. When I realised what I was doing, I made a conscious decision that my behaviour was unethical so I was able to get back into being a therapist without muddling my focus . . . (Petra).

Another story revealed feelings of regret about responding to a client's invitation to extend professional boundaries by accepting her phone calls. Despite these being focused on issues related to therapy, he thought 'it became more than therapy for her; she was getting something from me that she didn't have from the partners in the past . . . and she became more dependent' (Tim).

Illustrations of misinterpretations and misconceptions of the therapeutic context as sexual were shared. Some therapists spoke of clients' sexualized ideas about therapy leading to their decision to discontinue after therapists' clarification of boundaries. As one therapist recalled, a first meeting revealed that the client assumed therapy involved something physical, openly acknowledging her sexual arousal in the room. A therapist recounted a client who brought a book to the first session: 'She said I should read this because it says the therapist's job is to have sex with clients to help them' (Dan). Another recalled a client telling of her sexual experiences in such a way that the therapist felt as if it was intending to arouse. A therapist working in a medical setting was left feeling grossly misunderstood when a connection he made with a young autistic client was interpreted as sexual:

> This girl wouldn't communicate with anybody and most of my colleagues were frustrated. One day I was exhausted after many attempts to engage her and I spontaneously started doing what she was doing; looking at the floor . . . then she started moving her arms and I was moving mine . . . One of the colleagues noticed this and I was immediately taken off the case. The psychiatrist thought I was being seductive sexually and that the patient may develop an unhealthy attachment to me. That was classified as sexual but it was beautiful; it did feel like attraction but not sexual, I was trying to communicate through her channels with her. We started to develop some form of communication and she was guiding me . . . (Adam).

Movement in Boundaries Should Be Ethics Led

Many accounts captured the importance of clarity of boundaries and therapists' transparency. Dina hypothesized whether, if a client expressed his/her sexual attraction to her, it would mean that 'therapeutic boundaries became too permeable'. Tom referred to his previous experience in social work as a resource for managing such situations:

> Working with vulnerable families I learned never to blur these boundaries. I used to do home visits to single mothers and some women would invite me into a relationship. In order to protect myself, I used to stick to a script.

While all therapists saw ethics as paramount, their understanding of what constitutes ethical behaviour widely differed. Discussing hypothetical and lived instances of mutual sexual attraction brought forth

another spectrum including contradictory ethical beliefs. Some participants formulated exclusive narratives about personal relationships
between therapists and clients as never being ethical under any circumstances, emphasizing differences in power above all. This was portrayed
by the following accounts: 'Taking advantage of a vulnerable person is
never right' (Emma); 'Because of the power differential it is wrong to start
a personal relationship' (Sonia); 'It is always unethical . . . as the context
of therapy is well defined; codes of ethics and practice are very clear and
predetermined' (Vera). On the other hand, two examples of mutual attraction continuing onto a personal relationship between a therapist and an
ex-client unfolded. I had prior knowledge of these situations and have
purposefully selected these therapists to be part of my participant group.
Both stories involved clients' keen initiative after the end of therapy and
therapists' thorough consultations with their colleagues, supervisors and
professional bodies. A male therapist has been married to his ex-client for
11 years now and they have two children. He insisted that during therapy,
his sexual attraction to the client was not on his mind; he was noticing
her beauty, but the focus was on his professional role as a helper. Before
entering into a personal relationship, he undertook thorough consultations with his colleagues, supervisors and professional bodies. A female
therapist had a personal relationship of several years with her ex-client,
which ended around 20 years ago:

> He spoke so openly about his feelings of attraction. I felt sexual energy
> myself . . . It's a stimulation of a very challenging piece of work which was
> highly emotionally and intellectually charged. When he said to me he was
> attracted to me and wanted to go out with me, I went to the registration
> body, the supervisors and the UKCP; they all concluded, with therapy finish-
> ing, there were clear boundaries.

These experiences offered a narrative that mutual attraction between
therapists and clients can lead to a personal relationship if extensive
professional consultations considering the particular circumstances were
undertaken. Petra's phrase, 'movement in boundaries should be ethics
led', highlights how careful and ethically coherent management of therapeutic boundaries needs to be. Yet, the absence of explicit ethical guidelines seems to be contributing to the ambiguity in the field. This ambiguity
is reflected in the story of a therapist who expressed his uncertainty as
to how to depict some forms of clients' response to him and described
that sometimes his conversations with clients 'move into a borderline'
(Robert).

Plentiful Resources within the Systemic Approach Are Underused

Therapists found it relatively easy to make relevant connections between systemic theory, practice and hypothetical situations of sexual attraction in therapy. For example, they pointed at the benefits of developing systemic hypotheses, keeping an open mind and holding onto uncertainty. Co-constructing the meanings 'without having to label or pathologise or having to use certain words', and systemic concepts of 'neutrality' (Cecchin, 1987) and 'not knowing' (Anderson & Goolishian, 1992) linked to 'therapists' use of self'; 'an openness to listening', 'learning from clients' and 'monitoring own assumptions', all came up as strong resources. Systemic sensitivity to the power differential in therapeutic relationships was given major importance. A fundamental systemic principle of meaning being determined by the context was seen as helpful in questioning the meaning of sexual attraction and exploring its interpersonal relevance in therapy. The social constructionist concept of 'multiple context levels' (Cronen & Pearce, 1985) closely related to those mentioned earlier includes 'familial and cultural differences, similarities, expectations and assumptions' (Petra). Isomorphism was depicted as useful in 'exploring which experiences are they trying to replicate with me, which domain of their life could this be coming from' (Olga). The concept of love as described by Maturana in a recent workshop, 'you only learn from those you fall in love with' had a major impact on Tim, who described his approach to clients as 'I try to connect with something I can love about them'. Self-reflexivity in terms of reflecting on therapists' impact on clients was regarded as crucial (Hoffman, 1992). Many therapists felt that relational reflexivity (Burnham, 2005), a concept also discussed by Smith-Pickard in Chapter 5, was a great resource; for example, in relation to a client's expressed sexual interest in her, Emma would explore, 'How does he want me to hear it?' A strong set of stories emerged about the advantages of systemic circular and reflexive questioning (Tomm, 1987) in exploring 'the quality of the therapeutic relationship; the kind of attraction; the clients' and the therapists' narratives about attraction' (Petra).

Discussion

The narratives contained in this study can be encapsulated by the following themes.

Sexual attraction as a social construct

Many accounts in this research confirmed that therapists' stance has a major influence on clients' experiences. Certain themes, even feelings and thoughts, are likely to be a product of therapists' preferred ideological frame of practice. Comparisons and, often, contrasts between psychodynamic and systemic approaches highlighted the impact that therapists' theories, methods and techniques have on the occurrence of sexual attraction in therapy.

What emerged from such accounts is sexual attraction as a social construct, drawing attention to the impact therapists and their working frameworks have in bringing this phenomenon forth (Anderson, Goolishian, & Winderman, 1986; Mendez, Coddou, & Maturana, 1988). While recognizing that the diversity of therapeutic approaches enriches the field of psychotherapy, it also raises ethical questions about therapeutic responsibility and the power to shape and even dominate clients' experiences.

Sexual attraction as a taboo

Sexual attraction emerged as a subject highly emotionally and morally charged, often surrounded by anxiety, apprehension, threat and stigma as barriers to professional discussions about it and for fear of being seen as an abuser. Therapists considered sexual attraction as a taboo stemming from cultural, familial, legal, social and institutional contexts and reflected on the oppressive power of these contexts to define the issues and govern the course of action. Replicating social and cultural patterns of 'cover-up' in therapy, to some extent, seemed to have contributed to moralistic, pathologizing and one-dimensional interpretations of sexual attraction. This is consistent with Luca and Boyden's findings in Chapter 13.

Sexual attraction as a spectrum

Therapists' narratives revealed many different spectrums of understandings and responses to sexual attraction, from it being a sign of a problem to the other end of the spectrum where reflexive conversations about it positively contributed to therapeutic outcomes. This spectrum opened up space to consider an overlap between feelings of sexual attraction and feelings of a positive working relationship. Other spectrums that emerged include dimensions of sexual attraction such as its intensity, nature, direction, shape, frequency and meaning.

Implications of the study

A wealth of stories was obtained about the meaning of sexual attraction in therapy, the implications for theory, practice and ethics, and the limitations within professional support systems. At the same time, there was an overwhelming recognition of great potential within the systemic approach to address the issues of sexual attraction. It transpired that systemic theories, concepts and techniques could be resourcefully used as a multidimensional framework to grasp the issue of sexual attraction in its complexity and its many forms of expression.

Research material brought into focus a range of clinical implications which are listed subsequently as clinical strategies.

Clinical Strategies in Working Systemically with Sexual Attraction

- *Taking a proactive attitude.* In addition to training courses and supervisors devoting more attention to this topic, clinicians of all levels of expertise could be more proactive in raising the subject in various professional contexts. More discussions and debate, sharing of practice and research involving case studies would contribute to further development of constructive reflective practices.
- *Considering sexual attraction as a multifaceted phenomenon.* Conceptualizing attraction as multidimensional could support normalization of its different forms and qualities and reduce pressure to give particular definitions, or make quick decisions and judgments. Exploring the meaning of it at societal, familial, cultural and gender levels, both for therapists and for clients, could facilitate more fruitful and constructive therapeutic outcomes.
- *Appreciating the therapeutic relationship as a unique form of intimacy.* Therapists could be more open to considering some expression of attraction by clients, even if there is some resemblance with sexual attraction, within the context of a well-established working connection, and not necessarily a sign of the broken therapeutic boundaries.
- *Reflecting on own stories about sexual attraction.* The importance of therapists challenging their conceptions, monitoring their judgments and assumptions, and recognizing their limitations, preferences and values appears crucial in expanding therapists' ability to talk about these issues and deal with them effectively.

- *Appreciating the relatively rare occurrence of sexual attraction in systemic work as to an extent related to the nature of the approach.* It appears important to understand the unique qualities of the systemic approach, in particular, a self-reflexive stance regarding the co-construction of the therapeutic relationship, as the theoretical and methodological reasons why this phenomenon does not feature typically in systemic therapy sessions.
- *Considering the therapeutic potential of sexual attraction.* Approaching this phenomenon without pathologizing or problematizing it would contribute to the development of more constructive therapeutic practices and potentially enhance the quality of the therapeutic relationship.
- *Considering doing nothing about sexual attraction.* Therapists' decision to deal with this internally and not address it in any way with clients should be based on their clinical judgement and included as a valid intervention within the repertoire of possible therapeutic responses.

References

Anderson, H., & Goolishian, H. (1992). The client as the expert: A not knowing approach to therapy. In S. McNamee & K. Gergen (Eds.), *Therapy as a social construction* (pp. 25–39). London: Sage Publications.

Anderson, H., Goolishian, H., & Winderman, L. (1986). Problem determined systems: Towards transformation in family therapy. *Journal of Strategic and Systemic Therapies*, 5(4), 1–11.

Bakhtin, M. (1981). *The dialogic imagination: Four essays.* Austin and London: University of Texas Press.

Brock, G. W., & Coufal, J. C. (1994). A national survey of the ethical practices and attitudes of marriage and family therapists. In G. W. Brock (Ed.), *AAMFT ethics casebook* (pp. 27–48). Washington, DC: AAMFT.

Burnham, J. (2005). Relational reflexivity. A tool for socially constructing therapeutic relationships. Chapter 1. In C. Flaskas, B. Mason, & A. Perlesz (Eds.), *The space between: Experience, context and process in the therapeutic relationship.* London: Karnac Books.

Cecchin, G. (1987). Hypothesising, circularity and neutrality revisited: An invitation to curiosity. *Family Process*, 26(4), 405–413.

Cronen, V. E., & Pearce, W. B. (1985). Toward an explanation of how the Milan method works: An invitation to a systemic epistemology and the evolution of family systems. In D. Campbell & R. Draper (Eds.), *Applications of systemic family therapy: The Milan approach* (pp. 69–86). London: Grune & Stratton.

Farris, J. (2002). Some reflections on process, relationship and personal development in supervision. In D. Campbell & B. Mason (Eds.), *Perspectives on supervision*. London: Karnac Books.

Harris, S. M. (2001). Teaching family therapists about sexual attraction in therapy. *Journal of Marital and Family Therapy*, 27(1), 123–128.

Hoffman, L. (1992). A reflexive stance for family therapy. In S. McNamee & K. Gergen (Eds.), *Therapy as a social construction*. London: Sage.

Lieblich, A., Tuval-Mashiach, R., & Zilber, T. (Eds.) (1998). *Narrative research: Reading, analysis and interpretation* (Applied Social Research Method Series). London: Sage Publications.

Maturana, H. (1985) KCC Oxford Summer School, workshop.

Mendez, C. L., Coddou, F., & Maturana, H. R. (1988). The bringing forth of pathology. *Irish Journal of Psychology*, 9(1), 144–172.

Nickell, N. J., Hecker, L. L., Ray, R. E., & Bercik, J. (1995). Marriage and family therapists' sexual attraction to clients: An exploration study. *American Journal of Family Therapy*, 23(4), 315–327.

Tomm, K. (1987). Interventive interviewing: Part II. Questioning as a means to enable self-healing. *Family Process*, 26(2), 167–183.

Epilogue
Meta-reflections on Sexual Attraction

Maria Luca

The journey into the heart of sexual attraction in therapy is now ending by reflecting back. What the book has claimed is that the passionate parts of therapy, not merely those pertaining to love as *agape* (Greek word for tenderness or selfless love) but *Eros* as romantic or sexual desire, reveal themselves in therapy more often than we are prepared to acknowledge. An important message arising from the minds of contributors in this book is that when Eros presents itself in the therapy dyad, we need not fear it, that it is meaningful and potentially healing, that it requires understanding and professional handling, and that dialogue or therapist disclosure does not necessarily lead to sexual involvement as long as our language is sensitive and we are mindful and reflective of the impact therapist disclosures can have on clients. A key idea throughout the book is that therapist denial of, or avoidance in working with, sexual attraction, whether on the part of the client or the therapist, often carries within it a missed opportunity to deepen our work. In fact, increasingly modern perspectives on sexual desire postulate that 'The effectiveness of therapeutic action is in the stirring of desire' (Celenza, 2010, p. 182).

The purpose of the book has been to demystify and thus to normalize sexual attraction. The reader will have seen through the pages how desire leaps out in therapy relationships to surprise, frighten and delight. As therapists, we cannot predict how a therapy relationship will unfold, but we are required to approach each clinical situation with faith and

Sexual Attraction in Therapy: Clinical Perspectives on Moving Beyond the Taboo – A Guide for Training and Practice, First Edition. Edited by Maria Luca.
© 2014 John Wiley & Sons, Ltd. Published 2014 by John Wiley & Sons, Ltd.

confidence, so if desire appears, we can be ready to welcome it with curiosity, interest and the will to understand, just like we approach anger, hate, shame and guilt if we as therapists become the object of these emotions. The common thread bringing chapters together is that relationality in therapists is the bedrock of a successful encounter with sexual desire and that by being relational, therapists are not merely gazing at their clients' world through smoked glass but fully participate in it from this intersubjective position.

Psychotherapy encourages people to become aware of meanings they assign to their life, to become cognizant of how they live their life and to understand the perils of their destructive acts. Therapy does this through radical reflection. If our aim as therapists is to accompany our clients in their life journeys, we must ask ourselves what kinds of companions we are. We have an ethical responsibility to learn to tolerate even the rockiest journey, walk into territories we most fear, gaze at the darkest recesses of our clients' minds and concern ourselves with the desire to be there despite our fears and because of them. The book has been an invitation to therapists to ponder and deliberate on the landscape of sexual desire, consider its intentions, open themselves to the feelings it evokes in them and allow themselves to be inspired by its force, as a way of appreciating its true colours and learning to handle it appropriately.

Evidently, much has been written about clients' love or erotic desire for her/his therapist, but little on the therapist's erotic feelings for her/his client, which, according to Hirsch (1988), are 'probably inevitable in, and possibly essential for, fruitful long-term analytic experience' (p. 210). We would add that erotic feelings can and do develop in short-term therapeutic work. Celenza's (2010) paper title, 'The Guilty Pleasure of Erotic Countertransference: Searching for Radial True', captures one of the obstacles to therapists' moving beyond the taboo of sexual attraction, that is, the *guilt* from enjoying the Dionysian excess: 'The discomfort was more in the way of a nagging guilt was I enjoying him too much? Did our play cross over to flirtation in a way that seductively offered something I could not and would not deliver? Though he did not seem to mind, I did not know if this would always be true and more to the point, was I behaving with his best interests in mind?' (p. 181).

If love and eros have a legitimate place in human nature, it follows that they have a legitimate place in therapeutic practice. By default, what takes place in therapy relationships is a microcosm of the lived experience in the wider world, albeit with more focus and intensity on the internal, psychological aspects of human experience. What differentiates the terms of engagement between people in the wider world from those of clients and therapists is the professional and ethical responsibility we carry to do no harm and to be mindful of what would be in the best interests of our clients.

Contributors in various chapters have resolutely advocated from their unique perspective that this microcosm would be enriched through radical reflection on sexual attraction in therapy. In a common voice and through modality shaped vocabularies, contributors opened up a dialogue with readers on the promises, ambiguities and dangers of sexual attraction in therapy. The imagined reader posed the questions, expressed the fears, guilt, pleasure and anxieties and joy among other feelings, and the consulting rooms opened their doors through clinical material, with the view of illuminating the reader.

As a way of concluding, I would like to show some of the main features from the various chapters. Before this, I would like to say that a common view embedded in all chapters is that therapists should talk about their reactions in encountering sexual attraction to supervisors or colleagues. Speaking from relational vantage points, contributors have expressed personal views on how sexual attraction can be handled therapeutically. Clinical strategies were developed in each of the chapters, which are intended not as fixed ways of working, not as prescriptive truths, but as clinical considerations and types of interventions therapists can utilize fluidly and in a timely fashion. Application would depend upon therapists' judgement of where a client is at in the therapy process, as well as the readiness of the client to take on board sexual attraction. Fixing interventions would be prescriptive and a contradiction in terms of the relational focus, which is the hub of this book.

Now I should like to turn to Chapter 1, where we have seen how Michael Worrell's reflections on sexual attraction from a cognitive behavioural therapy (CBT) perspective are embedded in the notion that 'sexual drama infuses therapy'. He showed how the drama unfolds from the outset, before reminding us of the scarcity of CBT literature on the subject. The chapter advocated that the 'shutting down' of exploration and acknowledgement of sexual attraction evident among CBT therapists could be tackled through CBT practitioners having personal therapy and through advancing the model towards a more relational perspective.

In a similar fashion to Chapter 1, John Nuttall in Chapter 2 brought to the fore the relational aspects of sexual attraction captured in vignettes where eros was central. By exploring how sexual desire presents itself through Petruska Clarkson's five relationship modes, he highlighted the different aspects of sexual relating. He navigated, through the lenses of a personal integration and the foray of the consulting room, to capture the meanings of client erotic communications and therapist responses.

Michael Berry's existential approach to sexual attraction in Chapter 3 embodies most powerfully the idea of radical reflection mentioned earlier in this section. He situated this as a key principle in the service of an authentic and meaningful encounter. He concluded with the notion that 'the existential therapist must be prepared to address and discuss the meanings of a sexual attraction, insofar as her/his clinical practice is bound by genuine commitment to the other, and marked by authenticity', principles every existential therapist aspires to.

In Chapter 4, Doris McIlwain developed the notion of 'knowing desire but not showing it' as one would in real life. She stressed the importance of permitting desire to unfold rather than distorting it in defensive ways. McIlwain reminded us that if we fall for the perils of 'bystander, frightened abandoner, seduced authority who indulges in fantasies, smiling exploiter, briskly business-like overcompensator or intrusive policer of desire, chances are we are taking a stance someone else in the client's past may have taken. The chapter advocated the use of Facework, a reflective form of detachment and mindful partitioning that can be achieved through a reflective encounter rather than an expressive encounter with desire.

Paul Smith-Pickard's transcendental phenomenological therapy with sexual desire in Chapter 5 attempted to show therapists how to transcend shame, embarrassment, fear or any other negative feelings through dialogic relatedness and psychological proximity. Using the metaphor of therapist and client as the unconsummated lovers bound to each other by the desire to make a difference to each other, he argued that sexual attraction provides the therapeutic capital for authentic relatedness, a theme also highlighted by Michael Berry in Chapter 3. Negotiating relatedness for Paul Smith-Pickard is a talent and a commitment that requires Socratic questioning. One such question involves how close or how far should I, the therapist, situate my relatedness in order to achieve appropriate proximity or distance, where sexual attraction is present.

Richard Blonna in Chapter 6 explored and clinically situated the principles of acceptance commitment therapy (ACT) through discussing the importance in being mindful as therapists, accepting and coexisting with sexual desire as opposed to controlling, avoiding or attempting to eliminate it from our minds. The chapter assigned a natural state to sexual desire and part of the human condition, arguing that it cannot be regulated by ethical codes of conduct or professional boards. As he candidly stated, 'The responsibility for managing sexual attraction rests squarely on the shoulders of professionals entrusted with the care and nurturing of clients and students'. However, Blonna did not leave his argument there. He thoroughly expiates a navigation of ACT principles and applied these in helpful and practical step-by-step ACT practices enriched by situational examples, which illustrate how commitment is required in recognizing sexual attraction and how mindfulness (a moment-by-moment awareness) and acceptance (learning to coexist with uncomfortable emotions) are crucial in handling it.

The literature shows that discussing sexual attraction in supervision is avoided. Kirsten Murray and John Sommers-Flanagan in Chapter 7 have dealt with the role supervision as well as the training of therapists can play in dealing with sexual attraction. Consistent with conceptualizations in previous chapters, they have postulated sexual attraction as a common, natural and ordinary therapeutic occurrence, then endorsed and described processes where greater understanding and insight is used to reduce sexual thoughts and feelings. The authors recommend safe training environments that foster open discussion and normalization of sexual attraction, and emphasize that supervisors should develop collaborative and open relationships with supervisees.

Harris and Timm in Chapter 8 highlighted that conjoint therapy takes on additional levels of complexity because of the triad of relationships present in the room, and how the intensity of this can be heightened when it is fuelled by sexual attraction. The authors have drawn attention to how harder it is to address sexual attraction in conjoint therapy when the client's partner is also in the room. They endorse the approach developed in Chapter 7 by stating that if a therapist believes in honesty as a guiding principle (a subject explored in depth in Chapter 14), it is important that the therapist's honest feelings are filtered through a collegial consultation or clinical supervision.

Using the metaphor of Odysseus, who wanted to hear the Sirens' wonderful music but had his crew bound him hand and foot to the mast as his ship approached their island, psychoanalyst Andrea Sabbadini in Chapter 9 took us on a journey to show how the analyst handles the sweet music of erotic desire. Abstinence, Sabbadini argues, is neither about falling prey to the Sirens' 'honey-sweet tones' nor about refusing to hear it by plugging our ears with beeswax. It is about listening to the Sirens' song, learning from it, but at the same time remaining bound to the superego mast of our principles, if our ship is to take us safely to Ithaca through the perilous waters of the analytic journey.

In Chapter 10, Luca and Soskice opened the therapeutic stage of the love-obsessed clients who refuse to accept that the therapist will not be their lover. Stalking the therapist, although a rare occurrence, is challenging and at times traumatic for therapists. Client relational intrusion, the chapter argued, can be handled through carefully thought-out strategies, including talking to a supervisor and, where appropriate, reporting incidents to the police.

Part II of the book has provided a qualitative research arena where therapists, as research participants, expressed their views and experiences of sexual attraction to clinician/researchers. These research-informed chapters have brought to the fore actual encounters of sexual attraction in an attempt to bridge, in Castonguay et al.'s (2010) assertion that 'a gap exists between what researchers write about and what practitioners do in therapy' (p. xviii). Starting with a grounded theory study, Arcuri and McIlwain in Chapter 11 revealed the attributes that may render a practitioner more (or less) vulnerable to unbidden attraction while recommending the importance of further studies to explore the spectrum of complexities that arise in handling sexual attraction.

Penny and Cross in Chapter 12 presented a brief profile of typical offenders (from existing literature) who become sexually involved with clients, consisting of older males, people who were sexually abused in childhood, have insecure attachments and lack current intimate relationships. They illustrated how discourses of masculinity play an important part in the role and management of sexual attraction. The chapter challenged discourse that perpetuates the position that the client is the cause of the response the therapist feels.

Luca and Boyden's grounded theory study in Chapter 13 showed how experienced therapists were *thrown off balance* in encountering sexual desire, became avoidant, felt guilty about and frightened with the implication of not making effective use of it. Their study also captured the paradoxical attitudes of some therapists in the study who considered sexual attraction as potentially *relational and transformational* and therefore useful to the work, despite *feeling thrown off balance*. They concluded with clinical strategies that emerged from the study.

Marshall and Milton's interpretative phenomenological analysis study in Chapter 14, explored the therapeutic use of therapists' disclosures of their sexual feelings toward clients, suggesting that the need to be honest was found to influence therapists' decisions to disclose their feelings. However, they warn that the choice to disclose must be made with the client's best interests at heart.

Some clients, as Chapter 15 by Desa Markovic showed, erroneously believe that therapy includes sexual relations with the therapist and are surprised to learn that therapists are ethically bound to abstain from this.

The chapter captures systemic family and marital therapists' accounts of instances of sexual attraction in their work, including that it is a taboo subject and that it rarely manifests in family work.

The wisdom of scholars featured in this book is not purely an accumulation of academic research but one shaped by many years of clinical practice, which has been instrumental in formulating their ideas. I am indebted to them all for their intellectual rigour and commitment to advance knowledge beyond the taboo of sexual attraction.

References

Castonguay, L. G., Muran, J. C., Angus, L., Hayes, J. A., Ladany, N., & Andreson, T. (2010). *Bringing psychotherapy research to life*. Washington, DC: APA.

Celenza, A. (2010). The guilty pleasure of erotic countertransference: Searching for radial true. *Studies in Gender and Sexuality*, *11*(4), 175–183.

Hirsch, I. (1988). Mature love in countertransference. In J. Lasky & H. Silverman (Eds.), *Love: Psychoanalytic perspectives*. New York: New York University Press.

Index